DEMOCRACY, DECENTRALISATION AND DEFICITS IN LATIN AMERICA

Edited by

Kiichiro Fukasaku and Ricardo Hausmann

INTER-AMERICAN DEVELOPMENT BANK
DEVELOPMENT CENTRE OF THE ORGANISATION
FOR ECONOMIC CO-OPERATION AND DEVELOPMENT

ORGANISATION FOR ECONOMIC CO-OPERATION AND DEVELOPMENT

Pursuant to Article 1 of the Convention signed in Paris on 14th December 1960, and which came into force on 30th September 1961, the Organisation for Economic Co-operation and Development (OECD) shall promote policies designed:

- to achieve the highest sustainable economic growth and employment and a rising standard of living in Member countries, while maintaining financial stability, and thus to contribute to the development of the world economy;
- to contribute to sound economic expansion in Member as well as non-member countries in the process of economic development; and
- to contribute to the expansion of world trade on a multilateral, non-discriminatory basis in accordance with international obligations.

The original Member countries of the OECD are Austria, Belgium, Canada, Denmark, France, Germany, Greece, Iceland, Ireland, Italy, Luxembourg, the Netherlands, Norway, Portugal, Spain, Sweden, Switzerland, Turkey, the United Kingdom and the United States. The following countries became Members subsequently through accession at the dates indicated hereafter: Japan (28th April 1964), Finland (28th January 1969), Australia (7th June 1971), New Zealand (29th May 1973), Mexico (18th May 1994), the Czech Republic (21st December 1995), Hungary (7th May 1996), Poland (22nd November 1996) and the Republic of Korea (12th December 1996). The Commission of the European Communities takes part in the work of the OECD (Article 13 of the OECD Convention).

The Development Centre of the Organisation for Economic Co-operation and Development was established by decision of the OECD Council on 23rd October 1962 and comprises twenty-three Member countries of the OECD: Austria, Belgium, Canada, the Czech Republic, Denmark, Finland, France, Germany, Greece, Iceland, Ireland, Italy, Japan, Korea, Luxembourg, Mexico, the Netherlands, Norway, Poland, Portugal, Spain, Sweden and Switzerland, as well as Argentina and Brazil from March 1994. The Commission of the European Communities also takes part in the Centre's Advisory Board.

The purpose of the Centre is to bring together the knowledge and experience available in Member countries of both economic development and the formulation and execution of general economic policies; to adapt such knowledge and experience to the actual needs of countries or regions in the process of development and to put the results at the disposal of the countries by appropriate means.

The Centre has a special and autonomous position within the OECD which enables it to enjoy scientific independence in the execution of its task. Nevertheless, the Centre can draw upon the experience and knowledge available in the OECD in the development field.

Publié en français sous le titre :

DÉMOCRATIE, DÉCENTRALISATION ET DÉFICITS BUDGÉTAIRES EN AMÉRIQUE LATINE

 THE OPINIONS EXPRESSED AND ARGUMENTS EMPLOYED IN THIS PUBLICATION ARE THE SOLE RESPONSIBILITY OF THE AUTHORS AND DO NOT NECESSARILY REFLECT THOSE OF THE OECD OR OF THE GOVERNMENTS OF ITS MEMBER COUNTRIES.

*
* *

Foreword

This volume represents the deliberations of the November 1997 eighth joint OECD Development Centre and Inter-American Development Bank annual conference of the "International Forum on Latin American Perspectives". The conference falls into the context of the Development Centre's research programme entitled "Reform and Growth of Large Developing Countries" and is part of the Centre's external co-operation activities.

Table of Contents

PART TWO

PRACTITIONERS' VIEWS

Preface

The annual Inter-American Development Bank–OECD Development Centre *International Forum on Latin American Perspectives* has become a valuable platform for dialogue between policy makers in OECD and Latin American countries since its inception in 1990. This volume presents the proceedings of the eighth annual Forum which took place in Paris in November 1997.

The theme of the 1997 Forum was "Democracy, Decentralisation and Deficits in Latin America", reflecting two major political and economic trends in Latin America: the consolidation of democracy and fiscal decentralisation. The combination of these trends will have a significant impact on the region's future fiscal performance. Democratic decision-making in taxation and public expenditure involves the process of collective action; a process with potential pitfalls which, in the absence of an appropriate institutional structure, could lead to undesirable outcomes including a "deficit bias" in public finance, a destabilizing "procyclical" response to economic shocks and fluctuations, and a tax and spending cycle associated with elections. Decentralisation compounds the pitfalls associated with fiscal management by devolving taxing and spending powers to lower levels of government.

The Forum was divided into two sessions: an experts' meeting and a policy-dialogue panel session, and the presentation of this publication reflects that structure. Many of the chapters highlight the fact that designing the institutional arrangements needed to ensure sound fiscal outcomes in the increasingly democratic and decentralised budget process is both important and complex. The recent experience of Latin American countries reviewed in detail here suggests that the region's budgetary arrangements and institutions, including the degree and form of fiscal decentralisation, must be consistent with the overall objectives of strengthening democratic institutions, increasing the effectiveness and transparency of the budget process and promoting an appropriate fiscal stance at all levels of government.

This volume will stimulate further debate on fiscal policy in Latin American countries and contribute to the formulation of policies aimed at achieving sound public finances.

Jean Bonvin
President
OECD Development Centre
Paris

Enrique V. Iglesias
President
Inter-American Development Bank
Washington, D.C.

February 1998

Opening Remarks

Jean Bonvin

Every year since 1990, the Inter-American Development Bank and the OECD Development Centre have jointly organised an International Forum on Latin American Perspectives. The success of this annual event owes much to the very nature of this Forum. Indeed, it is a unique forum for addressing the emerging issues faced by policy makers in Latin America. The topics chosen and the participants invited to past meetings all point to the relevance of this International Forum as a platform for policy discussion by senior government officials and opinion leaders in Europe and Latin America.

This year's Forum follows that tradition. Today's topic is a very timely one. Over the last few years, research has shed new light on the interactions between decentralisation and government finance in OECD and non-OECD countries. Growing interest in these interactions suggests that important changes have taken place in the mainstream perception of the role of the government in the economy. It also reflects increased awareness that managing fiscal policy in the democratic decision-making process has become a major challenge for many countries, including those in Latin America.

This Forum provides an excellent opportunity for senior officials of OECD and Latin American countries and international experts to have an exchange of views on this emerging policy issue. Learning from others' experiences is an important exercise in policy making. In other words, to use public finance terminology, I am sure this Forum will generate strong positive externalities.

To set the ball rolling, I would like to make three observations regarding the topic of this year's Forum.

First, in the context of Latin America, macroeconomic stability and sustained growth depend to a large extent on fiscal consolidation and disciplined public finances. Recent stabilization programmes in this region have been successful in that any disarray in public finances has been eliminated or kept under control. On the other hand, fiscal decentralisation has raised some concern over the ability of local governments to manage larger resources and to deal effectively with public expenditure management and tax collection. Concern has also been expressed over the availability and efficiency of fiscal instruments to attain these goals. Given the disparities in social and economic development within the region, particularly in the case of large countries, the potential scarcity of local managerial expertise may also constitute a constraint to fiscal decentralisation. Recent research from the perspective of public choice also emphasises that different levels of government may have different incentives, or disincentives, in respect to fiscal consolidation. Moreover, they may face different constraints in terms of indebtedness and access to alternative sources of finance.

Second, this Forum also draws attention to the importance of the interrelationship between electoral systems and budgetary institutions and their implications for the fiscal outcome. As you know, the issues involved are very complex and politically sensitive. Yet, at the same time, this is one of the areas in which Latin American countries may learn useful lessons from the experience of OECD countries.

Third, I would like to highlight one more general issue that is relevant for the future in Latin America. That is the need for more effective co-ordination of fiscal policy as well as the harmonisation of tax systems across trading nations, in the light of recent trends in the globalisation of production and investment, and the creation of regional free trade areas. As you know, MERCOSUR is one of the most successful such areas to be established in recent years. The pursuit of stability in exchange rates and international relative prices is a basic requirement for deeper integration among trading nations. Given today's increasingly liberalised international capital markets, this requirement has placed greater emphasis on the conduct of fiscal policy because the member countries forfeit, to varying degrees, their ability to conduct an independent monetary policy. Monetary integration within the European Union is a case in point. As our economies become more and more inter-connected, it seems to me that the important task of ensuring overall macroeconomic stability is now being placed in the realm of fiscal policy.

PART ONE

DEMOCRACY, DECENTRALISATION AND FISCAL PERFORMANCE

Fiscal Institutions for Decentralising Democracies: Which Way to Go?

Ricardo Hausmann[1]

Introduction

Latin America is becoming more democratic. Of the 26 borrowing member countries of the Inter-American Development Bank only 13 had democratic governments in 1980. Now, all of them do. Democratic institutions are also becoming more decentralised. While only three countries in 1980 had direct elections for mayor, now 17 do, and mayors in six other countries are appointed by elected municipal councils. This process has been accompanied by a decentralisation of spending: the share of government spending by local State and local governments has increased from about 15 per cent to 20 per cent in the last decade. This democratic trend has been consistent with improved fiscal discipline. While only four countries in 1983 had deficits below 3 per cent of GDP, now 16 countries do. Deficits in the region averaged less than 2 per cent of GDP in 1996. Moreover, deficits in the 1990s have been well below the average levels observed in industrial countries.

Hence, the fears that democracy might lead to less fiscal discipline are hard to square with recent Latin American experience. However, such concerns cannot simply be disregarded, for collective decision making is full of dangers that should not be overlooked. In fiscal and other matters, governments must deal with at least four types of problems: *aggregation of preferences, co-ordination, agency and commitment*, and they must deal with them using rules and procedures that regulate the interaction between the different players involved.

If Latin America has been able to achieve sound outcomes it is precisely because it has found ways to deal with some of these hazards, but it has not been able to deal with all of them. In particular, while Latin American countries have been able to limit the *deficit bias*, at least by OECD standards, not all of them have been equally successful. Hence, controlling the natural penchant of political systems towards debts and deficits should always be an area of concern. In Latin American countries this vigilance needs to be greater because fiscal accounts are subject to significantly more *volatility*[2]. Shocks to revenue and non-discretionary expenditure are several times greater than those observed in industrial countries. Hence, institutions must deal with more dynamic challenges. Research[3] shows that countries have been coping with this volatility in a highly *procyclical* fashion, a fact that could only worsen the initial volatility. Finally, there is strong evidence of an *electoral budget cycle*[4] in which the deficit rises significantly in an electoral year, requiring major cutbacks in the following year.

Hence, the challenge for Latin American countries is to improve the institutional setting of their decision-making processes so that they can cope with these problems while strengthening democracy.

The Four Central Problems of any Public Institution

Aggregation of Preferences

How are social choices derived from individual preferences? Ever since Arrow's impossibility theorem showed the complexities of this process, much economic theory has been developed to understand its implications. In a direct democracy, people vote for specific choices. In representative democracies, people vote for those who are supposed to express their preferences. The vote may be cast for an individual (e.g. a president) or a group (e.g. a parliament, legislative assembly or congress with two houses). Electoral systems and legislative systems reflect some mapping between individual preferences and social choices. Some systems may favour simple majorities, while others imply a stronger bias towards the *statu quo* by requiring larger majorities for certain decisions. Still other systems reflect a concern for regional balance (for example, the US Senate). Concerns for the rights of the minorities are often expressed in constitutional provisions that restrict the type of decisions that political representatives can make.

The rules of aggregation are like a mapping function between individual preferences and social choices and have fundamental effects on the working of political systems and hence on fiscal decision making.

For a given division of votes, some rules of aggregation may give rise to large majorities, while others may lead to many small parties which need to govern through coalitions. For example, consider an election in which the three main parties win 45 per cent, 40 and 10 per cent of the votes respectively. A first-past-the-post system may create a very large majority, as the Labour Party achieved in the United Kingdom in 1997. In fact, if the vote were homogeneously distributed throughout the country, the first party would win all legislative contests. By contrast, under a system of proportional representation the two smaller parties may be able to form a coalition and control the parliament.

Another dimension of this problem is the degree of political decentralisation of public decisions. For some electoral results, a system in which investments in roads are determined by locally-elected governments will lead to an allocation of resources very different from that which may have been adopted by federal congress. One of the driving forces behind the current movement towards decentralisation is precisely the fact that it allows a closer match between local preferences and public decisions.

Moreover, the rules of aggregation themselves may affect the number of parties that coexist. Proportional representation and two-round electoral systems tend to generate political systems with a larger number of parties, while first-past-the-post systems lead to fewer parties. Hence, the electoral system affects a country's political structure and, in particular, the possibility of minority or coalition governments.

The choice of a political system represents a selection between different trade-offs. From the point of view of the issues that will be discussed below, one important trade-off is between inclusiveness and decisiveness. For example, some systems lead to coalition governments that are forced to find common ground in order to satisfy the preferences of a larger electoral base; other systems might generate large majorities but at the cost of incorporating the preferences of fewer voters.

In particular, systems with a larger degree of proportional representation tend to have a larger number of parties and smaller government majorities in parliament.

Co-ordination

Once political representatives are chosen and they appoint the relevant government officials, this group of politicians and civil servants must interact according to a set of rules and procedures. This interaction may lead to distortions arising from the interconnected nature of their decisions. One such distortion is known as the *commons problem*, which is exemplified in the following hypothetical situation.

A restaurant offers only two dishes: chicken for $10 and lobster for $50. Chicken is more popular because the $40 premium is quite steep. Consider the case of nine friends who expect to share the bill. If all but one ask for chicken, then the ninth one has the choice of ordering chicken and paying $10 or asking for lobster and paying only $14 (i.e. 9 times 10 plus 50, divided by 10). The temptation is to order lobster. Now imagine that all others plan to order lobster. The choice is then: lobster for $50 or chicken at $46! (i.e. 9 times 50 plus 10, divided by 10). The best choice is still lobster. Hence, no matter what others plan to do, the best economic choice is always lobster for the last one to order in the group, even if he or she would have individually preferred chicken.

Collective choice has its perils and this example illustrates just one of them. They are caused by the way social interactions distort decisions, making them inefficient. The possibility that each participant can shift the burden of decision onto others makes everybody worse off. These problems are critical for fiscal decision making because all participants are allocating a common pool of tax resources. The problem is potentially more serious with decentralisation, since it allows one jurisdiction to shift the tax burden onto others.

Government revenue can be thought of as a common resource that is perceived as underpriced and hence is subject to overutilisation. If some participants have common interests, they will ask for spending on the programmes they want, with the costs borne by all taxpayers. If many groups do this, there will be a tendency towards excessive spending. This same logic may lead to overindebtedness since each group may prefer to postpone the burden of taxation through deficits, given that each will only pay for a small fraction of the additional debt.

Another related issue is the *dynamic commons problem*[5]. Suppose that a country has just suffered a positive and temporary shock, for example, due to an improvement in the terms of trade. Most groups would agree to the proposition that the resulting fiscal windfall should be saved to protect spending programmes in less favourable times. However, if some groups fear that others will use their acquiescence to grab the resources, then they will have an incentive to do the same. The lack of a co-ordination mechanism, which ensures that resources will be carried over to another day, leads to their immediate dissipation.

A third issue is that of *delayed adjustment*[6]. When heterogeneous collective bodies must act on difficult but necessary measures, there may be a tendency to delay action in order to wait and see if some other group is willing to bear the burden of adjustment. As this process continues, economic costs often mount. Delayed adjustment is more likely when there is a divided government, a situation that is influenced, as mentioned above, by the electoral system.

Co-ordination problems can be addressed either by *delegation* or *rules*. By delegating to a single authority, the externality involved in the commons problem can be internalised. Alternatively, if the commons problem is expected to cause excessive spending or borrowing, explicit rules that limit such choices can be adopted.

Agency

In a representative democracy, the public at large delegates choices to elected officials who then recruit a set of appointees. Both politicians and bureaucrats are supposed to act with the best interests of the electors in mind, but they obviously might have incentives to put their own interests first. This is the essence of the agency problem[7].

This problem is most acute when agents have considerable discretion, leaving them free to choose among a large set of actions, or when their choices are not easy to observe.

Some institutional arrangements are better than others for coping with this problem. Disclosure requirements may reduce the information asymmetry which agents exploit in order to hide their actions. A free press and a credible judicial system may be sufficiently dissuasive to keep agents honest. The ability to reward and punish politicians, which is affected by the structure of government and the competitive nature of the political process, may constrain agents. First-past-the-post systems allow electors to discipline politicians. Systems with proportional representation that use slates of candidates must rely on party discipline.

One common justification for decentralisation is that it allows electors to discipline top local officials who perform functions that would be carried out by low-level bureaucrats in a centralised system.

One form that the agency problem might take affects the electoral budget cycle. An unchecked executive may exploit the inability of the public to distinguish between healthy economic expansion and an artificial and unsustainable fiscal stimulus to create an election-year boom which, once the election is over, may require cutbacks.

The agency problem can be tackled in several ways, as the ample literature on corporate governance has discussed. First, making the actions of the agent as observable as possible limits the ability to exploit advantages. Hence disclosure is critical. That is why corporations have their financial position assessed by autonomous auditors who inform shareholders independently of management. In transparent judicial systems, acts of judges must be made public and higher courts given the power to review their decisions.

Aligning the interests of managers with those of the principals through compensation schemes or other mechanisms may also help. For example, many corporate executives are paid in stock options. In New Zealand the salary of the Governor of the central bank is linked to the achievement of the agreed inflation target.

Those who are pessimistic about the possibility of solving the agency problem in government would opt for minimising government activities. This has been one of the arguments in favour of privatisation.

Commitment

Economic decisions involve a calculation about the future. In that calculation, the future course of economic policy becomes an important element, since it can significantly affect the absolute and relative attractiveness of different projects. However, in a democracy, future governments will, to a large extent, decide the future course of economic policy. Current governments might want to acquire certain commitments about future policy choices so as to assure current investors. But future governments may abandon these commitments. The credibility of current explicit and implicit commitments will then become an important determinant of investment. This problem is especially severe if there is a time-inconsistency problem, i.e. a situation in which it is optimal to promise something now, where later it becomes optimal to renege on it[8].

This logic is particularly applicable to government debt. In order to issue bonds, governments have incentives to promise that they will make good on their commitment to service these obligations. Once issued, there are incentives to repudiate those obligations either explicitly, by a payment moratorium, or implicitly by a surprise devaluation and inflation[9]. Knowing this, investors will demand a large risk premium on these instruments, making it less attractive to issue them and more enticing to default on them. The market for debt may disappear altogether.

Latin America has had a relatively precarious access to capital. This may be the result of insufficient credibility. For example, a government may wish to borrow in bad times and repay the debt later in good times in order to smooth economic fluctuations and tax rates. However, if the government's commitment to pay later is in doubt, the markets will not be willing to finance the deficit and the government may be forced to cut spending and raise taxes during recessions, hence behaving procyclically.

One contributing factor to the ability to commit is the degree of polarisation in society. If economic policy has broad-based support then it will be more credible. But if the opposition is in sharp disagreement and has a good chance of winning an election, a policy reversal may seem more likely.

The traditional solution to commitment problems is the elimination of discretion by adopting rules or other so-called precommitment devices. The hands of future parliaments and policy makers can be tied by enshrining certain decisions in the constitution or permitting certain choices to be reversed only by two-thirds or larger majorities. Most rules, such as a balanced budget provision, are only second best, in the sense that other decisions would be more efficient in the absence of commitment problems. Hence, a Barro (1979) rule would involve stable tax rates and government spending programmes, but would let the deficit react to the business cycle. Preventing that adjustment implies inefficiency and a procyclical fiscal policy that would be proportional to the volatility of the environment.

Institutional Problems and Fiscal Symptoms

The four problems discussed above are closely related to the fiscal challenges that Latin American governments must face. As shown in Table 1, there are several channels by which co-ordination, commitment and agency problems can cause bias towards deficit, procyclical policies and electoral budget cycles.

Table 1. **How Problems Affect Fiscal Performance**

	Co-ordination	Commitment	Agency
Deficit bias	Commons problem leads to deficit bias.		Agents that benefit from being in power may accelerate spending and postpone taxes.
Procyclical responses	Inability to co-ordinate to save booms leads to procyclical responses in both good and bad times.	Inability to commit to future sustainable policies leads to poor access to financial markets in bad times.	Doubts about the preferences of the agent leads to procyclical response as a signalling device.
Electoral budget cycles		Doubts about whom will be in office leads to financial jitters at election time.	Risk of being out of office accelerates spending. Agents (e.g. the executive) may have incentives to expand fiscally during election years to stay in office.

The Trade-Off Between Problems

Any institutional design for fiscal policy involves choices over how to address them and other problems. However, it is interesting to note how much of the economic debate on policy and institutions has involved an excessive focus on only one of the core problems. Hence, those who focus on agency problems (e.g. the predatory State) would like to minimise government involvement. Authors concentrating on credibility want everything spelled out in the constitution. Those who are concerned with the commons problem focus on delegation. In the real world, however, we do not observe these corner solutions and the reason may be that there are trade-offs among these problems.

We have tried to capture these trade-offs in Table 2. Co-ordination and commitment problems may be addressed through rules, but not the same rules, creating a potential conflict. For example, some United States have tax boards that are empowered to adjust taxes in order to assure a balanced budget, after the assembly approves spending. This rule may make debt commitments more credible but may lead to excessive spending and taxes since it does not address the co-ordination problem per se. Co-ordination problems may be addressed by delegating some of the critical choices to an authority that can internalise the externalities, such as the executive. Many Latin American systems give the executive the power to choose the maximum level of spending and borrowing, and the legislature cannot amend these parameters. However, the executive may abuse these powers, given that it is subject to agency problems: it may use its discretion to manipulate the budget for electoral reasons.

Table 2. **The Trade-Off Between Problems**

	Co-ordination	Commitment	Agency
Aggregation	PR systems by increasing the effective number of parties may increase co-ordination problems. Party discipline may limit co-ordination problems by making the party internalise externalities, such as the commons problem. Plurality may limit party discipline in presidential systems.	Fixed rules may improve credibility but limit political participation by preventing the political system from changing the rules.	First-past-the post electoral systems may limit agency problems through voter punishment. Slate systems with party discipline may limit the ability of voters to punish politicians.
Co-ordination		Addressing co-ordination problems through delegation of authority may increase discretion and aggravate commitment problems. Moreover, rules designed to address co-ordination problems may be inadequate for commitment problems.	Co-ordination problems may be limited by delegation, but this may aggravate agency problems
Commitment			Adopting fixed rules can reduce commitment problems, but this limits flexibility. Flexibility opens the possibility of agency problems. Hence, more flexibility, more agency problems.

While IDB (1997) finds that more proportional representation leads to higher deficits, suggesting that co-ordination problems are more severe as the number of political parties increases, party discipline may reduce the effective number of agents and internalise the externality inherent in the commons problem, but party discipline is not independent of the political system. Table 3 suggests that plurality (i.e. first-past-the-post) systems lead to a lower number of parties, but presidential systems may lead to low party discipline since failure to co-operate does not bring down the president (e.g. in the United States). This creates a co-ordination problem, as each legislator is quite autonomous, in spite of the small number of parties. Party discipline may reduce co-ordination problems if the number of parties is not too large, as may be the case in Brazil.

Table 3. **Political Systems and Co-ordination Problems**

	Presidential	Parliamentary
Plurality	Few parties. Low party discipline.	Few parties. Moderate party discipline.
Proportional representation	Many parties. Low congressional support. Moderate party discipline.	Many parties. Coalition governments. High party discipline.

In general, institutional strategies can be considered in terms of rules, delegation and transparency/accountability. Table 4 presents a summary analysis of their impact on co-ordination, credibility, flexibility and agency. Co-ordination problems may be addressed through delegation, but this is likely to aggravate agency problems in the empowered authority. Moreover, it does not address commitment problems, as this authority is also subject to time-inconsistency problems. Commitment problems may be addressed through rules, but these are likely to be too rigid in a volatile environment, causing flexibility problems. If rules are made more complicated through the introduction of escape clauses, they are subject to interpretation and may become less credible; this can cause agency problems in those empowered to interpret the rules.

Table 4. **No Silver Bullet: Strategies vs. Problems**

	Co-ordination	Commitment	Flexibility	Agency
Rules-based strategies	Rules that address co-ordination problems may be inefficient or inadequate to address commitment problems.	Rules that address commitment problems may be inefficient or inadequate to address co-ordination problems.	Are unlikely to respond effectively in volatile environments unless rules are complicated. This may allow their abuse. Moreover, the rule itself may be inefficient.	Rule must be interpreted and agents can abuse the interpretation for their own interest, making the rule less credible.
Delegation to agenda setter	Agenda setter may co-ordinate efficiently.	Agenda setter may suffer from time inconsistency problems.	Agenda setter may use his discretion to adapt to changing circumstances.	Agenda setter may aggravate agency problems (e.g. electoral budget cycle).
Disclosure/ transparency	Co-ordination when the other's actions are unobservable may cause the collapse of co-operative equilibria.	Commitment to an unobservable behaviour may not be credible.	Credible information may be critical to distinguishing shocks from abuse.	In so far as it makes the agent's actions more observable it should reduce agency.

Only transparency seems to improve matters on all fronts. It makes co-operative equilibria more sustainable by making the behavior of others more observable. For example, the United States Congress recently adopted a rule whereby the Joint Tax Committee must flag any tax provision that affects fewer than 20 firms. In all likelihood, this will make it harder to cater to special interests. Transparency also makes credibility easier to establish. New Zealand adopted a system whereby the government sets its own targets, but the highly autonomous Treasury informs the public about its achievements. Markets have reacted very favourably.

Transparency may also facilitate the adoption of rules. Most rules are based on budget projections and these can be manipulated. In the United States in the 1980s the Gramm-Rudman deficit reduction provisions were made ineffective by overly optimistic projections. As a consequence, Congress took away from the Executive the power to make official budget projections and transferred it to the somewhat more autonomous[10] Congressional Budget Office.

Reforming Fiscal Institutions in Latin America: Some Proposals

In general, Latin American systems of representation are proportional, making co-ordination problems an important concern. Latin America is subject to great volatility, making flexibility important and procyclical policies all the more damaging and difficult to avoid. The region also has a history of inflation and debt problems, making credibility a critical concern. Hence,what types of institutional arrangements are likely to address these issues simultaneously?

Hausmann and Gavin elsewhere in this volume present some relevant stylised facts. Budget institutions that delegate more power to the executive and to the finance minister deliver lower average deficits. Unfortunately, these institutional arrangements seem to be insufficient to address the procyclical problem or electoral budget cycles. Proportional representation systems tend to have larger average deficits and more procyclical responses.

Given this background, how should the fiscal institutions of Latin American countries be reformed?

i) Choose fiscal institutions taking full account of the nature of the political and electoral system

While political systems (e.g. presidential vs. parliamentary) and electoral systems (first-past-the-post vs. proportional representation) have an impact on fiscal performance, it is unreasonable to expect them to be adopted on the basis of their fiscal impact. There are other considerations related to social cohesion that override narrow macroeconomic objectives. A more reasonable proposition is that budget institutions should be discussed and designed on the basis of desired fiscal outcomes, taking into account the political and electoral institutions. For example, New Zealand's Fiscal Responsibility Act of 1994 was approved in the context of an electoral reform that moved towards a system with more proportional representation. This connection is in line with Hallerberg and von Hagen (in this volume) and IDB (1997) who suggest that budget institutions can overcome some of the difficulties associated with electoral systems.

ii) Create autonomous scorekeepers to assure credible fiscal transparency.

Transparency is likely to improve credibility, agency and co-ordination problems under any arrangement, but for transparency itself to be credible the scorekeeping function must be autonomous. Otherwise, its numbers will be suspect. The autonomous scorekeeper must generate or audit not only the fiscal outcomes but also the projections, since it is based on these that allocative decisions are made. It should have autonomy over the definitions of the deficit, as changing financial and institutional arrangements are likely to require changing definitions.

To assure the scorekeeper's autonomy, the legislature should make long-term appointments by a super majority. The scorekeeper too must be kept accountable by making its information public, by requiring it to explain *ex post* the deviations between projected and actual values and by encouraging surveillance by the International Monetary Fund.

iii) Empower the autonomous scorekeeper with the role of calculating an underlying cyclically adjusted deficit.

The yearly budget deficit is a very poor indicator of the underlying fiscal position of a country, especially in volatile environments. Instead, an appropriate methodology should correct for the fiscal impact of the terms of trade, the current account, the real exchange rate, and interest rates if these variables are not at their equilibrium levels. It should also develop a methodology for dealing with contingent and pension liabilities. Medium-term projections could also be valuable in assessing the sustainability of the fiscal position.

Obviously, the calculation of a cyclically-adjusted deficit involves much discretion and many judgements. It is very easy to distort the assumptions to achieve any desired result. That is one more reason for providing the scorekeeper with credible institutional autonomy. Otherwise, it will be perceived as exploiting its discretion over budget assumptions to further some political agenda.

The calculation of an underlying deficit by a credible entity would signal the nature of the current deficit to markets. This would provide valuable information for determining whether the government's financial demands are an efficient use of its borrowing capacity or if they reflect an attempt to postpone inevitable adjustments.

Delegate the Choice of the Spending and Deficit Levels to the Executive

Delegating to the executive such aggregate choices as the total amount of spending and borrowing is a useful means of limiting the commons problem. The legislature should be allowed to cut these figures, but not to increase them. The legislature should also have the power to make budget reallocations between expenditure items. However, the autonomous scorekeeper should evaluate the actual changes in appropriations in order to prevent willful underestimation of commitments. Moreover, the executive should be empowered to cut spending unilaterally in order to permit it to adjust quickly to negative shocks. If the legislature fails to agree on a budget, the original draft should become law in order to prevent gridlock and to promote legislative agreements.

iv) Restrict the ability of the executive to propose and carry out spending and to create deficits which are consistent with intertemporal solvency.

Countries that have adopted the provisions suggested in the previous paragraph have not solved the procyclical or the electoral-budget-cycle problems. This suggests that more needs to be done.

Latin American countries need to save more during booms but probably do not do so because of the dynamic commons problem. Markets may be unwilling to finance stabilizing deficits in bad times because they might be unable to distinguish between a prudent response and a reckless one, given that they do not know with certainty whether the disturbance is temporary or more permanent. Lack of a credible commitment eventually to generate a surplus sufficient to pay back the additional debt may also be at work. Agency problems may also be at fault. The executive may choose too large a deficit because it wants to win elections, because it discounts the future too heavily, or because it derives private gains from it.

Adopting a rule that restricts the maximum allowable deficit may solve many of these problems. Putting a constraint on the underlying deficit would insure surpluses in good times and would limit electoral deficits. It would also permit efficient adjustment to bad shocks.

v) Empower the autonomous scorekeeper with the role of monitoring fiscal rules.

Any rule, like any law, requires interpretation, but the interpretation must be made in a way that prevents those in charge of applying the law from interpreting it to their advantage. Also, it is important that whoever does the interpreting is somewhat sheltered from interest-group pressures. That is why the United States Supreme Court and not the Executive is charged with interpreting the Constitution and the laws. Provisions in antitrust legislation require the application of the rule of reason, a highly discretionary task. Autonomous antitrust agencies, but not ministries of trade and industry, are empowered to apply the rule of reason.

Any fiscal rule that could be adopted would require interpretation and it makes sense to use the autonomous scorekeeper for this purpose. The amount of power granted to the autonomous scorekeeper should probably depend on national characteristics.

If the political system and bond markets can provide sufficient discipline, better information may force all budget players to behave in a collectively responsible manner. In these countries, the autonomous scorekeeper should only be empowered to furnish information on the agreed performance targets. Other countries may want to go a bit further. If the budget is subject to large shocks and the political system is fragmented, the risk of a collapse in credibility because of fears of delayed adjustment may imply that markets will be very volatile. Also, such conditions may aggravate the dynamic commons problem by making it more difficult to save resources for a rainy day. Such countries may want to restrain themselves somewhat more to increase their credibility.

One alternative is a national debt board proposed by von Hagen and Harden (1995) for European countries and a national fiscal council (NFC) proposed by Eichengreen, Hausmann and von Hagen (1996) for Latin America. The latter could be considered a scorekeeper with enhanced powers. Not only would it calculate current and estimated future deficits and explain their significance by separating cyclical effects from longer-term considerations, but it would also be empowered to set a maximum allowable deficit that the legislature and executive could authorise. In other words, the maximum allowable deficit calculated by this institution would constitute a constraint on the political process, albeit a more flexible one than a traditional balanced budget rule.

In moving in this direction, the decisions of these entities could be restricted by forcing them to apply a rule, even one that implies significant discretion in its interpretation. The implementation of a target on the underlying cyclically-adjusted deficit is one way to narrow the scope of the autonomous entities.

These proposals may not be acceptable for several reasons. In practice, these agencies do not have direct control over the budget and hence must rely on the rule of law, the respect for institutions and a deep and widely-shared commitment to sound fiscal outcomes. Moreover, the law may intend to grant autonomy, but its effectiveness is not assured. Autonomous institutions such as independent central banks, utility regulators, bank supervisors and antitrust or anti-dumping authorities work better in some settings than in others depending on national, sectoral and design considerations as well as on the political culture of each nation[11]. Legislators may question whether the autonomous agencies can be trusted to carry out their assigned tasks without abusing or misusing their powers.

There are sufficient degrees of freedom in institutional design to adapt a simple scorekeeper body, or a national debt board or a fiscal council. Countries that have doubts about institutional capacity, accountability and autonomy may start out with formulations that are closer to a pure scorekeeper. Countries that value the credibility gains obtained by reducing the borrowing discretion of the political system and have confidence in the adequate functioning of such an institution would be willing to provide it with more authority.

An Agenda for Fiscally Sound Decentralisation

Decentralisation has the potential to improve on the aggregation problem by bringing decisions closer to voter preferences. It can also improve on the agency problem by making governments more accountable. However, by creating the possibility of interaction between different jurisdictions, decentralisation may lead to potential co-ordination problems that manifest themselves in soft budget constraints.

Stein (1997) and IDB (1997) find that decentralised governments tend to be larger. This result is consistent with several interpretations. One of them is that because local governments can be trusted to deliver public goods that are more in line with voter preferences, they are given more resources to manage. Hence, this result per se is no indication of inefficiency. However, Stein and IDB also found that the form of decentralisation also affects size. In particular, arrangements that are more likely to lead to soft budget constraints seem to be associated with larger size. This evidence is a clearer indication of political distortions at work.

To achieve a well-functioning system it is important that decentralisation be organised so that it can obtain better preference matching and government accountability without falling into the pitfalls of co-ordination failures. Achieving this involves *improving democratic institutions* and *hardening budget constraints*. Our next five proposals are related to these two issues.

vi) Improve Local Democracies... but

Decentralisation has a chance to improve fiscal performance if local democracy assures that public decisions follow social preferences and keep politicians and bureaucrats honest and accountable. This requires civic participation, clear rules for the financing of elections and political parties, a free, fair and competitive press, and a well-functioning judiciary. Otherwise, lobbies might find that it is possible and cheaper to exert undue influence on local governments, media moguls could become kingmakers, important areas of public life may escape social scrutiny, and the perception of impunity may have very corrosive effects. Well-functioning political systems are a must for well functioning governments, at any level.

...Harden Budget Constraints on Governments below the National Level

Soft budget constraints are the consequence of the interrelation between the power to tax, spend, and borrow and the nature of the transfer mechanism. Hardening budget constraints requires a consistent design in these four areas.

vii) Limit Vertical Imbalance Efficiently

Vertical imbalance, i.e. the dependence of local governments on transfers from the federal (or State) level, generates incentive problems in resource allocation at the local level because spending initiatives need not be put through the test requiring local citizens to pay for them. However, vertical imbalance is inevitable because many tax instruments are more efficiently managed in a centralised fashion. Centralisation may permit the achievement of economies of scale in collection, reduce distortions and inequities associated with assigning a geographical origin to tax bases and limit tax competition between different jurisdictions which may weaken tax capacity. Income taxes, the value added tax, taxes on foreign trade and payroll taxes are better left to the national government. State and local governments might piggyback on some of these taxes. Local governments should also be prevented from imposing taxes that are equivalent to an internal tariff or which limit internal trade.

Given the scarcity of tax instruments that can be efficiently used by State and local governments, every effort should be made by the central government to stop using them. Therefore, State and local governments should be allowed to use taxes that resemble user charges such as tolls, gasoline taxes or property taxes.

viii) Adopt Stabilizing and Non-Discretionary Transfer Rules.

Even after best efforts are made to increase the tax capacity of local governments, vertical imbalances will remain and the decentralisation process will need to define a system of transfers. Promoting stability and avoiding discretion are two important principles when doing this. Discretionary transfers create incentives for State and local governments to create pressure for additional transfers. Discretion is reduced if there are clearly-established rules that define both the total amount of the transfer and its regional distribution.

While it is common for transfer rules to be based on a share of the revenue collected either from specific taxes or total ordinary income, there are good reasons to avoid these formulas. First, they lead to transfers that are as unstable and procyclical as their source. This puts unnecessary strains on all State and local political systems, which are as likely to have problems dealing with fluctuations as is the national government. Hence, it is best to have the central government provide stabilization services instead of imposing this burden on each State and local government. Second, rules that are based on shares of revenue make it harder for the central government to close fiscal gaps, because they cause spending to increase automatically whenever revenue rises.

One alternative is to fix the overall transfer as a share of GDP. This will permit stability and limit discretion, and will not cause spending to rise when the federal government is trying to cut its deficit.

Transfers that are based on the principle of notional-cost reimbursement can be particularly effective for the financing of social services. If they are based on the principle of capitation, i.e. a fixed amount of money per person served, they define not only a clear rule but also provide an important price signal. This is a way to implement the principle that budgetary resources should follow outcomes, not inputs. Chile's educational transfers are a case in point. Moreover, these transfers incorporate a de facto stabilization principle.

ix)   Clarify Roles by Avoiding Concurrent Responsibilities.

Another mechanism whereby budget constraints are softened is the lack of a clear division of responsibilities between the central and State and local governments. In many countries, the decentralisation process has involved not an outright transfer of functions and accountability, but instead a shared arrangement where two or more levels of government end up providing the same service, be it primary education, housing or road maintenance. This mechanism allows local governments to extract resources from the central government by choosing to underprovide in areas of joint responsibility and compel the central government to make additional spending in their jurisdictions. For this reason, a clear separation of roles and responsibilities can permit a better control of central government budgets, better planning and provision of services, and a more transparent use of State and local resources.

x)   Set Tight Limits on the Borrowing Authority of State and Local Governments.

Another source of soft budget constraints is the ability of State and local governments to overborrow in expectation of a federal government or central bank bailout. In this respect, it is important to consider the following options.

Some governments, such as Chile's, have opted for prohibiting autonomous borrowing. This has the advantage of limiting co-ordination problems but at the cost of severely restricting the investment capacity of State and local governments unless funds are made available in some fashion. Other countries have opted for more autonomy. In this case, it is important that the budget institutions at the State and local level be properly designed. One critical element is the constraint on the deficit. We argued above that, for the case of national governments, fixed deficit provisions such as balanced budget rules are either inefficient or unworkable, given the amount of volatility that is common in Latin America. This would still be true at the State and local level if the central government were not provide a stabilized flow of transfers. However such stabilization mechanisms are implemented, tight limits on borrowing may be an efficient part of State and local budget institutions. In fact, in the United States, 37 States have freely adopted balanced budget rules.

Also, State and local governments either should not own banks or these institutions should be restricted from lending directly or indirectly to their owners. Otherwise, governments might be able to circumvent their own budget institutions and force the central bank into bailing them out, as has happened all too often.

Also, clear limits should be put on the ability of State and local governments to use their claims to future transfers as a guarantee for new loans. While such an arrangement may reduce the cost of financing by transferring the risk to that of the national government, it limits the ability of the market to signal the unsustainability of the fiscal position, until the guarantee is exhausted. By then, the government may be excessively overindebted.

Finally, a proper framework should be adopted to allow for project finance. State and local governments should be able to pledge the cash flow of a development project to secure financing. However, clear default rules should be enacted so as to clarify property rights and restrict the possibility of bailouts.

Concluding Remarks

For too long, fiscal policy discussions have been focused on targets and instruments and not on institutions and procedures. The 1990s have seen a change of focus. We still know too little to be too sure about what to do. The economics profession has barely scratched the surface of the interaction between political, electoral, fiscal, federal and financial institutions and it will take a long time to make as much progress here as has been made in other areas. However, as always in the policy world, action will be required before full clarity has been attained. This paper proposes a set of initiatives meant to start a debate, not to end it.

Notes

1. I have greatly benefited from interaction with economists and consultants who have worked for the Office of the Chief Economist of the IDB. I especially want to thank Michael Gavin, Ernesto Talvi, Ernesto Stein, Alberto Alesina, Barry Eichengreen, Jürgen von Hagen and Rudolf Hommes. The typical disclaimers apply.

2. The analysis of the impact of volatility on Latin America was studied in IDB (1995) and in Hausmann and Reisen (1996).

3. See Gavin, Hausmann, Perotti and Talvi (1996), Gavin and Perotti (forthcoming), Talvi and Végh (1996).

4. See Stein, Talvi and Grisanti (1997).

5. See Hausmann, Powell and Rigobon (1993) and Aizenman and Powell (1996).

6. See Alesina and Drazen (1991), Drazen and Grilli (1993) and Guidotti and Végh (1992).

7. For an excellent non-technical review of agency problems see Arrow (1985). A more technical treatment can be found in Hart and Holmstrom (1987).

8. The literature on credibility started with Kydland and Prescott (1977) and Calvo (1978).

9. See, for example, Bulow and Rogoff (1989) and Calvo and Guidotti (1993).

10. The majority party in Congress names the head of the Congressional Budget Office, giving it a partisan connotation, which would be avoided if the appointment required a larger majority.

11. See Eichengreen, Hausmann and Piras (1997) for a discussion of the factors that seem to affect the performance of autonomy in practice. This study is based on an IDB research network project which compared 18 autonomous institutions in five countries.

Bibliography

AIZENMAN, J. AND R. HAUSMANN (1995), "Inflation and Budgetary Discipline", *NBER Working Paper,* No. 5537.

AIZENMAN, J. AND A. POWELL (1996), "The Political Economy of Saving Behavior and the Role of Capital Mobility", manuscript, Dartmouth College and Central Bank of Argentina.

ALESINA, A. AND A. DRAZEN (1991), "Why Are Stabilizations Delayed?" *American Economic Review*, Vol. 81, December.

ALESINA, A., R. HAUSMANN, R. HOMMES AND E. STEIN (1996), "Budget Institutions and Fiscal Performance in Latin America", *NBER Working Paper,* No. 5586.

ALESINA, A. AND R. PEROTTI (1995a), "Fiscal Expansions and Adjustments in OECD Countries", *Economic Policy*.

ALESINA, A. AND R. PEROTTI (1995b), "Budget Deficits and Budget Institutions", manuscript, Harvard University and Columbia University.

ARROW, K. (1985), "The Economics of Agency", in J. PRATT AND R. ZECKHAUSER (eds.), *Principals and Agents: the Structure of Business*, Harvard Business School Press, Cambridge, Mass.

BARRO, R. (1979), "On the Determination of the Public Debt", *Journal of Political Economy,* 87.

BULOW, J. AND K. ROGOFF (1989), "A Constant Recontracting Model of Sovereign Debt", *Journal of Political Economy*, 97, No. 1.

CALVO, G. (1978), "On the Time Inconsistency of Optimal Policy in a Monetary Economy", *Econometrica*, 46, 6.

CALVO, G. AND P. GUIDOTTI (1993), "On the Flexibility of Monetary Policy: The Case of the Optimal Inflation Tax", *Review of Economic Studies*, 60.

DRAZEN, A. AND V. GRILLI (1993), "The Benefits of Crises for Economic Reform", *American Economic Review*, Vol. 83, June.

EDIN, P. AND H. OLHSSON (1991), "Political Determinants of Budget Deficits: Coalition Effects vs. Minority Effects", *European Economic Review*, 35.

EICHENGREEN, B. (1992), "Should the Maastricht Treaty be Saved?", *Princeton Studies in International Finance*, No. 74.

EICHENGREEN, B. AND T. BAYOUMI (1994), "The Political Economy of Fiscal Restrictions: Implications for Europe from the United States", *European Economic Review*, 38.

EICHENGREEN, B., R. HAUSMANN AND C. PIRAS (1997), "Autonomia Administrativa de las Instituciones Gubernamentales", Regional Research Network, Inter-American Development Bank, Washington, D.C.

EICHENGREEN, B., R. HAUSMANN AND J. VON HAGEN (1996), "Reforming Fiscal Institutions in Latin America: the Case for a National Fiscal Council", manuscript, Office of the Chief Economist, Inter-American Development Bank, Washington, D.C.

FEREJOHN, J. AND K. KREHBIEL (1987), "The Budget Process and the Size of the Budget", *American Journal of Political Science*, 31.

GAVIN, M., R. HAUSMANN, R. PEROTTI AND E. TALVI (1996), "Managing Fiscal Policy in Latin America: Volatility, Procyclicality and Limited Creditworthiness", Inter-American Development Bank, *OCE Working Paper* No. 326.

GRILLI, V., D. MASCIANDARO AND G. TABELLINI (1991), "Institutions and Policies", *Economic Policy*, 6.

GUIDOTTI, P. AND C. VÉGH (1992), "Losing Credibility: The Stabilization Blues", *Working Paper* 92/73, International Monetary Fund, Washington D.C.

HALLERBERG, M. AND J. VON HAGEN (1997), "Electoral Institutions, Cabinet Negotiations, and Budget Deficits within the European Union", *CEPR Discussion Paper*, No. 1555.

HART, O. AND B. HOLMSTROM (1987), "The Theory of Contracts", in T. BEWLEY (ed.), *Advances in Economic Theory*, Fifth World Congress, Cambridge University Press, Cambridge.

HAUSMANN, R., A. POWELL AND R. RIGOBON (1993), "An Optimal Spending Rule Facing Oil Income Uncertainty", in E. ENGEL AND P. MELLER (eds.), *External Shocks and Stabilization Mechanisms*, IDB-Cieplan.

HAUSMANN, R. AND E. STEIN (1996), "Searching for the Right Budgetary Institutions for a Volatile Region", in R. HAUSMANN AND H. REISEN (eds.), *Securing Stability and Growth in Latin America*, OECD-IDB, Paris.

KYDLAND, F. AND E. PRESCOTT (1977), "Rules Rather than Discretion: The Inconsistency of Optimal Plans", *Journal of Political Economy*, 85,3.

LIJPHART, A. (1994), *Electoral Systems and Party Systems*, Oxford University Press, Oxford.

RODRIGUEZ, E. (1997), "El Ciclo Politico-Fiscal en Costa Rica", manuscript.

ROGOWSKI, R. (1987), "Trade and the Variety of Democratic Institutions", *International Organization*, 41, No. 2.

ROUBINI, N. (1991), "Economic and Political Determinants of Budget Deficits in Developing Countries", *Journal of International Money and Finance*, 10.

ROUBINI, N. AND J. SACHS (1989), "Political and Economic Determinants of the Budget Deficits in the Industrial Democracies", *European Economic Review*, 33.

SAINT-PAUL, G. (1994), "Monetary Policy in Economic Transition: Lessons from the French Post-War Experience", *European Economic Review*, 38.

TALVI, E. AND C. VÉGH, (1996), "Can Optimal Fiscal Policy be Procyclical?", manuscript, Office of the Chief Economist, Inter-American Development Bank and UCLA.

VON HAGEN, J. AND I. HARDEN (1995), "Budget Processes and Commitment to Fiscal Discipline", *European Economic Review*, 39.

Fiscal Performance in Latin America: What Needs to be Explained?

Michael Gavin and Ricardo Hausmann

Introduction

While democratic forms of decision making possess crucial advantages over the alternative — providing legitimacy, mechanisms for the revelation of the preferences of the citizenry, and ways to discipline unresponsive governments — it is also true that democratic decision making about public spending and taxation involves a process of collective choice that carries with it potential pitfalls. These do not pose insuperable problems — indeed, we shall document that in some key dimensions, fiscal outcomes have been improving dramatically as the region has become more democratic. But in the absence of appropriate institutional arrangements, the interplay of interests that determines fiscal outcomes in a democratic polity can lead to poor results.

The purpose of this volume is thus to contribute to our understanding of fiscal outcomes in Latin America, and in particular to how they have been influenced by the political and institutional arrangements that define the fiscal decision-making process in each of the varied democracies of the region. This requires first taking stock of fiscal policy making in the region. Towards that end, the stage is set for further discussion by laying out some stylised facts about fiscal outcomes in Latin America.

The objective is in part merely descriptive. But these descriptions also serve a diagnostic purpose, highlighting the special challenges for the management of fiscal policy that are posed by the structure of the Latin American public sector and the characteristics of the Latin American macroeconomic environment, and identifying areas where fiscal policy may not have met these challenges as effectively as might be feasible. Here the focus is on three main diagnostics:

i)   have Latin American governments exhibited a "deficit bias", thus leaving their economies with larger public debts than might be optimal?

ii) how well has fiscal policy been managed in a "cyclical" context? That is, has fiscal policy "leaned against the wind" of economic shocks and fluctuations in the way that theory suggests that it should, or has it instead amplified them?

iii) and, finally, have fiscal outcomes displayed an important tendency to be influenced by political pressures associated with elections?

We find that, while Latin America shares similar political institutions and decision making structures with the industrial economies, the economic context within which Latin American institutions much operate is very different, and is in fact substantially more demanding. A highly volatile macroeconomic environment generates large fluctuations in fiscal revenue, and frequently creates the need for very large fiscal adjustments, while relatively small budgets reduce the fiscal room for manoeuvre. We find, moreover, that the volatility of fiscal outcomes is more than just a passive response to macroeconomic shocks in Latin America, and in contrast to the industrial economies, fiscal outcomes have displayed an important "procyclicality", with public spending expanding in economic good times and collapsing in bad times, thus amplifying rather than absorbing shocks to the economy. Finally, and again in contrast with the industrial economies, we find evidence of a large electorally-motivated fiscal "cycle", suggesting that politically-motivated fluctuations in fiscal policy have been a problem in at least some countries.

After laying out these stylised facts on fiscal performance, we summarise some evidence on linkages between key institutional arrangements and fiscal outcomes. Here we focus on two factors, one related to the electoral system and the other to the arrangements that surround the budgetary decision making process. The concern with electoral systems arises because systems that result in the representation of large numbers of political parties in the legislature may increase co-ordination problems, thus providing the advantage of enhanced representation of various political interests at the potential cost of reduced decisiveness, with adverse consequences for fiscal outcomes. Our concern with budgetary institutions is motivated by the now substantial body of evidence that the rules under which budgets are formulated and moved through the political process can have important consequences for fiscal outcomes over the long term.

Previous research on the impact of electoral systems and budgetary institutions on fiscal outcomes has focused mainly on the problem of deficit bias[1]. We extend that evidence here, showing that political fragmentation is associated with larger fiscal deficits and higher public spending in Latin America. The evidence also suggests, consistent with previous research, that strong budgetary institutions are associated with greater fiscal discipline. However, we find that such budgetary institutions do not solve, and may indeed aggravate, key fiscal problems in Latin America, notably the problem of procyclical fiscal policy.

Thus, while Latin American democracies share similar political institutions with the industrial economies, these institutions operate in a very different and in many ways less forgiving context. This may give rise to problems in fiscal performance such as the ones that we identify here. But, as recent Latin American experience has shown us, these problems can be overcome with appropriate institutional adaptations to the more complex environment.

Size and Structure of the Latin American State

Governments are small. The first and perhaps most obvious difference between governments in Latin America and the industrial countries is their size. The public sector of the typical Latin American country spends roughly 25 per cent of GDP, approximately half of the almost 50 per cent of GDP spent by the typical industrial-country government.

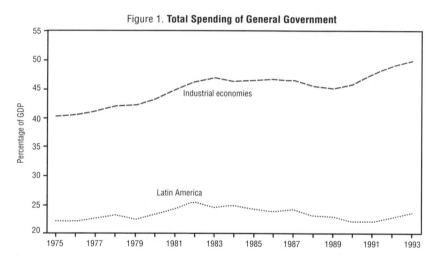

Figure 1. **Total Spending of General Government**

It is striking to note that, unlike in the industrial economies, Latin American governments have not grown, on average, since the 1980s. Indeed, despite some recovery in the mid-1990s, public spending in Latin America remains below the peak attained in the early 1980s, while public spending by the industrial economies has grown dramatically over the same period.

35

Even more dramatic has been the decline in spending by public enterprises (not included in the above figures) which, measured as a share of GDP, has fallen from a peak of roughly 20 per cent of GDP in 1981 to roughly 10 per cent of GDP in 1993, reflecting the privatisations and rationalisation of public enterprises throughout the region.

Public spending is very different. The structure of public spending in Latin America also differs in important ways. The most notable difference between Latin America and the industrial countries is in the size of spending on social security systems, where industrial-country spending of over 15 per cent of GDP dwarfs Latin America's average of 2.5 per cent of GDP.

Table 1. **Non-financial Public Sector Spending, 1990-95**

	Industrial economies	Latin America
(Percentage of GDP)		
Social security payments	16.4	2.5
Interest payments	3.6	3.8
Public investment	1.9	6.6
"Core" functions	24.2	15.2
Total	45.7	27.8
(Percentage of total spending)		
Social security payments	35.9	9.0
Interest payments	7.9	13.7
Public investment	4.2	23.7
"Core" functions	53.0	54.7

Source: Inter-American Development Bank (1997). For public enterprises only capital spending is included. Figures represent simple averages of individual country data.

This is mainly due to the fact that the region's population is still relatively young; less than 5 per cent of the Latin American population is over the age of 65, compared with nearly 15 per cent of the population in the industrial countries.

Latin American governments are, however, small in every dimension. Most notably, and despite the privatisations of the 1980s and 1990s, they typically spend much more on public investment — over 6 per cent of GDP compared with less than 2 per cent in the industrial economies.

Nor are all governments of the region equally small — there is enormous variation in the size of Latin American governments, especially among the smaller and poorer countries of the region. Public spending in Barbados amounts to 35 per cent of GDP, while spending in Bolivia, Trinidad and Tobago, Uruguay, Honduras, Jamaica, Brazil, and Venezuela has averaged 30 per cent of GDP or more during the 1990s.

At the other extreme, public-sector spending in Haiti and Guatemala amounts to only 12 per cent of GDP, while spending in the Dominican Republic, El Salvador, Paraguay and Peru has averaged well under 20 per cent of GDP.

Differences in government size are partly attributable to differences in per capita income — around the world, wealthier countries have tended to have large governments, and Latin America is no exception. The Latin American economies with the lowest per-capita income spent, on average, roughly 20 per cent of GDP, while the richest countries of the region spent an average of nearly 30 per cent of GDP.

However, income explains only part of the variation in government size in the region. As Figure 2 illustrates, while there is a tendency for governments to be larger in wealthier countries, a number of low-income economies, most notably Belize, Guyana, Nicaragua and Suriname, are much larger than might be expected on the basis of their relatively low income. By the same token there are other economies, notably the Bahamas and to a lesser extent Chile, where on the basis of their relatively high income levels, the public sector is substantially smaller than would be expected. We will explore the relationship between income and government size in more detail below, where we note that the relationship between income and government spending differs greatly for different kinds of government activity.

Figure 2. **Government Expenditures in Latin America (Consolidated public sector, in percentage of GDP); 1990-95**

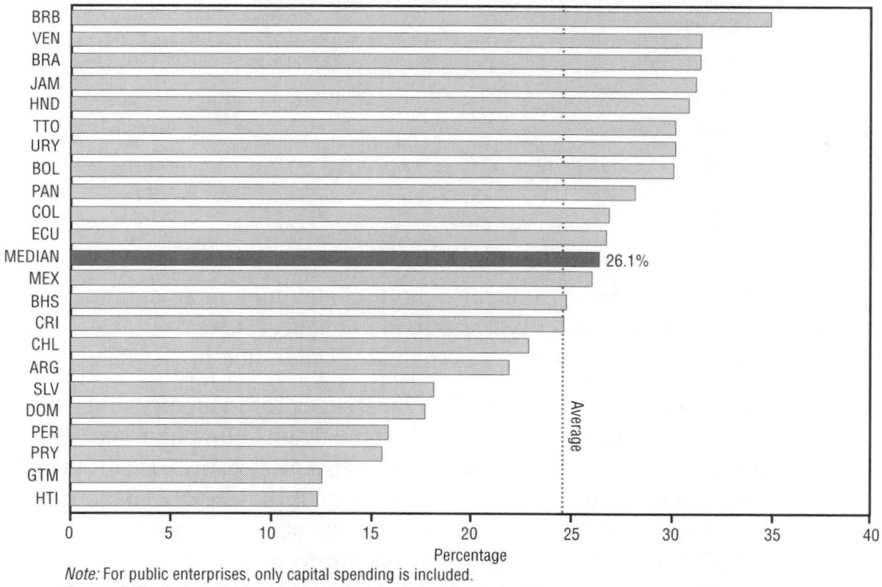

Note: For public enterprises, only capital spending is included.
Source: OCE calculations based on Recent Economic Developments, IMF.

Small governments reflect limited fiscal capacity. The small size of Latin American governments reflects the fact that governments of the region possess a much more limited capacity to raise revenue to finance public spending than do industrial-country governments. This limited fiscal capacity stems from large informal sectors that exist in much of the region and which largely escape direct taxation, and a more

37

limited bureaucratic capacity to collect taxes. As a result, to finance even the relatively small states that exist in the region, governments have had to impose relatively high rates of tax on those businesses and individuals that do pay taxes. In many cases, this has resulted in taxes comparable to those observed in the industrial economies.

This means that many governments of the region have relatively limited scope to increase revenue simply by adjusting tax rates upwards, which could prove both politically and economically counter productive. This point has important implications for the management of the large fiscal shocks that affect the region, as we discuss below.

Revenue structures pose challenges for fiscal management. Several features of Latin American revenue structures increase the vulnerability of the public finances to macroeconomic shocks. First, governments in Latin America are substantially more reliant upon non-tax revenue sources than are industrial-country governments, reflecting the importance of natural-resource rents and income from state owned enterprises in total revenue.

Table 2. **The Structure of Fiscal Revenue in Latin America**
(Consolidated central government, 1990-94)

	Industrial economies	Latin America
(Percentage of total revenue)		
Nontax revenue	8.1	15.9
Tax revenue	90.2	71.8
Income tax	35.0	20.4
Social Security contributions	32.2	23.5
Indirect taxes	20.4	26.3
Trade taxes	1.0	5.2

Source: Gavin, Hausmann, Perotti and Talvi (1996). All figures refer to population-weighted averages of country data.

Latin American governments are also more reliant upon indirect taxes, and most notably trade taxes, and substantially less reliant upon direct taxes — taxes on income and contributions to the social security system — than are the industrial economies.

This revenue structure poses important challenges for the management of fiscal policy in Latin America. As we shall describe in more detail below, non-tax and indirect taxes are particularly volatile revenue sources in Latin America, because the underlying bases are relatively volatile. The structure of fiscal revenue thus exposes national budgets to larger shocks than they would face with a revenue structure more like that of the industrial economies, requiring the political system to cope with the need to bring about frequent, large fiscal adjustments. What follows describes some of the factors surrounding the democratic decision-making process that may impede timely fiscal adjustment, and institutional structures that can improve the capacity for democratic decision making to cope with the required fiscal adjustments.

Debt and Deficits

Debt and deficits have not been particularly big in Latin America... or have they? It is commonly believed that fiscal deficits and resulting public debts have been much larger in Latin America than they have been in the OECD countries. There are indeed some economies of the region in which this is true, most notably in Guyana and Nicaragua where during the 1990s public debt averaged five and seven times the gross domestic product respectively. Setting aside these unrepresentative cases, however, fiscal deficits and the resulting public debts have been quite similar in Latin America and the industrial economies, if measured as a share of GDP. Over the 1970-94 period, central government deficits have averaged about 3.8 per cent of GDP in the OECD and 3.9 per cent of GDP in Latin America.

Figure 3. **Fiscal Deficit**

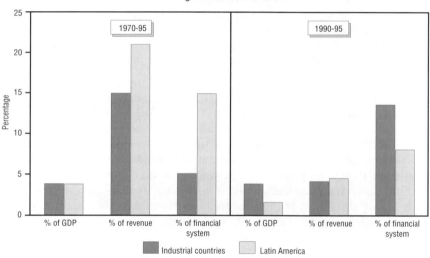

However, this average masks the profound fiscal consolidation that has taken place during the past decade. Indeed, during the 1990s fiscal deficits have been much lower, averaging only about 2 per cent of GDP, about half the size of those recorded in the industrial economies.

The stock of public debt, of course, is the result of the deficits that are recorded over the long term, and the typical Latin American government possess a public debt of around 56 per cent of GDP, somewhat below the industrial-economy average of 68 per cent. Despite this, most Latin American governments are widely perceived to be less creditworthy than are most industrial-economy governments, as evidenced by the generally lower bond ratings and higher interest rates demanded by investors to hold Latin American debt. Guatemalan government bonds, for example, are widely perceived as a more risky investment than Italian bonds even though Guatemala's public debt, at about 24 per cent of GDP during the 1990s, is much lower than in Italy, where the public debt is well over 100 per cent of GDP.

One reason for this apparent anomaly is that GDP provides an incomplete and potentially misleading ruler with which to measure the macroeconomic costs of fiscal deficits and debt. The overall size of the economy is a sensible metric when the objective is to measure how large a portion of national income is being allocated by the state. However, it is less adequate when the question is whether a given fiscal position is sustainable or not. Here a more appropriate metric may be a government's tax capacity. By this metric, Latin America's fiscal performance during the 1990s has roughly matched that of the industrial countries, but performance over the past 25 years appears somewhat less impressive. Latin American governments possess a much more limited tax capacity than do industrial country governments, and as a share of government revenue fiscal deficits have been significantly higher than in the industrial economies. Similarly, the public debt of Latin American governments now averages about 2.5 years of tax revenue, compared with an average of 1.6 years in the industrial economies.

Another important consideration is the depth of the domestic financial system that may be called upon to finance a fiscal deficit. A fiscal deficit may generate relatively little economic and financial disruption if it is being absorbed by a very deep financial market, such as the ones that are typical of industrial economies. If, however, domestic financial markets are shallow, a deficit of the same size — measured as a share of GDP — may be highly disruptive. Financial markets are still relatively shallow in Latin America, though they have been expanding in the 1990s. Nevertheless, even by this metric, Latin American deficits have been smaller than those of the industrial countries during the 1990s, but if measured relative to the size of domestic financial markets, fiscal deficits have been approximately three times as large during the past 25 years as they were in the industrial economies.

In short, by all of these metrics the deficits of the 1990s have been small by comparison with the industrial economies. During the past 25 years deficits have of course been larger. Even the deficits and the public debts that they have left behind have not been particularly large by the standards of the industrial economies, if measured as a share of GDP. However, if measured as a share of fiscal revenue or the size of the domestic financial system, they have been from two to three times as large as in the industrial economies; while deficits have been small in the 1990s the existing public debt, the legacy of many years of fiscal outcomes, remains substantially larger than that of the industrial economies if measured relative to the government's tax capacity or the size of the domestic financial system.

Have fiscal deficits been excessive? We see that, according to some relevant measures, Latin America's fiscal deficits and public debt have tended to be higher than those observed in the developing economies, and in some countries debt and deficits are substantially higher than those observed in the industrial economies. Is this healthy, or does it mean that fiscal deficits have been excessive? Has the political system in countries of the region displayed a significant bias toward deficit finance, to the detriment of economic progress in the region?

No matter which metric is used, simple comparisons with the industrial countries can shed limited light at best on this question. A judgement ultimately rests upon an answer to the question of whether the deficits have generated costs that exceed the benefits that may have been associated with the deficit spending. A complete assessment is beyond the scope of this chapter, but enough evidence has been accumulated to suggest that the costs have been substantial. Large and volatile fiscal deficits have been implicated in the region's history of economic and financial instability, including highly disruptive collapses of the exchange rate regime, and the fact that larger fiscal deficits appear to have complicated the cyclical management of fiscal policy and contributed to the destabilizing, "procyclical" fiscal adjustments that have been typical of the region. These costs suggest that the fiscal deficits that have characterised the region during much of its recent history have been regrettable, that the much more modest deficits that most countries have run during the 1990s are a positive thing, and that countries would have been better off on balance if the political system had run similarly modest deficits during previous decades.

Fiscal Outcomes have been Volatile in Latin America

We have examined the average behaviour of fiscal outcomes, but an equally important aspect of fiscal policy lies in the variability of outcomes, including in particular the question of how fiscal policy has reacted to shocks and fluctuations in the macroeconomic environment — has it been a stabilizing or a destabilizing influence? In this section we explore these issues. We find that fiscal outcomes have been highly volatile. This volatility is related to the volatility of the underlying macroeconomic environment, but this is only part of the story. In Latin America, the volatility of fiscal outcomes does not reflect a passive response to a volatile economic environment, but rather a tendency for fiscal policy to amplify shocks in a "procyclical" manner.

Fiscal balances have been highly volatile in Latin America. We have seen that assessments of the size of Latin America's debt and deficits depend upon some thinking about the appropriate metric to use in comparisons with industrial economic experience. In other equally important dimensions no such subtle judgements are required. By any metric, fiscal outcomes in Latin America have been very volatile, fluctuating from year to year to a much greater extent than has been typical of the industrial economies (Table 3).

For example: if the fiscal balance is measured as a share of GDP, the typical change in the balance from one year to the next has been about 3 per cent of GDP in Latin America, about twice the typical change of 1.5 per cent in the industrial economies[2]. If the primary surplus, which excludes interest payments, is compared the difference is even more pronounced; the typical change in this variable is 3.4 per cent of GDP in Latin America, compared with 1.4 per cent in the industrial economies.

Table 3. **Macroeconomic Volatility in Latin America**
(Standard deviation of percentage change)

	1970-92		1991-95	
	Latin America	Industrial economies	Latin America	Industrial economies
Real GDP	4.7	2.2	3.2	2.1
Real private consumption	5.6	2.1	5.1	
Terms of trade	15.1	8.9	4.9	1.3
Real exchange rate	13.4	4.8	12.7	4.0

Source: Inter-American Development Bank (1995). All data are population-weighted averages of the underlying country volatilities.

If measured as a share of fiscal revenue or as a share of the financial system these fiscal "shocks" are even larger. The typical change in the fiscal balance amounts to roughly 20 per cent of fiscal revenue in Latin America, four times that observed in the industrial economies. If measured as a share of the domestic financial system that must absorb fiscal shocks, the volatility of fiscal outcomes has been roughly ten times as large in Latin America as it has been in the industrial economies.

Fiscal volatility is associated with high volatility in the underlying economy. The instability of fiscal outcomes in Latin America is, to some extent, a reflection of the volatility of the underlying macroeconomic environment, which creates major instability in the tax base and, thus, in fiscal revenue. In Latin America, as in the industrial economies, tax revenue depends upon real output and income, which determine the base for income taxes and payroll taxes, and upon private spending, which determines the base for expenditure taxes such as value-added or sales taxes and import duties. As we have noted, Latin American budgets are more sensitive to fluctuations in private spending, because they rely more heavily upon indirect, expenditure-based taxes than do the industrial economies. The tax base is also affected by changes in the terms of trade; an improvement in the terms of trade will increase non-tax revenue directly if natural resource exports are in the public sector, and will affect income taxes indirectly if the higher income from higher export prices accrues to the private sector.

Public spending is also influenced by fluctuations in the macroeconomy. For example, fluctuations in the real exchange rates or world interest rates have created instability in the real value of international debt service. The budget is thus in many cases also affected by the real exchange rate, although the sign of the effect depends upon the structure of the public sector's income and spending commitments[3].

The economies of Latin America have been substantially more volatile than those of the industrial economies in all of these dimensions. The volatility of real output growth and changes in the terms of trade has been roughly twice as high as in the industrial economies, and the volatility of private consumption growth and the real exchange rate has been nearly three times as high. Note that in Latin America, unlike in the industrial economies, private consumption has been even more volatile than has been real GDP growth. This is significant, because it means that the expenditure-based taxes upon which Latin American governments rely heavily are particularly unstable sources of revenue.

How much of the volatility in the fiscal balance is attributable to the volatility of the underlying macroeconomic environment? After all, if Latin American deficits were volatile merely because they respond passively to fluctuations in output and other determinants of tax revenue, there may be little to worry about. However, macroeconomic fluctuations are not the primary reason for the higher volatility of Latin American fiscal deficits. To show this, we constructed a measure of fiscal "shocks", which is the standard deviation of changes in the primary deficit after accounting for the typical impact on the deficit of fluctuations in real output, the terms of trade, private consumption, and the lagged deficit. As Table 4 indicates, these factors explain only a small fraction of the volatility of the primary deficit in Latin America, and the remaining volatility is still three times as large in Latin America as in the OECD, when measured relative to GDP.

Government revenue and spending are even more volatile than deficits. Table 4 also documents the volatility of revenue and spending in Latin America. The volatility of fiscal revenue, measured as the standard deviation of percentage changes in inflation-adjusted revenue, is three times as high as in the industrial economies. This higher volatility is due in part to the region's higher reliance upon volatile non-tax revenue and indirect taxes, which are substantially more volatile than direct taxes in both regions. But it also reflects a higher volatility of every major form of revenue, the consequence of higher volatility in the underlying macroeconomy, documented above.

The volatility of Latin American fiscal expenditure is also striking. Capital spending is twice as volatile as in the OECD, wage payments are four times, non-wage purchases of goods and services are six times, and transfer payments are nearly nine times . How much is too much volatility in public spending? There are no precise answers, but the available rough guidelines suggest that the very high volatility that we observe in Latin American public spending is cause for concern. For example, under plausible conditions one should expect current public expenditure to adjust in line with permanent national income, implying a volatility not much greater than that of permanent income[4]. And indeed, in the OECD the volatility of current fiscal expenditure is not much higher than that of GDP growth. The 15 percentage point standard deviation in Latin America's current expenditure — roughly four times the volatility of GDP growth — would seem excessive by this standard. As noted above, it also seems plausible that these extreme fluctuations in public spending have an adverse effect on the efficiency of public spending programmes.

These costs might be worth paying if the fluctuations in public spending represented counter-cyclical movements in the budget that stabilize the economy, and therefore reduce the macroeconomic costs of shocks to the economy as a whole. However, the evidence suggests that the opposite is true; public spending in Latin America has in fact been highly procyclical, thus amplifying rather than absorbing shocks. To document this fact and draw out some implications, we now turn to some evidence on the cyclical properties of fiscal policy in Latin America.

Table 4. **Volatility of Various Fiscal Aggregates, 1970-94**
(Standard deviation of inflation-adjustment growth rates)

	Industrial economies	Latin America
Measures of the fiscal balance (per cent of GDP)		
Change in total surplus	1.5	3.0
Change in primary surplus	1.4	3.6
Fiscal "shock"	1.0	3.3
Total revenue	5.2	15.2
Nontax revenue	19.6	40.6
Tax revenue	5.0	16.7
Income tax	7.4	18.2
Social security	5.6	18.5
Indirect taxes	9.9	24.8
Trade taxes	30.1	32.4
Total expenditure	3.9	15.7
Capital expenditure	17.6	34.6
Current expenditure	3.8	15.3
Wage payments	4.5	17.0
Other purchases	7.4	45.4
Transfer payments	5.4	46.9
Interest payments	11.9	30.8

Source: Gavin, Hausmann, Perotti and Talvi (1996). Variables are standard deviations of percentage changes in the real value of the indicated variable. All variables are deflated using the GDP deflator. All figures refer to population-weighted averages of underlying country data. In some countries data are missing for some years, in which case all available observations in the relevant time period were used.

Procyclical Fiscal Policy

While different schools of economic thought diverge in many of their policy prescriptions, there is general agreement that fiscal policy should respond to transitory macroeconomic fluctuations in a counter-cyclical manner, running fiscal surpluses in good times and deficits in bad. Neoclassical approaches emphasize that if fluctuations in the budget are due to factors that are at least partly transitory, such as a change in the terms of trade that is expected to be reversed or a transitory recession, it is efficient to maintain rough stability in tax rates and spending programmes, thus generating fiscal surpluses when the economy is booming and deficits when it is in recession. When Keynesian considerations are introduced, the case for a "counter-cyclical" fiscal policy like this is strengthened. Fiscal authorities would want to cut taxes or increase spending during bad times, to reduce the magnitude and duration of the associated recession, thus generating an even larger fiscal deficit during bad times than would occur if fiscal authorities held tax rates and spending levels constant. The same logic justifies a fiscal contraction, and thus even larger surpluses in good economic times.

An important and highly relevant caveat applies to this discussion. As has recently been emphasized by Giavazzi and Pagano (1990), changes in fiscal policy may have opposite effects if the initial fiscal position is very tenuous. For example, if a government is nearly insolvent, a fiscal expansion may create such fear of a fiscal crisis that it will lead to a collapse of confidence, thus tending to reduce rather than expand domestic demand. Perotti (1996) presented evidence that suggests that this is a real possibility. Giavazzi and Pagano (1990) presented theoretical and empirical evidence that the converse can also happen, that fiscal contraction can have expansionary effects on the economy if it takes place when the government's fiscal position is very tenuous, and thus significantly reduces the probability of a fiscal crisis.

Thus, a "counter-cyclical" fiscal policy response to adverse shocks or a cyclical downturn of the economy applies mainly to governments for which there are no important concerns about solvency; a barely-solvent government may find it very difficult or impossible to implement such policy[5]. Such a government may instead find that it has little choice but to respond to adverse shocks with a fiscal contraction, hoping to restore confidence in the medium-term viability of the public finances, and keep the demand for financing consistent with the more restricted supply. As we shall discuss in more detail below, this appears to be an important part of the Latin American fiscal story, and the relevant question is how Latin American governments can manage fiscal policy to make a more stabilizing response to adverse shocks or cyclical downturns possible.

Fiscal balances display a procyclical pattern in Latin America. The *a priori* case for a counter-cyclical fiscal policy is thus well established. Unless fiscal policy has been so badly managed that doubts about the government's solvency preclude its being used as a response, an appropriate fiscal policy would display fiscal surpluses during good times and deficits during bad. This is more or less what we observe in the industrial economies, where the fiscal balance tends to move into deficit when output growth slows, and toward surplus when the economy grows more rapidly than normal. This is illustrated in Table 5, which provides estimates of the typical short-run impact on the fiscal surplus of higher real GDP growth in Latin America and the industrial economies.

The estimates[6] suggest that a one percentage point increase in GDP growth is associated with a movement toward fiscal balance of about 0.37 percentage points of GDP, indicating that in the industrial economies, fiscal policy has tended to be counter cyclical in the sense described above. Latin America, however, displays little or none of this counter-cyclicality — the fiscal balance is almost totally uncorrelated with cyclical fluctuations in output. As we shall see below, this reflects the fact that historically both revenue and spending tend to decline dramatically when the economy slows down, and to rise together when the economy recovers.

This is not the end of the story, for the fiscal response to economic fluctuations depends upon the nature of the shock. Table 5 also compares the fiscal response to cyclical fluctuations during "good times" and "bad times", where "bad times" are, roughly speaking, periods of recession, and good times are other times[7]. The industrial countries display a very interesting pattern. In periods of high growth the fiscal balance is only moderately sensitive to output shocks — increasing by about 25 cents for every dollar's worth of higher output. During bad times, however, the fiscal balance is highly sensitive to output fluctuations. During bad times, for example, the fiscal balance would deteriorate by roughly 90 cents if GDP were to decline by an additional dollar. This pattern is consistent with a world in which recessions are politically and/or economically more costly than economic booms, and tend therefore to elicit a much larger, counter-cyclical response.

Table 5. **Cyclical Properties of the Fiscal Balance**
(General government, share of GDP)

	Industrial economies	Latin America	Industrial economies	Latin America
Real GDP growth	0.368	0.042	–	–
	(10.5)	(1.10)		
Real GDP growth: good times	–	–	0.258	0.083
			(6.29)	(1.42)
Real GDP growth: bad times	–	–	0.944	-0.019
			(7.42)	(-0.25)
Per cent change in terms of trade	0.034	0.015	0.027	0.015
	(1.92)	(1.20)	(1.93)	(1.23)
Lagged fiscal balance	-0.174	-0.292	-0.173	-0.295
	(-5.64)	(-5.43)	(-5.80)	(-5.49)
Degrees of freedom	314	257	313	256
Adjusted R^2	0.286	0.084	0.331	0.084

Source: Gavin and Perotti (1997). Dependent variable is the change in the overall fiscal surplus, measured as a share of GDP. T-statistics are given in parentheses. Country dummy variables are included in all regressions and the sample period is 1970-94.

Almost precisely the opposite pattern is observed in Latin America. In good times the response of the fiscal balance to cyclical fluctuations is small though positive, but in bad times there is a weak tendency for the fiscal surplus to move in the "wrong" direction, with recessions' being associated with a decline in the fiscal deficit, rather than the reverse.

The pattern is even more striking if we confine our attention to deep recessions[8]. Figure 4 compares the cumulative change in real GDP with the cumulative change in the fiscal surplus during deep recessions. In the industrial economies we see a very consistent relationship: large recessions are associated with large movements in the fiscal balance toward deficit. No such pattern is observed in Latin America where, indeed, the average change in the fiscal balance in the 18 deep recessions illustrated in Figure 4 is positive, the "wrong" sign. This must have involved an enormous fiscal contraction, for the recession would have exerted a powerful tendency for the budget to move towards deficit if the fiscal policy stance had remained neutral.

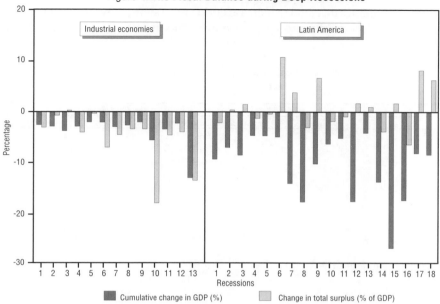

Figure 4. **The Fiscal Balance during Deep Recessions**

These episodes and the statistical evidence described above are all drawn from the 1970-94 period, most of which predates the fiscal consolidation of the 1990s. However, the experiences of Argentina and Mexico during the 1995 crisis provide cautionary evidence that the problem of procyclical fiscal adjustment remains relevant. Both countries fell into very deep recessions during 1995, during which a stabilizing fiscal policy would have been very valuable. However, policymakers in both countries felt obliged to respond to the crisis with major fiscal contractions including important reductions in public spending and increases in tax rates, and during the very sharp recovery that ensued, political debate soon turned towards tax cuts. The fiscal contraction was almost certainly the best available response to the crisis given the precariousness of the countries' access to credit markets. However, if not dealt with, that precariousness may continue to generate costly, destabilizing responses to economic shocks in the future.

Both revenue and spending are highly procyclical in Latin America. The failure of Latin American fiscal surpluses to move in a stabilizing manner is not due to a smaller sensitivity of tax revenue to the business cycle; indeed, tax revenue is even more sensitive to economic activity in Latin America than in the OECD countries, and if spending behaved similarly, Latin American budgets would be even more stabilizing. The key difference between Latin American and industrial-country fiscal outcomes lies in the cyclical behavior of public spending. In the industrial economies, total public spending is essentially uncorrelated with short-term fluctuations in output.

Transfer payments, which include spending on important income- and unemployment-sensitive programmes that tend to increase during recessions, move in a counter-cyclical fashion, and offset mildly pro-cyclical movements in other components of public spending.

Table 6. **Cyclical Properties of Revenue and Spending**
(General government, growth rates of spending and revenue)

	Real GDP growth	
	Industrial economies	Latin America
Total revenue	0.93	1.36
	(11.85)	(8.92)
Nontax revenue	0.29	0.88
	(1.01)	(2.21)
Tax revenue	0.96	1.51
	(9.44)	(9.44)
Total expenditure	0.09	1.09
	(1.23)	(6.85)
Capital expenditure	0.21	2.32
	(0.40)	(6.62)
Government consumption	0.30	1.24
	(4.24)	(7.98)
Subsidies and transfers	-0.24	0.58
	(-2.33)	(1.73)

Source: Gavin and Perotti (1997). The table reports the elasticity of the indicated budgetary aggregate with respect to GDP growth in a regression that also includes the growth rate of the terms of trade, the lagged fiscal balance, and country dummy variables. T-statistics are given in parentheses.

In Latin America, however, all components of the budget move in a pro-cyclical fashion, and sometimes dramatically so. A one percentage point increase in real GDP is, for example, associated with an increase in real public capital spending of over 2 percentage points, and in government consumption of over 1 percentage point.

The inflation tax reinforces fiscal procyclicality in Latin America. In the industrial economies inflation is procyclical, in the sense that it tends to increase during periods of economic boom and decline in periods of recession. In Latin America, however, the opposite is observed; inflation tends to be higher during bad economic times and lower when the economy is buoyant. In Latin America, then, the inflation tax tends to increase when times are bad and decline when they are good, reinforcing the procyclicality of fiscal policy. Unlike in the industrial economies, inflation in Latin America also tends to be higher when the previous year's fiscal deficit was higher[9].

These patterns suggest that inflation has acted much more like an instrument of fiscal policy in Latin America than has been the case in the industrial economies. This may be, but is not necessarily the result of a conscious choice by the policy makers to exploit inflationary finance when fiscal imbalances become very large. One scenario is that when the private sector becomes convinced that the political system will be unable to address rapidly a budgetary shortfall created by bad economic news, a loss

48

of confidence generates a run on the domestic currency, and the resulting depreciation generates a burst of inflation. This may address the fiscal shortfall, at least temporarily and partially, because the inflationary surprise will tend to erode the real value of non-indexed spending commitments[10]. The end result is that the inflation tax reinforces the procyclicality of the budget, rising when the economy moves into recession and declining in good times, thus tending to amplify economic fluctuations.

The cyclical management of fiscal policy varies greatly among economies of the region. Not all countries of the region display the same degree of procyclicality. If we measure the procyclicality of fiscal policy as the correlation between cyclical movements in government consumption and in real output, the Dominican Republic, Ecuador, Barbados, Bolivia, Argentina and Colombia display relatively low degree of procyclicality, roughly comparable to that observed in Germany, Italy and Japan

In Costa Rica, Mexico, Peru and Venezuela, on the other hand, the correlation between cyclical movements in government consumption and real output are roughly 0.8 or more, signifying a very tight relationship between economic fluctuations and government consumption (Figure 5).

Figure 5. **Procyclicality of Government Consumption (1970-95)**

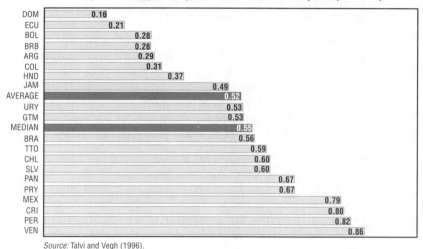

Source: Talvi and Vegh (1996).

Volatility and Procyclicality are Closely Related

Figure 6 suggests that fiscal procyclicality is associated with macroeconomic volatility, where volatility is measured as the degree of the standard deviation of real output growth. This statistical association is partly due to the fact that the large industrial economies are relatively stable and also tend to determine their fiscal policy in a relatively counter-cyclical manner.

Figure 6. **Volatility of Output and Procyclicality of Government Consumption**

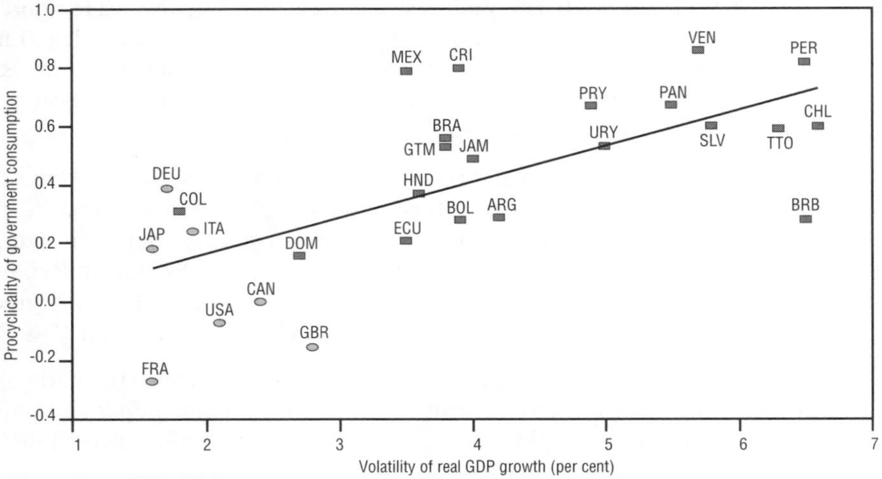

Source: Talvi and Vegh.

However, it is also true that the three Latin American economies with the lowest macroeconomic volatility, Colombia, the Dominican Republic and Ecuador, display much less procyclicality than do other countries of the region.

There are at least two plausible explanations for this statistical association. One explanation is that macroeconomic volatility is higher where fiscal policy is more procyclical because the procyclicality tends to amplify economic fluctuations, generating higher volatility. This is probably part of the story, but an equally plausible (and potentially complementary) explanation is that a highly unstable macroeconomic environment makes it difficult to manage a counter-cylical fiscal policy. We explore the impact of institutional arrangements on fiscal procyclicality below.

Fiscal volatility and procyclicality have been disruptive. The volatility and procyclicality of fiscal policy in Latin America have been costly. Not only has the "stop and go" nature of public spending almost certainly generated inefficiencies in the provision of public services, it has also contributed to macroeconomic volatility more generally. The contribution of fiscal volatility to the volatility of real output and the real exchange rate was documented in Inter-American Development Bank (1995), which also presented evidence that this macroeconomic volatility has lowered economic growth in Latin America by as much as a full per percentage point per year, has reduced investment, has undermined educational attainment, has worsened the distribution of income, and has contributed to higher poverty in the region. There is also a strong link between fiscal volatility and monetary and financial instability. The Inter-American Development Bank (1995) shows that fiscal volatility is associated with more unstable monetary outcomes, which undermines the domestic financial system. Gavin and Perotti (forthcoming) show that fiscal booms are strongly associated with the abandoning of fixed exchange rate regimes in Latin America, and that these changes in policy have been highly disruptive for the economy.

50

Why is Latin American fiscal policy pro-cylical? As we have noted, the destabilizing, procyclical nature of fiscal policy in Latin America is most pronounced in "bad times", when fiscal policy is most counter cyclical in the industrial economies. There is good reason to believe that this procyclicality has to do with a loss of access to non-inflationary sources of finance during bad economic times. This helps to explain why inflation tends to increase during bad times; if we view inflation as a fiscal resource of last resort, then sudden bursts of inflation offer support for the idea that alternative financing sources have become more scarce. It is also consistent with the evidence that Latin American governments' recourse to IMF credit and "extraordinary" sources of international financing tends to increase during bad economic times[11].

All of this suggests that the procyclical behavior of fiscal policy during bad times is the best response available to the authorities, given the somewhat precarious nature of their access to non-inflationary sources of finance. This suggests, in turn, that improving the fiscal response to bad times cannot be achieved simply by deciding to relax fiscal policy during such periods — as we have seen, this could promote a collapse of confidence in the viability of the public finances and an even larger crisis. Instead, emphasis has to be placed on managing fiscal policy during the "good times", ensuring that the fiscal position is sufficiently solid that the fiscal implications of an adverse shock or economic downturn will not generate fears about the viability of the public finances, thus ensuring that the financing required to implement a more stabilizing, counter-cyclical response to the "bad times" will be available.

This idea that a more stabilizing response to bad times can be achieved by maintaining a more solid fiscal position during good times is supported by the evidence for Latin America. Gavin and Perotti (1997) show that Latin American countries that enter period with a strong fiscal position have tended to display a substantially lower degree of fiscal procyclicality, as measured by the response of the fiscal balance to changes in real economic activity, than do countries in the region that enter the period with large fiscal deficits[12]. One interpretation of this finding is that countries that enter a period with a fiscal position strong enough to weather an adverse shock without falling into a potentially unmanageable fiscal deficit do not suffer the loss of confidence that would otherwise enforce a procyclical adjustment to adverse shocks, and are therefore able to manage a more stabilizing fiscal response to economic downturns.

The question then becomes, why has it proven so difficult to achieve the required management of fiscal policies during good times? This would require that governments save a large portion of the temporarily high revenue that they receive, thus running large fiscal surpluses when times are good. It may be much harder for Latin American governments to do this precisely because the economic booms and fiscal shocks are so large; it is very difficult to "hide" very large fiscal surpluses from participants in the fiscal decision-making process, and it may be individually rational for all participants to spend a transitory boom in fiscal revenue, even though everyone would be better off if there were some way to commit all participants to a co-operative strategy that enforced more saving of the boom income[13]. The collective nature of decision making about fiscal policy thus tends to promote an overspending of income during economic booms, which is procyclical in itself and also sets up the economy for an even more procyclical reaction to economic downturns.

In a highly volatile economic environment, there is thus a potential vicious circle which is related to the political "distortions" that are discussed in more detail below. Countries may be forced into procyclical fiscal adjustments during bad times because they lose access to financial markets. This loss of market access occurs because the very large fiscal shocks raise doubts about the political feasibility of the required adjustment. The resulting procyclical fiscal response exacerbates the problem of macroeconomic volatility. This vicious circle could be broken if the government could find a way to commit itself to saving enough during good times to ensure a viable fiscal position even after a large adverse fiscal shock, but for reasons that are discussed in more detail below, it has generally proven as difficult in Latin American democracies as it been in the industrial economies to maintain large fiscal surpluses during good times. The difference is that the costs of this failure are much higher in the volatile Latin American environment.

This makes the management of fiscal policy very challenging in Latin America, substantially more so than in the industrial economies. It requires much larger and more costly adjustments, and the tackling of a more complex problem of cyclical management, all of which is must be undertaken through a democratic decision-making process. The challenge, discussed in more detail below, is to organise that process so that the democratic process can respond more effectively to the special challenges that face the region.

Electoral Budget Cycles

Nowhere is the potential interaction between democratic politics and fiscal outcomes intuitively easier to grasp than around the time of elections, when governments are often believed to relax fiscal policy with the aim of pleasing — or at least trying to avoid alienating — important constituencies in the run-up to an election. Of course, tax cuts or extra spending in the pre-election period will have to be covered, with interest, by tax increases or spending cuts in the post-election period, and if they are large enough they may even destabilize the economy. The strategy may nevertheless be attractive to a government, because the potential macroeconomic costs will generally be borne, and the required fiscal correction will generally take place, after the election, by which time they may, after all, be some other government's problem.

Figure 7 illustrates the typical evolution of Latin American budgets around the time of an election[14]. During election years spending tends to be higher than usual and fiscal revenue lower, with the result that the deficit is typically about 1.3 percentage points larger than during non-election years. In the year after the election, public spending goes back to normal, and revenue rises, and the fiscal balance tends to be roughly 1.3 percentage points above normal, implying an apparently election-related swing in the fiscal balance of more than 2 percentage points of GDP.

Figure 7. **Fiscal Outcomes and Elections — Latin America, 1980-96**

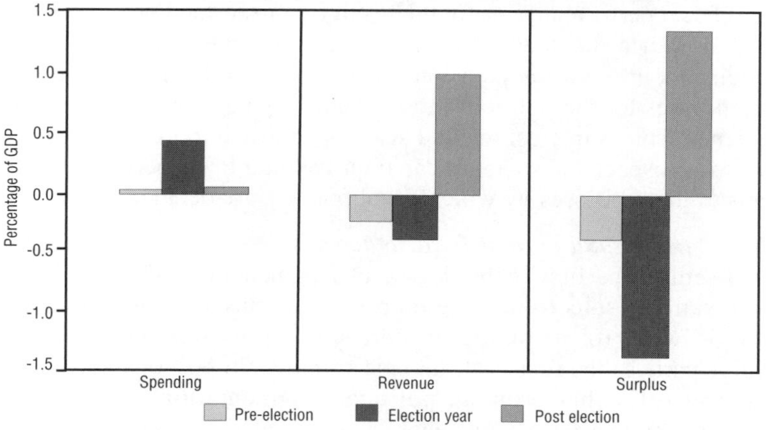

Pre-election　Election year　Post election

If it exists at all, this fiscal response to elections is much more subtle in the industrial-economies; there appears to be no systematic relationship between elections and fiscal outcomes in the industrial-country data. This suggests that the strategic use of fiscal policy to enhance electoral prospects of the governing party is more pervasive in Latin America than in the industrial economies.

Why might this be true? One possibility is suggested by evidence that the depth of the "electoral budget cycle" in Latin American countries is correlated with the volatility of the underlying macroeconomic environment[15]. This correlation has two plausible explanations. One is that those countries whose political systems have managed to constrain the fiscal response to elections have avoided the destabilizing consequences of the fiscal response, and for that reason possess more stable economies. Another, potentially complementary explanation is that in countries with substantial macroeconomic volatility, and therefore large shocks to the budget, it may be easier to indulge in election year fiscal expansions, which are less visible amidst the noise created by the economic environment, and therefore less exposed to the harsh light of scrutiny by the public and opposition politicians.

The Role of Institutional Arrangements

To summarise, we have found that over the past decades, fiscal outcomes in Latin America have been characterised by an important deficit bias, procyclical and thus destabilizing reactions to economic fluctuations, and a pronounced fiscal cycle associated with elections. From the mid-1980s as the region has become more democratic it has made remarkable progress in reducing fiscal deficits, but the problems of procyclicality and electoral fiscal cycles have not been eliminated.

What are the underlying causes of these unresolved problems? Systematically sub-optimal fiscal performance is not the result of uninformed or irrational individual behaviour, but, rather, the undesired consequence of strategic interactions among the many participants in the fiscal decision making process. If this is so, then countries with different rules for the political and budgetary "game" ought to display different fiscal outcomes. This is interesting, and also potentially important for policy, because it holds out the prospect that societies can improve their fiscal performance by making adjustments to the processes by which fiscal policies are decided.

Political fragmentation and fiscal outcomes. We focus on two aspects of the institutional setup. The first is the degree of fragmentation of the political system. This fragmentation results from electoral rules that translate votes into congressional representation with, for example, proportional-representation systems generally yielding more parties than first-past-the-post systems. Proportional representation and other electoral rules that promote political fragmentation are not accidents of history, they arise from a desire to increase the representativeness of the political system, by making space in the legislature for smaller parties that represent smaller constituencies that might be under-represented in a first-past-the-post system.

However, this representativeness may come at a cost. A political system with lots of parties increases the likelihood of minority governments and the need for coalition governments. And with many parties, each representing a small and particular constituency, individual parties may be less likely to internalise the social cost of a common resource like fiscal revenue, and may be tempted to ask for spending that they like, with the costs to be borne by taxpayers as a whole. This may promote excessive public spending, and deficit bias, since the party's constituency will only pay for a small fraction of the additional debt service. Also when fiscal adjustment is required, there may be increased temptation to delay adjustment in the hope that some other interest group will be held responsible for the effects after a change in government.

In short, co-ordination problems in the fiscal decision making process may be aggravated by high degrees of political fragmentation. Such systems may also be characterised by increased political turnover. This may aggravate credibility problems that arise because current governments cannot commit future governments to any course of action. This may contribute to the problem of procyclicality. For example, a government may wish to borrow in bad times and repay the debt in good times in order to smooth economic fluctuations and tax rates. However, if the government's commitment to pay later is in doubt, the market may not be willing to finance the deficit, and the government may be forced to cut spending and raise taxes in bad times, as has been typical of Latin America[16].

The measure of political fragmentation that we use is "district magnitude", which measures the average number of representatives elected per district in each of 26 Latin American and 15 European countries. In a pure first-past-the-post system this would, of course, be equal to one, while it may be a very large number in a system of proportional representation. This variable is positively related to the number of parties represented in the legislature, and negatively related to the share of government seats in the legislature. It is therefore a useful summary of the structural tendency for the political system to generate fragmented and divided governments.

Budgetary institutions. The second aspect of the institutional setup that we explore is budgetary institutions — the set of rules and procedures by which budgets are drafted in the executive branch, modified and approved by congress, and then carried out. There are three broad classes of such rules: rules that impose constraints on the deficit; procedural rules that govern the preparation of the budget; and rules that affect the transparency of the budgeting process.

There are several links between such rules and fiscal outcomes in theory. It is easy to believe, though not obviously true, that numerical rules on permissible spending and deficits will affect those decisions, even if the limits are not respected without exception. There is also good theoretical reason to believe that hierarchical budgetary rules that give a player some primary or agenda-setting powers on the budget will help to resolve some of the co-ordination problems that can lead to excessive spending and deficits. For example, rules that give relatively more power over formulation of the budget to the finance minister are likely to provide greater fiscal discipline than do rules and procedures that give relatively equal powers to all ministries. Similarly, it seems likely that budgetary procedures that favour the executive over the legislature will be conducive to fiscal discipline, since single-district representatives may push for programmes that benefit their constituency, while the executive is more inclined to internalise the overall constraints.

A detailed description of these institutional arrangements in Latin America is provided in Inter-American Development Bank (1997) and Stein, Talvi and Grisante (1997). Here we will confine ourselves to a summary of the evidence on the relationship between these institutional arrangements and fiscal outcomes. The index of budgetary institutions that is utilised is a composite index based upon a number of characteristics of the budgetary process, and is designed to measure the degree to which the process is constrained by numerical limits, hierarchical, and transparent. A higher value of the index represents "stronger" institutions, that are more constrained, hierarchical and transparent.

Institutional influences on spending and deficits. In Table 7 we summarise evidence on the institutional determinants of government size, measured as total spending by the consolidated public sector during the 1990-1995 period. The sample is a cross-section of 21 Latin American countries and 14 industrial economies.

Government size is very strongly and positively related to a country's openness to international trade[17], to the share of the elderly in the population, and to the initial debt/GDP ratio. After controlling for these factors, there is very strong evidence that in countries with larger district magnitudes public sectors tend to spend more than in countries with smaller district magnitude. The point estimate of the impact of district magnitude on government size is even larger in a sample of Latin American economies, although with a much smaller sample size, the statistical significance of the estimate is much reduced.

Table 7. **Electoral Arrangements and Government Size, 1990-95**

	Full sample		Latin America	
	(1)	(2)	(3)	(4)
Dependent variable: Total public spending				
District magnitude	1.48	1.43	1.85	2.24
	(1.94)	(1.71)	(1.10)	(1.34)
Initial (1989) debt/GDP	1.58	1.65	1.33	1.46
	(2.28)	(2.19)	(1.81)	(2.00)
Openness	8.51	8.87	13.03	15.17
	(2.41)	(2.33)	(2.95)	(3.36)
Share of population above 65	1.90	–	1.43	–
	(7.28)		(1.92)	
GDP per capita	–	1.52	–	1.69
		(6.38)		(2.11)
Adjusted R^2	0.75	0.71	0.46	0.48
Degrees of freedom	30	30	16	16

Source: Inter-American Development Bank (1997). Dependent variable is total expenditure of the consolidated public sector during the 1990-95 period, measured as a share of GDP. The explanatory variables are described in the text. T-statistics are given in parentheses.

This evidence supports the idea that political systems which promote more political fragmentation tend to generate the sort of pressures for higher public spending that were described above. Interestingly, there seemed to be no discernible relationship between the index of budgetary institutions and government size.

Institutional arrangements appear to have even more powerful effects on the fiscal deficits and debt emerging from the political decision-making process. As columns (1) and (3) of Table 8 indicate, district magnitude is strongly associated with large fiscal deficits, both in the full sample of Latin American and industrial economies and, even more strongly, in the sample of Latin American economies.

There is a positive, though somewhat weaker, association between public debt and district magnitude. These results support the idea that political fragmentation aggravates problems with deficit bias.

The results also indicate, however, that "strong" — that is, constrained, hierarchical and transparent — budgetary institutions can effectively offset this tendency. When fiscal deficits and public debt are explained by both district magnitude and budgetary institutions, budgetary institutions are strongly associated with smaller fiscal deficits and lower public debt. These results are even stronger if public debt is measured as a share of fiscal revenue rather than GDP.

This is an optimistic message because it suggests that with appropriate budgetary institutions, countries can enjoy the increased representativeness provided by proportional representation systems without paying a higher price in terms of increased deficit bias in fiscal decision making.

Table 8. **Institutional Arrangements and Deficit Bias**

	Full sample		Latin America	
	(1)	(2)	(3)	(4)
Dependent variable: overall fiscal balance				
District magnitude	-0.76	0.04	-1.71	-0.61
	(-2.31)	(0.16)	(-2.57)	(-1.07)
Budgetary institutions - Latin America	–	0.14	–	0.11
		(4.81)		(2.03)
Budgetary institutions - Industrial economies	–	0.07	–	–
		(2.89)		
Adjusted R^2	0.11	0.53	0.20	0.23
Degrees of freedom	36	29	22	16
Dependent variable: public debt				
District magnitude	0.14	0.02	0.62	0.02
	(1.17)	(0.59)	(2.21)	(0.22)
Budgetary institutions - Latin America	–	-1.01	–	-0.66
		(-2.96)		(-0.86)
Budgetary institutions - Industrial economies	–	-0.68	–	–
		(-2.40)		
Adjusted R^2	0.01	0.24	0.15	0.03
Degrees of freedom	36	29	22	16

Source: Inter-American Development Bank (1997). Dependent variables are total expenditure of the consolidated public sector and total public sector debt during the 1990-95 period, measured as a percentage of GDP. The explanatory variables are described in the text. T-statistics are given in parentheses.

Institutions and procyclicality. As we have noted, Latin America has made important progress in controlling deficit bias in the 1990s. However, the problem of a procyclical reaction to economic shocks persists. Is this problem related to institutional arrangements? Table 9 suggests a positive answer. This table investigates the statistical association between district magnitude and the procyclicality of fiscal outcomes, where procyclicality is measured as the correlation between the detrended components of government consumption and real GDP.

The table reveals that procyclicality is strongly related to macroeconomic volatility, but after controlling for this volatility, there is also a strong association between district magnitude and the procyclicality of public spending, suggesting that fragmented political systems have a harder time responding to shocks in a counter-cyclical, stabilizing manner. This may be related to the previous finding that political fragmentation promotes deficit bias, since it is obviously much harder to allow the deficit to rise after an adverse shock if it was already very large upon entering the period[18]. It may also be that, for reasons discussed above, in fragmented political systems governments may lack credibility, since turnover is high and there is no guarantee that future governments will run the fiscal surpluses required to finance large deficits during bad times.

Table 9. Institutional Arrangements and the Procyclicality of Public Spending

	G7 and Latin America	Latin America
District magnitude	0.08	0.12
	(2.99)	(2.22)
Real GDP volatility	14.59	10.24
	(4.91)	(3.00)
Adjusted R^2	0.51	0.32
Degrees of freedom	20	16

Source: Inter-American Development Bank (1997). Procyclicality of public spending is measured by the correlation between public consumption and real GDP, where each variable has been detrended using the Hodrick-Prescott filter. The volatility of real GDP is measured by the standard deviation of the detrended real GDP. T-statistics are given in parentheses.

Perhaps of equal importance is the finding that the index of budgetary institutions was not associated with either more or less procyclicality. If anything, the evidence suggests that "strong" budgetary institutions were associated with increased procyclicality in public spending. Also, budgetary institutions were not significantly related to the depth of the electoral fiscal cycle.

This is important because it suggests that institutional arrangements that address one problem, such as the problem of deficit bias, may be ineffective remedies for other problems, and may indeed aggravate them. For example, a very hierarchical budgetary process that gives great leverage to the finance minister may promote fiscal discipline on average, but it may also permit substantial leeway for the minister to temporarily respond to the electoral pressures facing his government or himself temporarily, thus aggravating the electoral fiscal cycle.

Concluding Remarks

In this paper we have reviewed some stylised facts about fiscal performance in Latin America. We found that fiscal outcomes have differed in important ways from the industrial-country experience. While fiscal performance in recent years has been exemplary in some respects, most notably in the substantial reduction in the region's fiscal deficits over the past decade, we have identified important problems that remain. First, a tendency toward deficit bias over the longer term has left the region with large deficits. Second, fiscal outcomes have been highly procyclical, particularly in bad economic times, when a stabilizing fiscal response would have been most valuable. Third, the data shows a clear and disturbing fiscal "cycle" associated with elections.

We also explored the question of whether electoral arrangements and budgetary institutions are systematically related to fiscal outcomes. The answer is "yes": we found that countries with proportional representation systems tend to have greater political fragmentation. They also tend to have larger governments that run bigger deficits and that behave more pro-cyclically than countries with less fragmented political systems.

We also presented evidence that budgetary institutions which embody stricter restrictions on deficit financing, greater transparency in the budgeting process, and more hierarchical budgetary procedures tend to reduce deficit bias, especially in countries with proportional representation systems. This holds out the prospect that appropriate institutional arrangements can offset potentially adverse effects of proportional representation, thus permitting countries to combine the greater inclusiveness of such systems with fiscal discipline. However, such institutions seem to have no discernible effect on the problems of procyclicality or the electoral fiscal cycle — and the electoral cycles may even be larger in countries with "better" budgetary institutions. This highlights the fact that the design of budgetary institutions may involve a number of different dimensions, and that there may be trade-offs among them. This leaves us with the research and policy agenda of understanding better the ways in which measures to promote transparency, hierarchical procedures, and restrictions on deficit financing interact, and can be combined to assure better fiscal outcomes in all the relevant dimensions.

Notes

1. For example, Roubini and Sachs (1989) provide evidence that countries characterised by the presence of large numbers of parties in the ruling coalition tend to experience larger fiscal deficits, while Grilli, Masciandaro and Tabellini (1991) suggest that fiscal indiscipline is associated with proportional representation systems. On the impact of budgetary institutions, von Hagen and Harden (1995) and Alesina and Perotti (1995) provide evidence that weak budgetary institutions are associated with larger fiscal deficits in the industrial economies, Poterba (1996) presents similar evidence for US states, and Alesina, Hausmann, Hommes and Stein (1996) provide evidence for Latin America.

2. Here and elsewhere in this chapter we measure volatility by the standard deviation of the underlying variable. For brevity, we often use the term "typical change" as a synonym for the more precise but less user-friendly "standard deviation of changes".

3. For example, if a government received much of its income in the form of income from an internationally-traded good, and most of its spending commitments are on domestically produced non-traded goods, a real exchange rate depreciation will tend improve the fiscal balance. (This is the case, for example, of Venezuela.) If, on the other hand, the government's income is more closely tied to domestic prices while it has large expenditures on imported goods and foreign-currency denominated debt, a real exchange rate depreciation will tend to generate a deterioration of the fiscal deficit. In either case, volatility in the real exchange rate will be translated into instability in the fiscal deficit.

4. See e.g. Wildavsky (1986). A more complete analysis would separate military from non-military expenditures, since the former category is clearly subject to political shocks exogenous to the domestic economy. However, this has not been important in Latin America.

5. A second caveat has to do with lags in the implementation of counter-cyclical policies. If it takes a long time to move counter-cyclical fiscal policies through the political process, the response to recession may arrive after the recovery has begun, thus amplifying the cycle rather than dampening it. This introduces an important note of caution in attempts to introduce *discretionary* changes in fiscal policy, but it does not provide a rationale for the procyclical fiscal policy that is documented below.

6. The results in Table 5 apply to the general government, which is the consolidation of central and sub national levels of government but excludes public enterprises. Gavin and Perotti (1997) investigate the cyclicality of fiscal outcomes at different levels of government, including the non-financial public sector (which includes general government

and non-financial public enterprises.) As one might expect, they found little evidence of counter-cyclical fiscal policy by local governments. They also found that in Latin America, public enterprises have tended to reinforce the procyclical fiscal patterns that are observed at the central government level. One interpretation of this is that public sector pricing, employment, and other decisions have been used by governments for purposes, and under constraints, very similar to those of the central government.

7. More precisely, "bad times" are defined as years during which real GDP growth in a country falls more than one standard deviation below the average. Similar results were obtained when "bad times" were defined as years during which real GDP declines.

8. These are defined as periods during which real GDP declines at least 4 per cent (Latin America) or 1.5 per cent (industrial economies).

9. See Gavin and Perotti (forthcoming) for a more detailed discussion.

10. Persson and Svensson (1996) argue that the impact of an unexpected increase in inflation on the fiscal balance is large and positive in Sweden. This need not be the case, because an increase in inflation may also have a large negative effect on fiscal revenue.

11. See Gavin and Perotti (forthcoming). "Extraordinary" financing includes arrears, IMF credit and special financing operations such as the United States' Treasury's support for Mexico during 1995.

12. See Gavin and Perotti (forthcoming). A "low" fiscal deficit was defined as a deficit less than 3 per cent of GDP. Gavin and Perotti (1996) also present evidence that the private, as well as public sector of Latin America is affected by the loss of market access during bad economic times.

13. See Lane and Tornell (1996) for a more extended discussion of these "voracity effects". Talvi and Végh (1997) argue that procyclical fiscal policies can in fact be optimal in highly volatile environments when fiscal surpluses generate strong pressures for wasteful public spending.

14. Figure 7 is based upon a statistical analysis of election years and fiscal outcomes that also controls for (i) the previous period's fiscal balance, (ii) the growth rate of real GDP and the terms of trade, (iii) country dummy variables that control for unobserved country-specific factors, and (iv) dummy variables for each year of the sample period, which control for unobserved factors that vary over time, but are common to countries of the region. The estimated impact of the election year and the post-election years are statistically significant at the 5 per cent confidence level, but the estimated impacts on revenue and expenditure are less precisely estimated.

15. Volatility was measured as the standard deviation of real GDP growth, and the depth of the electoral budget cycle was measured as the estimated impact on the fiscal surplus of election years, after controlling for the previous period's fiscal balance, the growth rate of real GDP and the terms of trade, country dummy variables that control for unobserved country-specific factors, and dummy variables for each year of the sample period.

16. Saint-Paul (1994) argues that in the context of asymmetric information about the government's intentions, the authorities may choose a very procyclical fiscal reaction in order to signal their commitment to fiscal discipline. Moreover, he points out that this result is most likely to be obtained in volatile and highly indebted countries.

17. Rodrik (1996) argues that this reflects the fact that open economies are more exposed to external shocks, and need larger public sectors to provide social protection against the implied risks.

18. Gavin and Perotti (forthcoming) provide evidence that, in Latin America, countries that entered a period with smaller fiscal deficits were able to respond to shocks in a less procyclical manner than were countries that entered with large deficits. This was not the case in the industrial economies, where loss of market access during bad times seems to be a less important feature of fiscal management.

Bibliography

ALESINA, A., R. HAUSMANN, R. HOMMES AND E. STEIN (1996), "Budgetary Institutions and Fiscal Performance in Latin America", *NBER Working Paper* No. 5586.

ALESINA, A. AND R. PEROTTI (1995), "Budget Deficits and Budget Institutions", manuscript, Harvard University and Columbia University.

BARRO, R. (1979), "On the Determination of the Public Debt", *Journal of Political Economy,* 87.

EICHENGREEN, B., R. HAUSMANN AND J. VON HAGEN (1996), "Reforming Fiscal Institutions in Latin America: The Case for a National Fiscal Council", manuscript, Office of the Chief Economist, Inter-American Development Bank, Washington, D.C.

GAVIN, M., R. HAUSMANN, R. PEROTTI AND E. TALVI (1996), "Managing Fiscal Policy in Latin America: Volatility, Procyclicality and Limited Creditworthiness", Inter-American Development Bank, *OCE Working Paper* No. 326.

GAVIN, M. AND R. PEROTTI (1996) "Fiscal Policy and Private Saving in Good Times and Bad", in R. HAUSMANN AND H. REISEN (eds.) *Promoting Savings in Latin America,* IDB and OECD, Washington, D.C.

GAVIN, M. AND R. PEROTTI (forthcoming), "Fiscal Policy in Latin America", in J. ROTEMBERG AND B. BERNANKE (eds.) *Macroeconomics Annual, 1997,* MIT Press, Cambridge, Mass.

GIAVAZZI, F. AND M. PAGANO (1990), "Confidence Crises and Public Debt Management", in R. DORNBUSCH AND M. DRAGHI (eds.) *Public Debt Management: Theory and History,* Cambridge University Press, Cambridge.

GRILLI, V., D. MASCIANDARO AND G. TABELLINI (1991) "Institutions and Policies", *Economic Policy,* 6.

HAUSMANN, R. AND E. STEIN (1996), "Searching for the Right Budgetary Institutions for a Volatile Region", in R. HAUSMANN AND H. REISEN (eds.) *Securing Stability and Growth in Latin America,* IDB and OECD, Paris.

INTER-AMERICAN DEVELOPMENT BANK (1995), "Overcoming Volatility in Latin America", Chapt. 3 of *Report on Economic and Social Progress in Latin America, 1995,* Johns Hopkins University Press for the Inter-American Development Bank, Washington, D.C.

INTER-AMERICAN DEVELOPMENT BANK (1997), "Fiscal Stability with Democracy and Decentralization", Chapt. 3 of *Report on Economic and Social Progress in Latin America, 1997,* Johns Hopkins University Press for the Inter-American Development Bank, Washington, D.C.

LANE, P. AND A. TORNELL (1996), "Power, Growth and the Voracity Effect", *Journal of Economic Growth,* 1.

LONDOÑO, J.L. AND M. SZÉKELY (1997), "Income Distribution and Poverty in Latin America During 1970-1995: Some Basic Facts", manuscript, Inter-American Development Bank, Washington, D.C.

PEROTTI, R. (1996) "Fiscal Policy When Things Go Badly", mimeo, Columbia University.

PERSSON, M., T. PERSSON AND L. SVENSSON (1996), "Debt, Cash Flow and Inflation Incentives: A Swedish Example", *NBER Working Paper* No. 5772.

POTERBA, J. (1996), "Budget Institutions and Fiscal Policy in the U.S. States", *American Economic Review,* 86(2).

RODRIK, D. (1996), "Why do More Open Economies Have Bigger Governments?", *NBER Working Paper* No. 5537.

ROUBINI, N. AND J. SACHS (1989), "Political and Economic Determinants of Budget Deficits in the Industrial Democracies", *European Economic Review,* 33.

SAINT-PAUL, G. (1994), "Monetary Policy in Economic Transition: Lessons from the French Post-War Experience", *European Economic Review,* 38.

STEIN, E., E. TALVI AND A. GRISTANTE (1997), "Institutional Arrangements and Fiscal Performance: The Latin American Experience", manuscript, Inter-American Development Bank, Washington, D.C.

TALVI, E. AND C. VÉGH (1997), "Can Optimal Fiscal Policy be Procyclical?", mimeo, Inter-American Development Bank, Washington, D.C.

VON HAGEN, J. AND I. HARDEN (1995), "Budget Processes and Commitment to Fiscal Discipline", *European Economic Review,* 39.

WILDAVSKY, A. (1986), *Budgeting: A Comparative Theory of Budgeting Processes,* Transaction Books, New Brunswick.

Electoral Institutions and the Budget Process

Mark Hallerberg and Jürgen von Hagen

Introduction

Large and persistent government budget deficits are a concern in most OECD countries as well as in other regions. In the United States, balancing the budget has gained political priority, although the two political parties have different views on how to reach this goal. In Europe, the failure to reduce large budget deficits puts the eligibility of several countries for the European Monetary Union at risk, and the Maastricht Treaty commits the governments of the European Union to avoiding "excessive deficits". One reason for a renewed commitment by politicians to reduce deficits is the recognition of the negative economic effects of chronic deficits and high public debts: higher risk premia in interest rates, lower economic growth, a restriction on public spending on valued public services, and, outside the OECD, the general financial and economic instability experienced by countries facing problems to service their debts regularly.

The renewed focus on reducing deficits and debts in the 1990s follows a period of twenty years of rising public debts. Debt ratios to GDP trended upwards in almost all OECD countries after 1970, the United Kingdom and Luxembourg being the noticable exceptions. Even if one concedes that governments may have underestimated the effects of the oil price shocks in the 1970s, the observation of a large increase in public debts during times of peace is hard to square with standard views of the role of deficit financing in economics, such as tax smoothing and optimal stabilization policies[1]. At the same time, states have had varying levels of success in keeping deficits low. In Europe, the United Kingdom and France have managed to maintain relatively low deficit and debt levels, while others, such as Italy, Greece, and Belgium, have suffered under chronic deficits and/or debt levels. Alesina *et al.* (1996) show that there are noticeable differences in the debt performance among Latin American countries as well. This poses the question (Alesina and Perotti, 1995; von Hagen, 1992) why countries in the same region and exposed to similar economic shocks responded in such remarkably different ways.

Recent research has focused on political economy to provide an answer. One strand of literature argues that the root of the deficit problem lies in the democratic process of party competition for political power, and that differences in deficit performance can be explained by the characteristics of national electoral systems. Another strand of literature argues that the root of the problem lies in institutional deficiencies of the government budget process, and that differences in fiscal performance can be explained by differences in the ways governments formulate their budgets, pass them through parliament, and implement them.

In the first branch of that research, the consensus is that electoral systems of proportional representation (PR) are a cause of large deficits and debts. PR systems are commonly regarded as producing governments that are inherently less stable than the governments produced by pluralist electoral systems. Furthermore, PR systems typically produce coalition governments among politically heterogeneous parties, while plurality systems produce single-party governments. While there are various versions of the argument, the essence is that governments are more inclined to run large deficits if their prospect to remain in power is uncertain, and if there is disagreement within them over the distribution of the cost of adjustment to negative shocks over different groups in society. While the theoretical work in this area has sparked considerable interest, empirical work lends only weak support for these arguments[2].

The other branch of the literature focuses on the institutional rules, formal and informal, under which the decisions relating to government budgets evolve within the executive and the legislative branches of government[3]. These institutional rules determine the distribution of power among the participants and regulate the flows of information among them. Building on a tradition in American political science, this literature views the government budget process as a common pool resource problem. Politicians representing different groups in society spend money taken out of a general tax fund on transfers to or projects benefiting their constituencies[4]. The incongruence between the incidence of the costs and benefits of these transfers and projects in society creates a tendency to overestimate the net marginal benefit from spending. As a result, government budgets grow too large, and deficits and debts become excessive[5]. The more fragmented a budget process is, i.e. the larger the number of participants that can influence the outcome and the weaker the institutional mechanisms co-ordinating their actions, the larger the deficit and the resulting debts. Conversely, von Hagen and Harden (1994a, b) using European data and Alesina et al. (1996) using Latin American data show empirically that elements of centralisation in the budget process are important to secure fiscal discipline.

Hallerberg and von Hagen (1998) bring the two strands of literature together arguing that electoral systems, indeed, are important in this context, as they constrain the availability of institutional mechanisms to reduce the fragmentation of the budget process. Specifically, they argue that each of the two main mechanisms identified by von Hagen and Harden (1994*a*, *b*), namely the delegation of strategic powers to a finance minister acting as the fiscal entrepreneur of the executive, and the commitment to numerical fiscal targets through a contract among the members of the executive, is appropriate for only one type of government: delegation for single-party governments (most common in plurality countries) and contracting for coalition governments (most common in PR countries).

We further develop their argument and bring in the distinction between parliamentary systems, the prevalent form of government in Europe, and presidential systems, the most prevalent form of government in Latin America. The following section lays out a model explaining the problem of collective action in government budgeting and shows how the resulting deficit bias is determined by two important political factors, the electoral system and the difference between presidential and parliamentary democracies; it also characterises political systems in terms of the number of veto players. Two institutional approaches to solving the collective action problem are then presented and the choice of institution is determined by the number of veto players explained. The concluding sections present empirical evidence supporting the relevance of institutional solutions to the problem of large and persistent deficits.

Where possible, we use data from current democracies that are Members of the OECD to illustrate our arguments. We pay particular attention to the subset of OECD countries that compose the European Union. From a policy perspective, these states are of interest because of the Maastricht Treaty's provisions concerning yearly deficits and aggregate debt. If certain institutions have been effective in some states, they may provide a way for high debt states to bring their fiscal policies in step with the Maastricht Treaty's guidelines. At different stages, we will also consider the implications of our work for Latin America.

The Budget Process and the Deficit Bias

A general characteristic of modern public finance is that public spending is targeted more narrowly at specific groups in society than is taxation. Public monies are spent on transfers and public policy projects that benefit well-defined sectors of society, while the bill is paid by the general tax payer. Examples are infrastructure investments with limited geographical benefits, subsidies to individual industries, or to specific groups such as farmers, families with children, and the like, paid for from a general tax fund. In all such cases, there is an incongruency between the incidence of the benefits and the costs of the programme with important implications for the budget process. The budget process can be understood as a bargaining process in which the different interests regarding public spending and taxation compete.

Decentralisation: The Fiefdom Approach

Both the executive and legislative branch affect the shape of the budget. We begin first with the executive. The executive's role in this process is in formulating and implementing the budget law. It consists of a number of spending departments, each of which caters to one or several different interest groups in society.

Consider, first, a completely decentralised, or fragmented process. Each participant represents the spending interests of a spending department. In presenting the bid, each participant has to weigh the benefits for his constituency against the tax burden borne by it. While this is, of course, a gross simplification, it seems plausible that an agricultural minister, for instance, would be more concerned about the services and goods provided to farmers and the taxes paid by them, than the minister of industry. In this situation, the incongruency between the incidence of the benefits and the incidence of the costs of public spending implies that each participant fully appreciates the marginal benefit of an additional dollar spent on the department's activities, but only that part of the marginal cost borne by the constituency. There is, therefore, a systematic overestimation of the marginal net benefit of each public policy programme. In a completely decentralised process, where each participant bids for the funds equating the marginal benefits and perceived marginal costs of spending of the department, taking the bids of all other participants as given, the decision making rule is simply to aggregate the individual bids to a total budget. This overestimation implies that the budget, and the budget deficit with it, will grow too large. Thus the "common pool" property of the general tax fund creates a positive spending and deficit bias.

We label this completely decentralised process the "fiefdom" approach[6]. Ministers set policy and budgets on their turf without much explicit interference from other ministers, including the prime minister[7]. Note that the outcome of a spending and deficit bias holds even if the ministers possess *identical* spending preferences — it is the difference in the consideration of the tax burden that drives the result[8].

The role of the legislature in the budget process is to scrutinise the executive's plans, to amend them, and to authorise public spending and taxation. The parliamentary part of the budget process can be interpreted as a bargaining process between the executive and the legislature. In this process, the executive's relative power depends critically on the scope of permissible amendments by the legislature, which is often formally restricted by law, and may be practically restricted by the executive's information advantage. Since the incongruence between the marginal benefit and the perceived marginal cost of an extra dollar spent on public activities is generally even larger for individual members of parliament, the spending and deficit bias tends to increase with the relative power of the legislature in the budget process. In particular, restrictions on parliamentary amendments to the executive's budget bill often lead to greater fiscal discipline (von Hagen, 1992; von Hagen and Harden, 1994a).

Political Determinants of the Number of Players in the Budget Process

The analogy with a common pool problem suggests that the number of players matters for the size of this bias: a larger number implying a larger deficit bias[9]. Within the executive, there are generally two levels of budget negotiations: those among members of the same party; and those between different political parties. A good starting point is to begin with party actors, i.e., to identify players with parties in government, since this is also what matters critically in the relationship between the executive and the legislature.

Electoral Institutions

Electoral institutions strongly influence the number of party players in government. One important factor is the number of parties that gain legislative seats; if there are few parties, there is a higher chance that one party can win an absolute majority, and an absolute majority is a virtual certainty in two-party systems. Several studies indicate that the number of parties in a given system is strongly and positively correlated with the number of representatives elected from each electoral district. This number is generally known as *district magnitude* (Duverger, 1954; Taagepera and Shugart, 1989, 1993). Electoral systems with low district magnitudes distribute seats less proportionately than those with large district magnitudes, and lower proportionality favours larger parties. An example of this comes from France, where, under a two-stage plurality system with a district magnitude of 1, the conservative parties won just 44 per cent of the total votes cast in 1993 but over 80 per cent of the National Assembly seats. This disproportionality can exist even in proportional representation states if the district magnitude is low — in Spain, for example, where the average district magnitude is just 6.7, the Socialist party was able to win 44 per cent of the popular vote in the 1986 national elections but 52 per cent of the seats in the Congress of Deputies[10]. At the other extreme, the Netherlands has only one electoral district composed of 150 seats for the entire country, and a party that wins less than one percent of the national vote can gain seats in parliament[11].

Plurality systems, which elect only one representative per district, encourage a two-party system, and they are consequently most likely to have one-party majority governments. Proportional representation (PR) systems have more variation in their district magnitudes, though the magnitudes are always larger than those found in plurality systems. They tend to have a larger number of "effective" parties in parliament and are characterised by multi-party majority or either one-party or multi-party minority governments[12]. Empirical evidence has consistently supported this relationship, e.g. Lijphart (1984)[13]. Table 1 compares the electoral systems of most OECD countries. A few points require clarification.

Table 1. **Electoral Systems in 21 OECD Countries**

State	System	District Magnitude	ENPP	Effective Threshold	Years in the Lijphart Study	% One-Party Majority in Lower House
Australia	Alternative Vote	1	2.35	35	84-90	100
Austria	2-Tier PR, Remainder Transfers	20/91	2.42	2.6	71-90	44
Belgium	PR	23	4.63	4.8	46-87	17
Canada	Plurality	1	2.37	35	45-88	60
Denmark	2-Tier PR, Adjustment Seats	7/175	4.92	2	64-88	0
Finland	PR	13	5.03	5.4	45-87	0
France	Plurality	1	3.5	35	58-81	6
Germany	2-Tier PR, Adjustment Seats	1/497	2.95	5	57-83	0
Greece	'Reinforced' PR	6	2.08	16.4	74-85	95
Ireland	STV	4	2.79	17.2	48-89	36
Italy	2-Tier PR, Remainder Transfers	19/625	3.62	2	58-87	0
Japan	SNTV	4	2.88	16.4	47-90	75
Luxembourg	PR	14	3.3	5.1	45-89	0
Netherlands	PR	150	4.59	0.67	56-89	0
New Zealand	Plurality	1	1.95	35	46-90	100
Norway	PR	8/165	4.23	4	89	0
Portugal	PR	12	3.05	5.7	75-87	33
Spain	PR	6	2.72	10.2	77-89	58
Sweden	2-Tier PR	11/350	3.4	4	70-88	10
United Kingdom	Plurality	1	2.1	35	45-87	99
United States	Plurality	1	1.92	35	46-90	100

Note: "PR" corresponds to "Proportional Representation", "STV" to "Single Transferable Vote", and "ENPP" to "Effective Number of Parliamentary Parties". All figures but those on one-party majorities come from Lijphart 1994, 17, 22, 31, 33-35, 44, 160-162; Lijphart's one party majority figures were supplemented with Woldendorp, Keman, and Budge (1993). Greece, Portugal, and Spain were not democracies during the entire period, and the years covered are, respectively, 1974-90, 1975-90, and 1977-90. This data is published in various issues of the *European Journal of Political Research*, and is based on the date of an election instead of the date of investiture used for the other countries. The figures for France are just for its Fifth Republic, or 1958-90, and include the period 1986-88 when the country used a proportional representation system. The Austrian, Irish and Portuguese data were not completely accurate in Woldendorp, Keman and Budge (1993). The authors supplemented the Austrian and Portuguese data themselves, while Jesse (1996) was used for Ireland for the period 1951-90. District magnitude figures are rounded to the nearest whole number. Brian Woodall provided data on one-party government in Japan.

First, PR systems do not translate the percentage of votes directly into the percentage of seats, and smaller parties often cannot gain entry into the legislature. We noted previously that district magnitude affects the number of political parties possible, and a logical comparison would be between this figure and the likelihood of one-party government. Yet such a comparison would be somewhat misleading — as the third column in Table 1 indicates, states sometimes have different district magnitudes at different levels of the allocation process. In addition, other factors that district magnitude does not measure, including legal thresholds (such as Germany's requirement that a party win either 5 per cent of the nation-wide vote or three seats by plurality vote) and rules for the allocation of seats (use of the D'Hondt method for allocating seats) favour larger parties over smaller ones. Arend Lijphart solves our problem of how to aggregate these institutional effects with his translation of such factors into an "effective threshold", which is the percentage of the national vote a party expects it must receive to gain any legislative seats.

Second, while France had a plurality system in all parliamentary elections but those held in 1986, its use of two rounds of voting increases the effective number of parties in parliament. Unless a given candidate wins an absolute majority in the first round, a second round of voting is held. This process encourages parties that ran candidates in the first round to form electoral coalitions for the second round. The predicted emergence of two strong blocks facing each other under plurality does still occur, however, since the UDF (Union pour la Démocratie Française) allies almost exclusively with the RPR (Rassemblement pour la République) while the Socialist Party works equally as often with the French Communist Party. France will therefore be treated as a "one-party government" in most cases later in this paper. Similarly, the United States is the only true presidential system in the dataset, and the statistics for one-party control of the House of Representatives do not indicate a one-party majority government.

Table 1 confirms the general link among electoral institutions, the number of parties, and the likelihood of a one-party majority government for the sample of OECD countries. The correlation between the effective threshold and the number of parties has the correct sign at -.59, and it jumps to -.69 if France is excluded from the sample. The most important figure is the correlation which links the occurrence of one-party majority governments with higher effective thresholds, and the correlation of .69 indicates that this relationship is relatively strong. Since states which have low district magnitudes also have higher effective thresholds, this result indicates that plurality elections or PR systems with low district magnitudes are likely to have one-party majority governments. In contrast, PR systems with high district magnitudes usually have either multi-party majority governments or minority governments.

Data from Latin America and the Caribbean reinforce this conclusion. Stein, Talvi and Grisanti (1997), in their examination of 26 countries from the two regions, report that the correlation coefficient between the district magnitude in the lower legislative house and effective number of legislative parties is .58, while the coefficient between the number of parties and the percentage of seats the sitting government possesses is even higher at .79.

Parliamentary vs. Presidential Forms of Government

A second factor that affects the number of party actors is the manner in which a country elects its executive. In parliamentary systems, which are most common within Europe, the executive is commonly determined by the legislature. Parties that form a majority coalition support the executive and commonly vote together on the executive's legislative proposals. The number of party players in the executive is, therefore, generally the same as the number of parties needed to pass legislation in parliament.

In contrast, a correspondence between the number of party players in the legislature and the executive is not guaranteed in the presidential systems that are common in Latin America. There, a population directly elects the leader of the executive. The legislature may have some limited powers to remove the president under extreme circumstances, but otherwise the president does not rely directly on the legislature for his position. Electorates can, and often do, support a president from one party while denying the party a majority in the legislature. In the United States, for example, a president has faced an opposition-controlled House or Senate 19 of the past 25 years. In Latin American and Caribbean countries during the period 1990-95, half of the twenty countries with presidential systems had presidents facing opposition-controlled lower houses (Stein, Talvi and Grisanti, 1997). There will then be at least two different party actors in the budget process. Whether the number is higher than two depends on the electoral system — in countries that elect their legislatures with proportional representation, it is likely that the number will be greater than two.

Party Players as "Veto Players"

"Veto players" are persons or groups whose agreement is required to pass any law. In practice, the number of veto players is equal to the number of parties whose consent is needed for a bill to become law (Tsebelis, 1995). The concept is useful because it simplifies the comparison of different types of political systems. In parliamentary systems with unicameral legislatures the number of veto players equals the number of parties that compose the government. In states with bicameral legislatures or where a president can veto legislation, the number of veto players can be larger, if different parties control the different institutions. In New Zealand, for instance, where one-party majority governments were the norm through 1994, there was usually just one veto player. In Italy in the 1980s there were a series of coalition governments composed of five parties (the *pentapartito*), and any proposal required in principle the approval of these five "veto players." In the United States, the consent of the House of Representatives, the Senate, and the President is required in most cases. However, there are only two parties that can control these institutions, so the maximum number of veto players is two.

Table 2 links the relationship between the type of electoral system and the type of executive system with the number of veto players. The number of veto players generally increases when one moves from a plurality to a PR electoral system and when one moves from a parliamentary to a presidential system.

Table 2. **Number of Veto Players**

	Electoral System	
Executive System	Parliamentary	Presidential
Plurality	1	1 or 2
Proportional Representation	2+	2+ or 3+

Tsebelis (1995), citing empirical evidence provided by Schick (1993), argues that increasing the number of veto players increases the size of budget deficits. McCubbins (1991) reports that divided governments in the United States lead to higher deficits than united governments in the period 1948-88. These observations are consistent with the "common-pool" interpretation of the budget process. To the extent that one can equate the number of players with the number of parties involved in budgetary decisions, the implication is that one-party governments should do a better job maintaining fiscal discipline than coalition governments in parliamentary systems. Electoral systems of PR, therefore, increase the likelihood of large deficits. Furthermore, presidential systems, since they may result in divided government, should on average run larger deficits than one-party, parliamentary governments.

However, the argument does not end here. If the number of "fiefdoms" within the executive matters, as argued above, it should do so even if all members of the executive come from the same party. Below we discuss two institutional approaches to limiting the spending and deficit bias. These approaches provide different co-ordination mechanisms among the players in the budget process in an attempt to solve the common pool problem. Based on that discussion we will then show that the number of veto players in the budget process determines the choice of institutional solution. Ultimately, it is the absence or presence of co-ordination, rather than the number of veto players *per se*, that determines the level of fiscal discipline.

Institutional Approaches to Centralising the Budget Process

A large literature exists examining the conditions under which the players will choose to co-operate with each other in common pool problems (Olson, 1965; Hardin, 1982; Ostrom, 1990; Ostrom, Gardner and Walker, 1994). All of these solutions involve the use of selective punishments or incentives and the monitoring of the actors. In the context of budgetary decisions, von Hagen and Harden (1996) identify two prototypes. The first involves delegation: one member of the executive is vested with special strategic powers that allow him to achieve a co-operative solution. The second approach involves fiscal contracts: playing a co-operative bargaining game at the outset of the budgeting process to agree on a budgetary pact allows one to reach the same goal.

Delegation and Contracts

With delegation, the executive lends authority to a "fiscal entrepreneur", whose function is to assure that all actors co-operate. To be effective, this entrepreneur must have the ability to monitor the others, possess selective incentives that he can use to punish defectors and/or reward those who co-operate, and have some motivation to bear the costs of monitoring himself (Olson 1965; Frohlich and Oppenheimer, 1978; Cox and McCubbins, 1993). Among the cabinet members, the finance minister often plays this role. His interests generally coincide with the interest of the general taxpayer more than with an individual spending constituency. This being the case, the finance minister is able to internalise the externalities involved in drawing money from the general tax fund. He has the responsibility to co-ordinate the formation of the budget, and, fair or not, the size of the budget deficit is often the principal indicator others use to judge his effectiveness. Finally, the finance minister's staff gives him the means to monitor the actions of the other ministries, and, since his prestige and hence his personal benefits depend on the effectiveness of his ministry, he has an incentive to guarantee that the monitoring occurs. The only question is whether the finance minister has the power to offer selective incentives and/or punishments to the spending ministers.

One practical way to implement delegation is for the finance minister to serve as an agenda setter in cabinet meetings where budget decisions are being made. The finance minister has the right to make the first proposal for the budget, and he has the power to constrain any amendments that the spending ministers might submit to his proposal. The stronger he is, the closer the outcome these negotiations must be to his ideal budget and the smaller is the deficit bias[14]. The larger the finance minister's agenda-setting power, the closer the deficit comes to the collectively optimal outcome. An alternative way to implement it is for the finance minister to have formal veto powers in the cabinet negotiations over the budget. Von Hagen and Harden (1996) show that the veto approach is less effective in reducing the deficit bias. In presidential systems, where the problem of co-ordinating different institutional actors is more acute, the congress can delegate authority to the president. "Fast track" authorisation on trade pacts in the United States, for example, allows the president to negotiate treaties and then to present them before congress in a take-it or leave-it vote. "Fast track" reduces the common pool resource problem in comparison to a vote with full amendment procedures.

Under the contract approach the executive agrees on a set of fiscal targets collectively negotiated at the start of the budgeting process. The emphasis here is on the multilateral nature of the negotiations. Through the exchange of information and co-operative bargaining, the process of negotiating budget targets forces all participants to consider the full tax burden created by additional spending, thus eliminating the externality causing the deficit bias.

The institutional choice between these two mechanisms to overcome the deficit bias depends critically on the number of veto players in a country's budget process. Our proposition is that delegation is the correct approach for governments that have just one veto player, but difficult for governments with more than one veto player. The use of contracts is the better approach for multi-veto player governments but more difficult to achieve for single veto player governments. In the context of parliamentary systems, the former is appropriate for single-party governments, the latter for coalition governments (Hallerberg and von Hagen, 1998).

This proposition hinges on two elements. First, members of the same political party are more likely to hold similar political views regarding the distribution of funds over the various spending departments than are members of different political parties. Conflicts of interest among members of the same political party in the executive therefore arise primarily from the common pool problem[15]. Specifically, the different ministers in a one-party government can be fairly sure that the finance minister holds more or less the same spending preferences as they do. In a coalition government, in contrast, cabinet members are likely to have different views regarding the distribution of government spending over the groups of recipients. Agreement on a budget, therefore, involves a compromise between the coalition partners regarding the distribution of funds for a given budget size.

Under such circumstances, delegating strategic powers to the finance minister is more difficult for a coalition government than for a single-party government, since the finance minister necessarily is a member of one of the coalition parties himself. For a coalition government, delegation then creates a new principal agent problem. This is because the finance minister can use his agenda setting or veto powers in the preparation of the budget bill not only to reduce the deficit bias, but also to influence the composition of the budget. Even if they recognise the desirability of a strong finance minister to reduce the deficit bias, the members of the other coalition parties must fear that, for a given size of the budget, the finance minister will abuse his powers to shift the distribution of transfers in the budget towards his own, preferred distribution, at the cost of the recipients favoured more strongly by themselves. These members will, therefore, be reluctant to vest the finance minister with strong agenda-setting powers. With limited agenda-setting powers, the finance minister becomes unable to achieve the collectively optimal decision. The same principal agent problem does not arise in the case of fiscal contracts, since the contracts are negotiated by all cabinet members. Thus, governments with two or more veto players are more likely to opt for the contracts approach.

Enforcement of the Budget: Monitoring and Punishment

The second factor in the choice between delegation and contracts is the enforcement mechanism. Even if the executive is able to agree on a budget with a small deficit bias, the agreement is unlikely to be effective unless it is enforced during the implementation of the budget law. A necessary condition for enforcement is that the financial activities of the spending departments be closely monitored during the budget year, usually a function of the finance minister. The more autonomy the spending departments have to determine the timing and size of financial transactions, the less the finance minister will be able to detect deviations from the budget agreement. Beyond that, particular interests will still prevail, if there is no real punishment for players who renege on the agreement. The two institutional solutions to the common pool problem require different enforcement mechanisms, which, again, reflect the number of veto players in the process.

Enforcement of the budget agreement can be based on two different types of threats. In one-party governments, the ultimate punishment is dismissal from office. Such punishment is heavy for the individual minister who overspends, but generally light for the government as a whole. It is based on the fact that prime ministers in one-party governments are typically the strongest members of their cabinets and have the power and authority to select and reshuffle their cabinet members. Such punishment is, therefore, relatively easy for the prime minister to execute. The prime minister is often also the leader of the governing party, a position that reinforces his power within the cabinet. Even in the United Kingdom, where the norm of "first among equals" is historically strong, the prime minister dictates the shape of the cabinet. In practice, the prime minister can delegate his enforcement powers to some extent to the finance minister, who will then represent a faithful "agent" of the prime minister[16].

In the case of coalition governments, punishment cannot be directed easily to the defecting minister by the prime minister. The distribution of portfolios is, as far as the sitting prime minister is concerned, exogenously given by the coalition agreement. The prime minister cannot easily dismiss or otherwise discipline intransigent spending ministers from a different party, since that would be regarded as an intrusion into the internal party affairs of his coalition partners. The most important punishment mechanism here is the threat that the coalition breaks up if a spending minister reneges on the budget agreement. Overspending by an individual minister from one party in the coalition implies a redistribution of public spending away from the transfer recipients most favoured by the others and, therefore, implies a cost of political support for the other parties in the coalition. This motivates the threat of breaking up the coalition. Thus, punishment leads to the death of the government rather than the dismissal of a single individual. The point is illustrated by the fact that fiscal targets are often part of the coalition agreement.

The credibility of the threat hinges on two important factors. It requires the existence of alternative coalition partners, and, if a new coalition cannot be formed and new elections are necessary, the anticipation of electoral results. If another partner exists with whom the aggrieved party can form a coalition, the threat to leave the coalition is clearly more credible. The number of parties in parliament is one obvious limit to the number of alternative coalition partners. Even among the parties which do exist, some may be undesirable for policy reasons or may not be considered *koalitionsfähig* such as the Italian Communist Party. Other parties may simply be impossible to exclude from the coalition formation process. A party is "strong" according to Laver and Shepsle (1996), if it can veto every potential cabinet, and coalition partners may not be able to punish a party that occupies such a dominant position. Yet, to the extent that there are several possible coalitions, reputations will be important. Parties which are known not to keep coalition agreements will have problems finding partners, and as long as parties anticipate that none of them has a reasonable chance of winning an absolute majority of seats in the future, they will value the possibility of co-operation in the future. The threat of new elections may also intimidate a defecting party into meeting its targets, if this party faces defeat if elections are called.

In conclusion, punishments directed at individuals are difficult to administer in governments with more than one veto player. The reverse also holds. Consider a single-party government where one spending minister continues to overspend his budget allocation despite admonition by the prime minister or finance minister. Threatening the end of the government to discipline the intransigent spending minister is not a credible strategy, since this would certainly put the entire government out of office, with no chance for the other ministers to continue in with another partner. If the prime minister is politically too weak to call the defector to order, the executive will ultimately simply ignore its original budget agreement and tolerate the lack of fiscal discipline.

Institutions outside the executive branch of the government can be used to help enforce the budget agreement of a coalition government. Parliamentary committees in particular often provide an information-collection function which can also be used to oversee the government (Krehbiel, 1991; Mattson and Strøm, 1995; Hallerberg, 1997). They hold hearings on the actions of the government and, in some cases, can call different ministers to justify their spending behavior. These committees are likely to be most effective when their area of expertise matches up with a particular ministry. They also function better when chairpersons come from a different party than the minister responsible for the given spending area[17]. In contrast, the role for parliament in a delegation context is much diminished. Strong information collection powers under a one-party government might undermine the power of the fiscal entrepreneur, and more generally would enable backbenchers to undercut the authority of the prime minister even in places lacking a fiscal entrepreneur.

Institutions outside the country can also serve as useful monitors for coalition partners. The OECD, for example, issues reports on every country that indicate likely spending and deficit levels. Elsewhere, the IMF provides this monitoring function (Fischer, 1997). In the context of European Monetary Union, the European Commission identifies countries running "excessive" deficits. Belgium, for example, which was not able to maintain a contract approach in the 1980s, used the opportunity of the convergence programmes demanded by the Maastricht Treaty to present a fiscal programme after 1992 that aimed to achieve the criteria for EMU by 1998. Portugal similarly attempted to go down the same path as Belgium with its Convergence Programme but was initially less successful. It failed to maintain the spending targets it had set out for itself, and deficits initially worsened. In 1993 it issued a revised programme and has since been able to maintain budgetary contracts. The example of the Maastricht requirements, and the fact that the attempt to reduce budget deficits though the imposition of fiscal targets from the outside failed in the large countries of the European Union (Germany, France, Spain and Italy) after 1992, also suggests that the effectiveness of outside actors in enforcing budget agreements depends critically on the importance of international organisations in domestic politics, which is plausibly a function of the size of the country (von Hagen, 1997).

Case Studies

Four case studies help illustrate the success or failure of the monitoring and punishment functions and how they are related to the number of veto players for the time period 1981-94. In the United Kingdom, the prime minister was exceptionally strong and could reshuffle the cabinet as well as appoint ministers almost at will. The chancellor of the exchequer was generally regarded as second in power only to the prime minister, and he was given the power to negotiate one-to-one with spending ministers about their budget allocations. If there was a dispute between the finance minister and a given spending minister, it went to a committee composed of senior ministers without portfolio known as the "Star Chamber"[18] for consideration and not to the full cabinet for resolution. These ministers do not have budgets of their own, and a log-rolling situation in favour of the spending minister is not possible. Since the senior ministers are appointed to consider the general interests of the cabinet as a whole, they usually support the finance minister (von Hagen and Harden, 1996).

In Greece one-party majority governments were also the rule, but in this case the government did not opt for a delegation solution. The country used a "preferential" form of proportional representation, which was designed to favour the largest parties in elections, and in practice only three parties usually win seats. The greatest distortion between the number of votes and number of seats occurred in the 1974 elections, when New Democracy received 54.4 per cent of the votes but 72 per cent of the seats (Alivizatos, 1990). Except during the short period when the conservatives allied with the small communist party, either the conservatives or the socialists have controlled the government with a one-party majority in parliament. Yet Greece did not develop a framework in which the finance minister has significant power over the spending ministers. The full cabinet made all major decisions related to the budget (von Hagen, 1992).

The Netherlands have the most representative system in the European Union, and as a consequence have never had a one-party majority government during the post-war period. In contrast to the United Kingdom, over the reference period the prime minister possessed little power. Negotiations among the parties during the formation of the coalition determine most items of importance, including the distribution of portfolios, and the prime minister consequently lacked the ability to remove defiant ministers. The prime minister also does not have the power to settle any disputes, and votes in cabinet meetings only in cases of a tie. Instead of using a strong finance minister, the coalition negotiations wrote explicit budgetary targets into the coalition agreement which constituted the fiscal contract among the parties. As expected, there were several institutional devices which enhanced the ability of parties to monitor each other's behaviour. The legislature in particular serves an important oversight role. Committee jurisdictions were matched with specific ministries, and the committee chair is required to come from a party other than the one which provided the minister (Andeweg and Irwin, 1993). Parties also had the means to punish defectors. The same parties were likely to be potential coalition partners again, and, since there was little likelihood that any of them could win an absolute majority, the parties anticipate the need for a multi-party coalition government in the future. There was also competition among them for positions in the government: with the exception of a few extremist parties which received almost no parliamentary seats, all of the parties were potential coalition partners, and a given party which violated a coalition agreement could be excluded from future governments. It was therefore in a party's best interest to cultivate a reputation for keeping its coalition agreements.

In contrast, Italy before 1994 had a similarly proportional representation electoral system, but no such contracts were negotiated among the coalition partners. Even if such agreements had existed, however, it is doubtful that they would have been credible.

(Strøm, 1990) indicates that the parliament did have some oversight powers, but the Italian coalition partners lacked an effective punishment mechanism to use even if they did detect defections. While no party could expect to gain an absolute majority under the proportional electoral system, there was also a low probability that a given party could be excluded from a future coalition. With many parliamentary seats going to extremist parties, whose share of seats reached a high of 40 per cent in the early 1970s, there were fewer coalition possibilities (*Ibid.*). Every government had to include the largest party in the centre, the Christian Democrats, in order to have any chance of passing legislation, and coalitions often were composed of the same parties as their predecessors. No party could credibly threaten the Christian Democrats as long as the political system remained in force.

Empirical Evidence from the European Union and Latin America

The previous section indicates that the number of veto players determines the choice of institutions strengthening fiscal discipline. Delegation coupled with enforcement directed at individual ministers is the adequate choice for governments with a single veto player, while contracts coupled with enforcement directed at the entire cabinet is the appropriate choice for governments with multiple veto players. In this section, we use empirical data from the European Union and Latin America to evaluate that prediction.

In the European context of parliamentary democracies, the distinction between single and multiple veto players is equivalent to the distinction between single-party and coalition governments. Table 3 reports the predicted and actual budgetary institutions based on the type of government in European Union countries from 1981 to 1994. Within this group, France, Greece, and the United Kingdom are states with one veto player; the others have more than one veto player.

Of the three states expected to use delegation, France and the United Kingdom did while Greece did not. However, Greece did not adopt an institutional solution to the problem of deficit bias at all. In this sense, the Greek case cannot be considered a misprediction. A similarly strong pattern emerges for the states where multi-party coalitions are common. Eight of the twelve states predicted to use a contracts approach did so at some point, while the remaining four states opted for neither of the solutions. Three of the four states which did not use one of the options were predicted to choose contracts, and four of the states that did negotiate contracts were not able to maintain them throughout the period. The sample size is too small to make any statistical comparison conclusive, but this high failure rate among states where one-party governments are not the norm is nonetheless noteworthy. One possible explanation is that the monitoring and punishment functions are more difficult to assure in multi-party governments than in one-party governments. Furthermore, the strong position of the finance minister can be enshrined in constitutional law, as it is in France and in the United Kingdom, where tradition serves the same purpose. In contrast, coalition agreements are more variable over time.

Table 3. **Predicted and Actual Institutional Solutions, 1981-94**

State	Predicted Institution	Actual Institution
Austria	Contracts	Contracts (1985-92)
Belgium	Contracts	Contracts (1993-94)
Denmark	Contracts	Contracts (1982-94)
Finland	Contracts	Contracts
Ireland	Contracts	Contracts (1987-94)
Luxembourg	Contracts	Contracts
Netherlands	Contracts	Contracts
Portugal	Contracts	Contracts (1994)
France	Delegation	Delegation
Germany	Contracts	Delegation
United Kingdom	Delegation	Delegation
Greece	Delegation	No Such Constraint
Italy	Contracts	No Such Constraint
Spain	Contracts	No Such Constraint
Sweden	Contracts	No Such Constraint

Note: Data for the incidence of contracts and delegation are from von Hagen and Harden (1996) with the exception of the data for Portugal, which comes from "The Economic and Financial Situation in Portugal". *European Economy. Reports and Studies I*. 1997. A state which almost always had one-party governments (p > .9) was coded as "delegation" as its predicted institution.

Germany is the difficult case in this sample. Germany's electoral system is based on a two-ballot structure that contains elements of both plurality and proportional representation, making a clear classification initially difficult. During the post-war period a major party (the CDU/CSU or the SPD) almost always formed a coalition with a smaller partner (either the FDP or the DP), the exception being the "grand coalition" of the two large parties from 1966 to 1969. However, in previous elections coalition partners usually pledged a continuation of the coalition, if together they received enough votes, and the Green Party made it clear that it would enter a coalition only with the SPD. This may explain why Germany also adopts a delegation approach, although it never had one-party majority government within the reference period. Note also that the partners of the grand coalition — each of which could expect to find a new partner should the coalition break up — introduced a medium-term fiscal strategy based on numerical targets as part of their coalition agreement. Thus, during the one period of a more typical scenario of two veto players in the executive, Germany's government reverted to a contract approach. Finally, the German finance minister's strategic role is considerably weaker than that of his counterparts in more typical delegation states.

Based on data from Stein, Talvi, and Grisanti (1997), we find similar results for Latin America, although our findings are necessarily more tentative because of data restrictions. Stein *et al.* construct a budgetary index based on answers to a survey sent to twenty countries in the region. They include ten characteristics covering three broad categories of budgetary rules: constraints on the size of the deficit, hierarchical rules, and the level of transparency[19]. Their index therefore does not correspond exactly to our division of budgetary institutions into three approaches, and in particular it is not possible to examine the incidence of budgetary pacts. We predict, however, that more hierarchical institutions would be most possible in countries where the president maintains a one party majority in the congress or where the number of veto players is equal to one. Indeed, based on their data, this seems to be the case. Table 4 compares the incidence of one-party government with the rankings of their countries in the index for the period 1991-95. In eight of the ten countries in the top half of their sample the president indeed enjoyed a one-party majority government and there was consequently just one veto player, while in eight of the bottom ten the president's party lacked a majority in the congress and there were therefore at least two veto players. The implication is that the states in the bottom half of their index lack hierarchical budget rules because parties that together can block any legislation are unlikely to delegate such powers to one single actor, the president, who is their political rival. Such states should instead rely on budgetary contracts to improve fiscal discipline.

Table 4. **Budgetary Institutions and Unified Government in Latin America**

State	Budgetary Institutions Index Rank	Does President Have Majority Support from his Party in the Lower House?
Colombia	1	Yes
Jamaica	2	Yes
Chile	3	Yes
Mexico	4	Yes
Panama	5	No
Uruguay	6	No
Trinidad and Tobago	7	Yes
Bahamas	8	Yes
Guatemala	8	Yes
Argentina	8	Yes
Costa Rica	11	No
Ecuador	11	No
Paraguay	13	Yes
Venezuela	13	No
Peru	15	Yes
Honduras	16	Yes
Brazil	17	No
El Salvador	17	No
Bolivia	19	No
Dominican Republic	20	No

Note: All the data are computed from Stein, Talvi, and Grisanti (1997). An explanation of the budgetary institutions index is provided in the main body of the our text.

Table 5 provides some evidence for the link between the information-providing capacities of parliamentary committees and the three budgetary institutions in current European Union countries. The first column of data indicates whether or not a committee's area of responsibility corresponds with a government ministry. If this correspondence exists, a committee will presumably have a greater capacity to monitor that ministry. The second category is the appointment process for the chairperson of the committee. If the chairs are distributed proportionally, it is likely that the chair will come from a different party than the respective minister, and it will be harder for the minister to conceal actions. The last two categories measure a committee's ability to compel either witnesses or documents from the government.

Table 5. **Comparison of Committee Monitoring Power and Budgetary Institutions**

State	Ministry Match	Chair Proportional	Compel Witnesses	Demand Docs	Total	Institution
Austria	1	0	1	1	3	Contracts
Denmark	1	1	1	0	3	Contracts
Finland	0	1	0	1	2	Contracts
Ireland	*	*	*	*	*	Contracts
Luxembourg	1	1	0	1	3	Contracts
Netherlands	1	1	0	0	2	Contracts
France	0	0	1	1	2	Delegation
Germany	1	1	0	0	2	Delegation
United Kingdom	0	0	0	0	0	Delegation
Belgium	1	1	0	0	2	Fiefdom
Greece	0	0	0	0	0	Fiefdom
Italy	1	0	0	0	1	Fiefdom
Portugal	1	1	1	0	3	Fiefdom
Spain	1	1	1	1	4	Fiefdom
Sweden	1	1	0	1	3	Fiefdom

Source: Hallerberg (1997). The respective variable is coded as "1" if the answer is "yes" and "0" if it is "no". The committee data is adopted from Mattson and Strøm (1995). The data on the budgetary institutions is from Hallerberg and von Hagen (1998). Ireland strengthened its committee structure significantly in 1993, but detailed data on the change does not appear in Mattson and Strøm (1995). Its committee attributes are therefore represented with a "*".

This data can only be suggestive; it does not assign priorities, nor are there enough cases to indicate statistical significance. With these qualifications in mind, it is clear that, as expected, the five states that used contracts had a higher average number of these institutions at 2.6, while non-contract states had an average of just 1.7. In addition, the two countries that had one-party majority governments and are hence most appropriate for delegation, Greece and the United Kingdom, also had the weakest institutional capacity to collect information[20].

Budgeting Institutions and Fiscal Performance

So far, we have argued that different types of governments, classified by the number of veto players, choose different types of institutional mechanisms to overcome the deficit bias resulting from the common pool nature of public budgeting. In this section, we provide evidence for the effectiveness of such mechanisms. The key issue is, of course, whether or not countries delegating significant strategic powers to a finance minister or relying on the contract approach to fiscal targets run systematically lower deficits.

Average Fiscal Performance

A first question we ask is whether these institutions improve the fiscal performance of governments on average over a longer period of time. To answer this, we take data from the 15 European Union states covering the period from 1981 to 1994.

Table 6 presents the results from a regression analysis. Our list of variables follows Roubini and Sachs (1989) and De Haan and Sturm (1994; and forthcoming) with the important distinction that we add dummy variables for the presence or absence of a strong finance minister or fiscal contracts[21]. There are two sets of variables. The first set of variables measure fluctuations in a given country's economy, and they are expected to have some impact on budget deficits regardless of the presence or absence of government policies meant to reduce public debt levels. Positive changes in GDP should improve the budget situation, while increases in the unemployment rate are likely to add to the size of the deficit due to automatic payments of unemployment compensation. In addition, changes in real interest rates affect the size of interest payments on the debt, and, if the real interest rate is higher than the real growth rate, interest payments will generally cause an increase in the total debt level. We therefore include a variable for the net change in debt servicing costs[22]. A lag for our dependent variable, which is the change in the debt level, is also included to reduce autocorrelation in the model.

The second set of variables covers some of the most frequently-cited political explanations. One way to conceptualise veto players is to think about the number of parties in the coalition. To make our work directly comparable with others (Roubini and Sachs, 1989; Edin and Ohlsson, 1991; De Haan and Sturm, 1994; and forthcoming, Franzese, 1996) we include dummy variables for the number of parties in a majority coalition government (either 2-3 parties or 4-5 parties) and for the presence of minority governments, with a one-party government equal to the case where the 2-3 party, 4-5 party, and minority government dummies all equal zero. If veto players matter, then one would anticipate that the presence of any of these dummies would positively affect the debt level, with coefficients that increase as one moves from 2-3 party majority government to minority government[23]. Our contention is that veto players affect only the type of budgetary approach that potentially solves the common pool problem and not the size of the deficit itself, and by including veto players in the regression along with dummy variables for delegation and contracts we test this directly. We also examine the role of changes in the government, both in terms of elections and actual changes and in terms of just election years. Finally, we also include the political composition of government.

Table 6. **Budgeting Institutions and Average Fiscal Performance, 1981-94**
Dependent Variable: Change in the Gross Debt Level as a Proportion of GDP (to Maastricht Definitions)

Variable	Coefficient	Std. Error	t-ratio	Prob
Constant	3.6	0.81	4.45	0.0001
Change in Debt t-1	0.30	0.05	5.62	0.0001
Change in GDP, Real Values	0.90	0.16	-5.46	0.0001
Change in Unemployment Rate	0.76	0.28	2.71	0.01
Change in Debt Servicing Costs	0.04	0.1	-0.38	0.70
Change in Govt.	1.57	0.44	3.55	0.0005
2-3 Party Majority Govt.	0.81	0.73	1.12	0.26
4-5 Party Majority Govt.	0.40	0.88	0.46	0.65
Minority Govt.	-0.52	0.86	-0.61	0.55
Left	-0.92	0.65	-1.43	0.15
Delegation	-1.95	0.73	-2.67	0.01
Contracts	-1.45	0.63	-2.30	0.02

R squared = 53.9%   R squared (adjusted) = 51.4%

Data Sources: European Commission (1995), De Haan and Sturm (1994), *European Journal of Political Research* (Various Years), Woldendorp, Keman, and Budge (1993), and von Hagen and Harden (1996).
Diagnostics: A lagged dependent variable was added to eliminate significant autocorrelation. The Lagrange multiplier statistic did not reject the null hypothesis of homoskedasticity. A comparison of the group-effects model with the standard OLS regression also indicated the lack of country-specific effects.

The results of the regression are encouraging. The variables for the two budgetary institutions are both significant and have the correct sign. None of the dummy variables for the number of veto players is significant, which confirms our argument that it is the budgetary approach rather than the number of veto players that matters. The measurement for partisanship is also not significant, although its sign indicates that left-wing parties are more likely to reduce the size of the debt burden. Only a change in government has a significant impact on the growth of debt.

Coping with Change

During a fiscal year political and economic circumstances may change in ways not fully anticipated when the budget was negotiated, and such changes may cause the executive to renegotiate the agreement. Such a situation would obviously give rise to the same type of co-ordination problems discussed earlier. A second way to test for the importance of budgetary institutions is, therefore, to see if they systematically affect the way governments react to political and economics changes.

One important event is a change in the players that negotiate the budget through elections or a break-up of the ruling coalition. Political-economy literature has often linked elections with government-inspired changes to the macroeconomy for short-term electoral gain at the expense of longer-term economic growth (Nordhaus, 1975; MacRae, 1977). The hope is that higher spending before an election will attract additional voters to the ruling government. The evidence for such "political business cycles" has been decidedly mixed. Even in the landmark article that began the debate, Nordhaus (1975) found evidence for such cycles in just four of nine cases he examined (see also Alesina, 1989; Davidson, Fratianni, and von Hagen, 1992; Alesina, Cohen, and Roubini, 1993; Clark and Reichert (forthcoming) find some evidence in states with dependent central banks).

Furthermore, if one expects to be replaced soon in the government one may not fear the punishment that either a finance minister (under delegation) or other coalition partners (under contracts) would levy on potential defectors (see especially Grilli, Masciandaro, and Tabellini, 1991). The expectation here is that deficits would increase both in election years and in years where there were changes in the coalition, and, following De Haan and Sturm, 1994, we consider a variable for years in which there was either an election or an actual change in the political parties that composed the cabinet.

To examine these arguments, Table 7 presents regression results that include both a variable for the year of an election and an interaction term for elections with the two budgetary approaches. The data indicate that contracts restrain the government while delegation does not. This makes intuitive sense — under fiscal contracts the players do not want to let their coalition partners gain an edge over them so they do not allow any slippage at all, while in a one party government a finance minister may allow some deterioration in the budget if he thinks it affects the very survival of the government.

Another important aspect concerns how well the various approaches perform when the economy worsens and economic growth is negative. Table 8 includes interactive terms for negative growth along with delegation and contracts. In this case, it is delegation, rather than contracts, that functions better. Under delegation it appears that deficits do not grow nearly as fast as under contracts, and, as the negative and significant coefficients for the two approaches show, under fiefdom deficits are even worse. A likely explanation is that finance ministers are able to react more quickly to economic downturns than the ministers of the cabinet.

Table 7. **Elections and Budgeting Institutions**

Variable	Coefficient	Std. Error	t-ratio	prob
Constant	3.4	1.2	2.8	0.01
Change in Debt t-1	0.3	0.06	5.4	0.0001
Change in GDP	-0.9	0.16	-5.3	0.0001
Change in Unemployment Rate	0.9	0.3	3.0	0.003
Change in Debt Servicing Costs	-0.02	0.1	-0.2	0.80
Election	2.8	0.8	3.6	0.0004
2-3 Party Majority Govt.	1	0.7	1.4	0.16
4-5 Party Majority Govt.	0.8	0.8	0.9	0.36
Minority Govt.	-0.3	0.8	-0.4	0.67
Left	-0.7	0.7	-1.1	0.29
Delegation	-1.7	0.9	-1.9	0.06
Contracts	-0.8	0.7	-1.2	0.24
Election*Delegation	-1.9	1.4	-1.4	0.13
Election*Contracts	-3.2	1.1	-2.8	0.005

R squared: 54.3%   R Squared (Adjusted) 51.3%

Table 8. **Recessions and Budgeting Institutions**

Variable	Coefficient	Std. Error	t-ratio	prob
Constant	4.4	1.2	3.6	0.0005
Change in Debt t-1	0.3	0.06	5.1	0.0001
Change in GDP	-1.0	0.2	-6.0	0.0001
Change in Unemployment Rate	0.9	0.3	3.0	0.003
Change in Debt Servicing Costs	-0.03	0.1	-0.3	0.74
Election	1.3	0.5	2.5	0.01
2-3 Party Majority Govt.	1	0.7	1.4	0.16
4-5 Party Majority Govt.	0.9	0.8	1.1	0.26
Minority Govt.	-0.4	0.8	-0.6	0.58
Left	-0.9	0.7	-1.3	0.18
Delegation	-1.9	0.8	-2.2	0.03
Contracts	-1.7	0.63	-2.7	0.01
Neggrowth*Delegation	-2.5	1.1	-2.2	0.03
Neggrowth*Contracts	-0.5	0.5	-1.1	0.28

R squared = 53.8%   R squared (adjusted) = 50.7%

Conclusions

A general characteristic of modern public finance is that public spending is targeted more narrowly than taxation. The incongruence in the incidence of the marginal benefit and the marginal cost of expanding public activities implies a common pool problem of public budgeting, with the result of a deficit bias in budgeting decisions. We have argued that this bias can be reduced by introducing institutional rules that promote centralisation of the budget process, i.e., that help the participants to internalise the externalities create by the common pool problem. Two approaches can be identified, delegation of strategic powers to a strong finance minister and commitment to fiscal targets through a contractual agreement among all participants. We have shown that the choice of institutional approach is determined by the number of party-veto players in the budget process which, in turn depends critically on two political factors: the electoral system and whether or not the chief executive is chosen in direct elections.

One-party governments are most suitable for delegation, while multi-party governments should rely on fiscal contracts. The comparison of the various systems and solutions which are now used indicates that, under certain circumstances, the use of delegation can be expanded to multi-party governments. The key is that all the parties in the government see their electoral fortunes as one, as in France and Germany. This indicates that delegation may also be a viable solution for Italy. The new electoral system introduced in 1994, which relies on the plurality method for 75 per cent of the seats in parliament, has led to two distinct constellations of parties. The presence of a centre-left minority government indicates that fiscal contracts may be the only feasible short-term solution, but if the electoral system continues to evolve and one of the two blocs can expect to win a majority of seats in future elections, a strong finance minister may become a better choice. Similarly, in New Zealand and Japan, which recently made their electoral systems more proportional, the result may be attempts to weaken the finance ministries in the respective countries.

This paper also carries an important implication for the future European Monetary Union. The Convergence Procedure prior to EMU and the Excessive Deficit Procedure under EMU can be read as versions of the contract approach with external enforcement. The fact that different countries in the more successful European groups used different approaches to achieve a greater degree of fiscal discipline should make us aware of an important question: is the contract approach really going to work for all states in the European Union? Our research suggests that the contract approach will not be effective in states where delegation is most appropriate. Indeed, it should come as no surprise that two delegation countries that are expected to form the core of EMU, France and Germany, have had trouble reaching the Maastricht criteria limits on yearly deficits and debt, while other states where contracts are expected to function well, such as Belgium and Portugal, have had greater success so far in meeting those targets.

Finally, there are some clear lessons for countries that are seeking to build institutions in new democracies throughout the world. The 1997 Inter-American Development Bank Report argues that "more hierarchical budget institutions that grant more power and responsibility to the finance minister (*vis-à-vis* other ministers) and to the executive (*vis-à-vis* congress) in determining aggregate spending and the fiscal deficit can contain deficit bias and lead to permanent and meaningful improvements in fiscal discipline". We agree with the conclusion that, all else being equal, more hierarchical rules do improve fiscal discipline, but not all governments are able to delegate decision-making powers to a central player like a finance minister. Yet all is not lost. In countries where multiple veto players prevail, fiscal contracts can serve as an effective solution to the common pool resource problem, and, as the last section demonstrated, they are even superior to a strong finance minister in preventing political business cycles. Greater weight should therefore be placed in such countries on the development of firm agreements among the relevant actors on fiscal targets, and on appropriate enforcement mechanisms for such contracts.

Notes

1. Barro (1979). See Alesina and Perotti (1995) for a review of theories explaining deficits and their empirical strength in the post-1970 period.

2. See Roubini and Sachs (1989), Edin and Ohlsson (1991), De Haan and Sturm (1994).

3. See von Hagen (1992), von Hagen and Harden (1994a, 1996).

4. Italy's experience with growing welfare payments is a prime example for this mechanism. Up to the mid-1990s, Italian politicians used the disability pension system quite openly to buy voter support. See *New York Times*, Sept. 19, 1997

5. See Velasco (1998), von Hagen and Harden (1996).

6. Readers should not confuse decentralisation of the negotiating process with decentralisation of spending and power in a given country. A highly "centralised" country like France can fall victim to the same decentralised bargaining problem as a more federal, and "decentralised," country like the United States.

7. The assumption that a given minister wholly determines policy for his ministry is standard in models of coalition formation. The best example is Laver and Shepsle (1996).

8. For a more formal treatment of the common pool problem in cabinets see Hallerberg and von Hagen (forthcoming).

9. See Perotti (1997) for empirical evidence confirming this suggestion.

10. Mackie and Rose (1991). The average district magnitude figures is reported in Lijphart (1994).

11. Other factors which affect proportionality include legal barriers which require a party to gain a certain percentage of the national vote to win legislative seats, the method used to apportion seats, and whether or not a second allocation of seats is used to reduce disparities at the district level. A succinct summary is found in Gallagher, Laver, and Mair (1992).

12. A reasonable measure for the number of parties considers the strength of parties as well as their absolute number. The measure that will be used here is for the effective number of parties in parliament and is taken from Mark Laakso and Rein Taagepera, as quoted in Lijphart (1994). It is calculated as $N = 1/S \, s_i^2$, where N equals the effective number of parties and s_i equals the proportion of seats party i possess in the legislature.

13. Other empirical studies that confirm this link include Lijphart (1994) and Taagepera and Shugart (1989 and 1993).

14. See von Hagen and Harden (1996) for a formal analysis.

15. Laver and Shepsle (1994), for instance, in summarising the findings of the case studies in their edited volume, note that the distribution of portfolios among members of the same political party has little effect on the policies which the government adopts; much more important is the distribution of portfolios among different parties.

16. Lupia and McCubbins (1994) indicate that an agent will choose the principal's optimal policy if two conditions are met: the principal understands the implications of maintaining the current policy or accepting the agent's proposal, and the policy that is most favourable for the principal is the one that the agent proposes. Especially in cases where spending cuts are needed, the prime minister can clearly see the implications of continuing spending at current levels or accepting the finance minister's negotiated settlement, and both principal and agent alike have the same interest to reduce the budget deficit. With both conditions met, the finance minister makes the same proposal the prime minister would have had better information been available.

17. More generally, there may be a greater desire to make budgetary procedures more transparent and more public in coalition governments that have negotiated budgetary targets than under one party governments. Mandatory reporting of expenditures reduces the costs for coalition partners to monitor each other. An aggressive press can then serve as a "fire alarm" to alert other coalition members of spending excesses (McCubbins and Schwarz, 1984).

18. The Star Chamber was dissolved in the early 1990s, however. Consistent with the argument presented here, the gross debt burden deteriorated after the weakening of the chancellor of the exchequer, from a gross debt of 35.7 per cent of GDP (Maastricht definition) in 1991 to 52.5 per cent in 1995 (European Economy 1995).

19. The rules for coding the data are found in Inter-American Development Bank (1997).

20. While these two results were consistent with the discussion presented above, there are also some surprises. Two countries which use delegation, France and Germany, also have some characteristics of target-based countries. They are also states which are characterised by coalitions which regularly align in elections, and this table suggests that the coalition partners may have some interest in monitoring each other even when budgetary targets do not form the basis of their system. Three states which use neither of the two institutional solutions, Portugal, Spain, and Sweden, do have committees with at least three of the information collection attributes, and they appear to be prepared to use commitment if they so chose.

21. There are also some differences in the countries and years covered in the respective studies. De Haan and Sturm base their regressions on the E.C. 12 from 1981 to 1989, while Roubini and Sachs consider 14 OECD countries from 1960 to 1985.

22. Following De Haan and Sturm (1994) we code this variable as (Nominal Long Term Interest Rate – Inflation Rate – Real GDP Growth Rate)*Debt Level (t-1).

23. Note that the conceptualisation of the number of veto players in minority governments is not clear. While Tsebelis (1995) argues that they should be treated as one-party majority governments, the fact that they must always find parties outside of the government to pass anything means that they resemble more multi-party coalition governments. Edin and Ohlsson argue that such governments are most prone to run large deficits, and for this reason we code them as a separate dummy variable.

Bibliography

ALESINA, A., R. HAUSMANN, R. HOMMES AND E. STEIN (1996), "Budget Institutions and Fiscal Performance in Latin America", *NBER Working Paper,* No. 5586

ALESINA, A. AND R. PEROTTI (1995), "Fiscal Expansions and Adjustments in OECD Countries", *Economic Policy.*

ALESINA, A., G.D. COHEN AND N. ROUBINI (1993), "Electoral Business Cycles in Industrial Democracies", *European Journal of Political Economy,* 9.

ALESINA, A. (1989), "Politics and Business Cycles in Industrial Democracies", *Economic Policy,* 8.

ALIVIZATOS, N. (1990), "The Difficulties of 'Rationalization' in a Polarized Political System: the Greek Chamber of Deputies", in U. LIEBERT AND M. COTTA (eds.) *Parliament and Democratic Consolidation in Southern Europe: Greece Italy, Portugal, Spain and Turkey,* Pinter Publishers, London and New York.

ANDEWEG, R. AND G. IRWIN (1993), *Dutch Government and Politics,* MacMillan, London.

BARRO, R. (1979), "On the Determination of Public Debt", *Journal of Political Economy,* 87.

BORRELLI, S.A. AND T.J. ROYED (1995), "Government 'Strength' and Budget Deficits in Advanced Democracies", *European Journal of Political Research* 28.

CLARK, W.R. AND U. NAIR REICHERT (forthcoming), "International and Domestic Constraints on Political Business Cycles in OECD Economies", *International Organization.*

COX, G.W. AND M. D. MCCUBBINS (1993), *Legislative Leviathan,* University of California Press, Berkeley and Los Angeles.

DAVIDSON, L.S., M. FRATIANNI AND J. VON HAGEN (1992), "Testing the Satisficing Version of the Political Business – Cycle 1905-1984", *Public Choice,* 73.

DE HAAN, J. AND J.-E. STURM (forthcoming), "Political and Economic Determinants of OECD Budget Deficits and Government Expenditures: A Reinvestigation", *European Journal of Political Economy.*

DE HAAN, J. AND J.-E. STURM (1994), "Political and Institutional Determinants of Fiscal Policy in the European Community", *Public Choice,* 80.

DUVERGER, M. (1954), *Political Parties. Their Organization and Activity in the Modern State,* Wiley, New York.

EDIN, P.-A. AND H. OHLSSON (1991), "Political Determinants of Budget Deficits: Coalition Effects Versus Minority Effects", *European Economic Review,* 35.

EUROPEAN COMMISSION (1995), *Statistical Annex of European Economy,* November.

FISCHER, S. (1997), "Capital Account Liberalization and the Role of the IMF", Monograph, International Monetary Fund, September.

FRANZESE, R.J. (1996), "The Political Economy of Over-Commitment: A Comparative Study of Democratic Management of the Keynesian Welfare State", Ph.D. Dissertation, Harvard University.

FROHLICH, N. AND J.A. OPPENHEIMER (1978), *Modern Political Economy.* Eaglewood Cliffs, Prentice-Hall, New Jersey.

GALLAGHER, M., M. LAVER AND P. MAIR (1992), *Representative Government in Western Europe,* McGraw Hill, New York.

GRILLI, V., D. MASCIANDARO AND G. TABELLINI (1991), "Institutions and Policies", *Economic Policy* 6.

HAHM, S.D., M.S. KAMLET AND D.C. MOWERY (1996), "The Political Economy of Deficit Spending in Nine Industrialized Parliamentary Democracies. The Role of Fiscal Institutions", *Comparative Political Studies* 29, 1.

HAHM, S.D. (1994), "The Political Economy of Deficit Spending: A Cross Comparison of Industrialized Democracies, 1955-1990", manuscript.

HALLERBERG, M. (1997), "A Theory for the Distribution of Committee Power in Parliamentary Systems", in L.D. LONGLEY AND A. AGH, (eds.), *Working Papers of Comparative Legislative Studies II: The Changing Roles of Parliamentary Committees.* Research Committee of Legislative Specialists, Appleton, Wisconsin.

HALLERBERG, M. AND J. VON HAGEN (1998), "Electoral Institutions, Cabinet Negotiations and Budget Deficits in the European Union." in J. POTERBA AND J. VON HAGEN (eds.), *Fiscal Institutions and Fiscal Performance,* University of Chicago Press, Chicago.

HARDIN, R. (1982), *Collective Action,* Johns Hopkins University Press, Baltimore.

HILDEBRAND, K. (1984), *Von Erhard zur Großen Koalition 1963-1969,* Deutsche Verlags-Anstalt, Stuttgart.

HUBER, J. (1996), "The Vote of No Confidence in Parliamentary Democracies", *American Political Science Review* 90, 2.

INTER-AMERICAN DEVELOPMENT BANK (1997), *Latin America After a Decade of Reforms,* Johns Hopkins University Press, Washington, D.C.

JESSE, N. (1996), "The Single Transferable Vote and Duverger's Law: Consequences for Party Systems and Elections", Ph. D. Dissertation, University of California, Los Angeles.

KATZ, R. (1980), *A Theory of Parties and Electoral Systems,* Johns Hopkins University Press, Baltimore and London.

KREHBIEL, K. (1991), *Information and Legislative Organization,* University of Michigan Press, Ann Arbor.

LAVER, M. AND K.A. SHEPSLE (1996), *Making and Breaking Governments,* Cambridge University Press, Cambridge.

LAVER, M. AND K.A. SHEPSLE (1994), "Cabinet Ministers and Government Formation in Parliamentary Democracies", in M. LAVER AND K.A. SHEPSLE, (eds.) *Cabinet Ministers and Parliamentary Government,* Cambridge University Press, Cambridge.

LAVER, M. AND N. SCHOFIELD (1990), *Multiparty Government, Comparative European Politics,* Oxford University Press, Oxford.

LIJPHART, A. (1994), *Electoral Systems and Party Systems: A Study of Twenty-Seven Democracies 1945-1990,* Oxford University Press, Oxford.

LIJPHART, A. (1984), *Democracies: Patterns of Majoritarian and Consensus Government in Twenty-one Countries,* Yale University Press, New Haven.

LUPIA, A. AND M.D. McCUBBINS (1994), "Who Controls? Information and the Structure of Legislative Decision Making", *Legislative Studies Quarterly,*19, 3.

MACKIE, T.T. AND R. ROSE (1991), *The International Almanac of Electoral History,* Third Edition, MacMillan, London.

MacRAE, D. (1977), "A Political Model of the Business Cycle", *Journal of Political Economy,* 95.

McCUBBINS, M.D. (1991), "Party Governance and U.S. Budget Deficits: Divided Government and Fiscal Stalemate", in A. ALESINA AND G. CARLINER (eds.) *Politics and Economics in the Eighties,* University of Chicago Press, Chicago.

McCUBBINS, M., AND T. SCHWARZ (1984), "Congressional Oversight Overlooked: Police Patrols vs. Fire Alarms", *American Journal of Political Science,* 28.

MATTSON, I. AND K. STRØM (1995), "Parliamentary Committees." in H. DÖRING (ed.) *Parliaments and Majority Rule in Western Europe,* St. Martin's Press, New York.

NORDHAUS, W.D. (1975), "The Political Business Cycle", *Review of Economic Studies.* 42.

OECD ECONOMIC SURVEYS 1994-95: Belgium/Luxembourg (1995), Paris.

OECD ECONOMIC OUTLOOK, 57 (1995), Paris, June.

OLSON, M. (1965), *The Logic of Collective Action,* Harvard University Press, Cambridge, Mass.

OSTROM, E. (1990), *Governing the Commons,* Cambridge University Press, Cambridge.

OSTROM, E., R. GARDNER AND J. WALKER (1994), *Rules, Games, and Common Pool Resources,* University of Michigan Press, Ann Arbor.

PEROTTI, R. (1998), "Fragmented Government", in J. POTERBA AND J. VON HAGEN, (eds.) *Fiscal Institutions and Fiscal Performance,* University of Chicago Press, Chicago.

PERSSON, T. AND L. SVENNSON (1989), "Why a Stubborn Conservative Would Run a Deficit: Policy with Time Inconsistent Preferences", *Quarterly Journal of Economics.*

ROGOFF, K. (1990), "Equilibrium Political Budget Cycles", *The American Economic Review,* March.

Roubini, N. and J.D. Sachs (1989), "Political and Economic Determinants of Budget Deficits in the Industrial Democracies", *European Economic Review,* 33.

Schick, A. (1993), "Government versus Budget Deficits", in Rockman, R. Kent and B.A. Weaver, *Do Institutions Matter?* The Brookings Institution, Washington, D.C.

Stein, E. E. Talvi and A. Grisanti (1997), "Institutional Arrangements and Fiscal Performance: The Latin American Experience", Paper Presented at the Conference on Budgeting Institutions and Fiscal Performance: Perspectives for EMU, Bonn, June 27-29.

Strøm, K. (1990), *Minority Governments and Majority Rule,* Cambridge University Press, Cambridge.

Taagepera, R. and M. Soberg Shugart (1993), "Predicting the Number of Parties: A Quantitative Model of Duverger's Mechanical Effect", *American Political Science Review,* 87, 2.

Taagepera, R. and M. Soberg Shugart (1989), *Seats and Votes: The Effects and Determinants of Electoral Systems,* Yale University Press, New Haven.

Tabellini, G. and A. Alesina (1990), "Voting on the Budget Deficit", *American Economic Review.* 80, 1.

Tsebelis, G. (1995), "Decision Making in Political Systems: Veto Players in Presidentialism, Parliamentarism, Multicameralism and Multipartyism", *British Journal of Political Science* 25.

Velasco, A. (1998), "A Model of Endogenous Fiscal Deficits and Delayed Fiscal Reforms" in J. Poterba and J. von Hagen (eds.) *Fiscal Institutions and Fiscal Performance*, University of Chicago Press, Chicago.

Von Hagen, J. (1992), "Budgeting Procedures and Fiscal Performance in the European Communities", *Economic Papers* 96.

Von Hagen, J. (1997), "The European Experience with Fiscal Initiatives: Fiscal Institutions, Maastricht Guidelines and EMU", mimeo.

Von Hagen, J. and I. Harden (1994*a*). "Budget Processes and Commitment to Fiscal Discipline", *European Economic Review.* 39.

Von Hagen, J. and I. Harden (1994*b*). "National Budget Processes and Fiscal Performance", in *European Economy. Reports and Studies* 3.

Von Hagen, J. and I. Harden (1996), "Budget Processes and Commitment to Fiscal Discipline", *IMF Working Paper.*

Weingast, B.R., K.A. Shepsle and C. Johnsen (1981), "The Political Economy of Benefits and Costs: A Neoclassical Approach to Distributive Politics", *Journal of Political Economy* 89, No. 41

Woldendorp, K., H. Keman and I. Budge (1993), "Political Data 1945-1990", *European Journal of Political Research.* 24.

Fiscal Decentralisation and Government Size in Latin America[1]

Ernesto Stein

Introduction

Latin America has had a long tradition of centralisation, which dates back to the period of colonial administration. After the independence movement, centralised fiscal structures remained in place, partly due to colonial inheritance, and partly to the need that countries had to keep distant provinces together under one power. Even today, when compared with the industrialised world, the region as a whole remains highly centralised. While sub-national levels of government are responsible for over 35 per cent of total government expenditure in industrialised countries, on average in Latin America the corresponding figure is less than 15 per cent.

However, during the past decade, together with the widespread return of democracy, several countries in the region have been going through significant processes of political and fiscal decentralisation. The increase in political autonomy of sub-national governments is reflected in Figure 1, which shows the number of countries in Latin America in which the local government executive authorities (mayors) are elected by the local population, as opposed to appointed by the central authorities. This number has grown from 3 in 1980, to 17 in 1995[2]. The trend toward fiscal decentralisation is illustrated in Figure 2, which shows the unweighted average and the median of the degree of expenditure decentralisation for fourteen Latin American countries, for which data was available for 1985, 1990 and 1995. The degree of expenditure decentralisation, measured as the proportion of total government expenditures executed by sub-national governments, increased by 4 percentage points during the last decade.

These figures suggest that, although the region remains highly centralised, the tendency toward decentralisation is quite strong: not only is a larger portion of the general government budget executed from the sub-national government levels; but the autonomy that these governments have in deciding how much to spend and what to spend on is increasing as well. In this context, a very important question is that of the possible effects of decentralisation on fiscal performance. In particular, in this paper we will concentrate on the effects on government size[3].

Figure 1. **Number of Countries where Mayors are Elected by the Population**

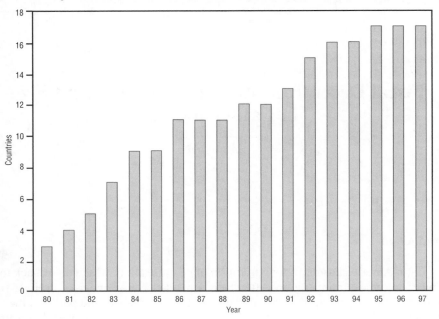

Figure 2. **Decentralisation Trends in Latin American Countries**

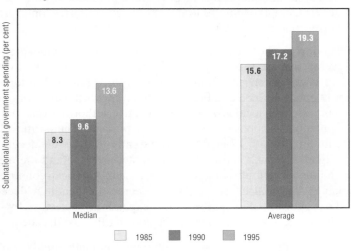

In contrast to the OECD countries where government size has experienced continuous growth in the last 35 years, reaching on average 49 per cent of GDP in 1995, its evolution has been uneven in Latin America. After very rapid growth through the 1970s and early 1980s, the size of governments in Latin America declined significantly in the late 1980s following the debt crisis, and has remained fairly stable since the beginning of the 1990s. The average size of government — as measured by the expenditures of the consolidated public sector — stands today at 28 per cent of GDP[4]. There are, however, very wide differences across countries in this respect. Government size ranges from 12 per cent of GDP in Guatemala and Haiti to numbers in excess of 40 per cent of GDP in Belize, Guyana, Nicaragua and Suriname. The average government expenditure of the consolidated public sector for each country in 1990-95 is presented in Figure 3.

Figure 3. **Government Expenditures in Latin America**
(Consolidated public sector, in percentage of GDP); 1990-95

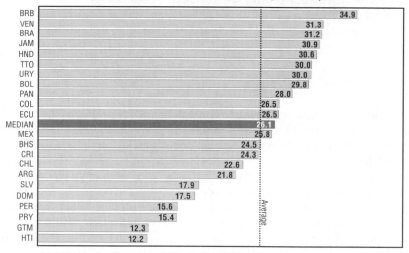

Note: For public enterprises, only capital spending is included.
Source: OCE calculations based on *Recent Economic Developments,* IMF.

The rationale for decentralisation is not generally one of improving fiscal discipline or reducing the size of government. Out of the three functions into which government activities are typically divided for conceptual purposes — the stabilization function, the redistribution function, and the allocation function — it is in the last one where most benefits of decentralisation emerge. Most authors agree that there are serious limitations regarding the ability of sub-national governments to provide stabilization and redistribution services. With regard to allocation, decentralisation can allow a closer match between the preferences of the population and the bundle of public goods and services chosen by government. If preferences are heterogeneous across jurisdictions, the decentralised decision maker can tailor the bundle of goods and services, in particular those whose benefits are geographically concentrated, to better suit the preferences of the population, instead of providing a "one size fits all" bundle for the country as a whole[5]. While this effect of decentralisation may have a very important impact on the efficiency with which public moneys are spent, it does not have a clear effect on aggregate fiscal performance variables such as government size and deficits. Decentralisation, however, can potentially have important effects on aggregate fiscal performance, because it can affect the degree to which government decisions are subject to agency problems, and to co-ordination problems.

Before discussing the different channels through which decentralisation can affect the size of government, it is important to point out that the issue of decentralisation is a very complex one, involving a variety of dimensions: the assignment of expenditure and revenue responsibilities among different levels of government, the degree of political autonomy enjoyed by lower levels, the nature of intergovernmental transfers, and the degree of borrowing autonomy granted to lower level governments. It is not only the degree of expenditure decentralisation, the most used decentralisation variable, that may have an impact on aggregate fiscal performance. The way in which intergovernmental fiscal relations are organised, i.e., the way in which the different dimensions of decentralisation are combined, may have an impact as well.

Decentralisation and Agency

Decentralisation can contribute to containing agency problems through different channels, by introducing elements of competition which increase the incentives of governments to do the right thing. If there are democratic institutions at the sub-national levels, and these work fairly well, decentralisation increases the visibility and accountability of government actions, and endows voters with more power to discipline public officials when they are acting according to self-interest[6]. The local population will be in a better position to discipline local public officials, rather than lower level bureaucrats of the central government which, under centralisation, would be responsible for similar tasks. To the extent that local services are financed by the jurisdiction's own revenues thereby closely linking the benefits provided by these services and the costs to the local tax-payers, citizens will have strong incentives to monitor the local authorities closely. Thus, decentralisation can lead to higher civic participation, and to better citizen control over the actions of the public officials. If in fact public officials have a preference for large governments, then decentralisation could, through this channel, lead to smaller governments.

There is some evidence that suggests that increased political participation is associated to smaller governments. Pommerhene and Schneider (1983) have explored the impact of direct democracy on government size for a sample of Swiss Cantons. Cantons that practice direct democracy, as opposed to representative democracy, have, other things being equal, smaller governments. This evidence is illuminating since, in the absence of agency problems, one might expect decentralisation and increased participation to have the opposite effect on government size. The argument has been made in Oates (1985), and goes as follows: under decentralisation, and in particular in cases where civic participation is high, the preferences of the population will be better taken into account than under centralisation, provided preferences within jurisdictions are more homogeneous than preferences across jurisdictions. If this is the case, it makes sense for people to entrust the government with more tax resources, since they know these resources are going to be spent in a way that closely matches their preferences[7]. Under this public-interest view of government, then, decentralisation would lead to larger governments, although in this case the increase in the size of government would obviously not be welfare-reducing.

Is Oates' argument incompatible with the evidence mentioned above? Not necessarily. Let us assume that, as in the Brennan and Buchanan view, public officials have a preference for larger government. In this case, a higher degree of participation (the highest possible being direct democracy) could have two different effects: on the one hand, it would increase the control of the population over the actions of the public officials, reducing the agency problem. This ensures that the *actual* size of the government will be closer to the population's *desired* size. But at the same time, it may increase the population's *desired* size, as suggested by Oates. Therefore, the effect on *actual* government size of an increase in political participation will be ambiguous.

But there are other ways in which decentralisation, by inducing competition, may reduce agency problems. Brennan and Buchanan (1980) have depicted the government as a monolithic "Leviathan" seeking to maximise revenues by exploiting its monopoly power over the tax base. Under decentralisation, mobility across jurisdictional borders assures some degree of competition for the tax base among governments, who compete to lure taxpayers into their territory by providing a more attractive fiscal bundle. This competition imposes constraints on the fiscal appetite of governments. In this way, mobility of individuals across jurisdictions brings the market for public goods and services closer to the "perfectly competitive" outcome. An important implication of the Leviathan hypothesis, then, is that "total government intrusion into the economy should be smaller, *ceteris paribus*, the greater the extent to which taxes and expenditures are decentralised" (Brennan and Buchanan, 1980, p.15). Naturally, this argument should be more powerful in societies where mobility of individuals across jurisdictions is high (as is the case in the United States), and less so in societies where mobility of individuals across jurisdictions is smaller, as is probably the case in most of the Latin American countries considered in this study.

Several authors have tested the "Leviathan" hypothesis, with diverse results. The original test was performed by Oates (1985), who explored the relationship between decentralisation and government size for a cross-section sample of 43 countries, as well as for the US states, and found no support for the Leviathan hypothesis. More recent studies such as Marlow (1988), Grossman (1989), and Ehadie (1994) do find support for the Leviathan. While Marlow and Grossman use a time-series approach for the United States, Ehadie explores the hypothesis in a cross section of 30 countries[8].

The studies by Grossman and Ehadie are particularly interesting, since they explicitly explore Brennan and Buchanan's caveat that the possibility of collusion among different units of government should be included among "other things equal[9]". Collusion, in this framework, is given by tax-sharing arrangements among different units of government. Consider a country where expenditures are fairly decentralised, but the central government collects all the taxes, which are then shared with lower level governments. This form of decentralisation would not be constraining the monopoly power of the taxing authority, since it introduces no competition for the tax base. To control for the possibility of collusion, Grossman includes in his analysis a variable which captures the degree of vertical fiscal imbalance of state and local governments: the share of grants-in-aid in their total receipts. He finds that the larger the share of grants, the larger the government, lending support to the hypothesis that decentralisation can restrain the behaviour of revenue-maximising governments, but tax-collusion can weaken this restraint. In contrast to Grossman's findings, in Ehadie (1994) the collusion variable does not have significant effects.

In summary, there are two potentially important channels through which decentralisation could lessen the effects of agency problems, thus reducing the size of government[10]. The first one involves increased political competition and participation. The second one involves tax competition. Interestingly, while through these two channels decentralisation will presumably have constraining effects on the size of government, these effects could disappear if the degree of revenue decentralisation is much smaller than that of expenditure decentralisation, i.e., if there is a large degree of vertical fiscal imbalance. In the first case, because the incentives for the population to closely monitor the performance of the local public officials will be much greater if the local government expenditures are financed through local taxes, people will be very interested in ensuring that the government does a good job in spending their money. They may be less concerned about the efficiency with which the government is spending other people's money (such as that which is transferred from the central government). Similarly, the degree of tax competition does not really increase if expenditures are decentralised, but revenues stay concentrated in the hands of the central government, who then shares the taxes with lower level governments via transfers.

Decentralisation and the Problem of the Commons

The control of the Leviathan has been the most widely studied link between decentralisation and the size of government. Another important way in which decentralisation could affect government size is through its effect on the problem of the commons. This problem arises due to an important characteristic of many government programmes: while they tend to generate benefits which are concentrated geographically (or sectorally), they are often financed from a common pool of resources. Under some institutional arrangements regarding the process of fiscal decision making, this can lead to over-utilisation of the common pool of resources, as those who benefit from the programmes fail to internalise their full cost. Weingast, Shepsle and Johnsen (1981), for example, have studied the commons problem at the level of the legislature, showing how it can lead to excessive spending due to the geographical interests represented by the legislators. Concentrating fiscal decisions in one central figure such as the Finance Minister, who typically responds to general interests rather than to geographical or sectoral interests, should reduce the extent to which fiscal decisions are subject to the commons problem[11].

How does decentralisation affect the degree to which an economy is subject to the commons problem? Consider first a country where all government programmes with national benefits (such as defence and foreign relations) are centralised, while all programmes with local benefits are decentralised. Assume also that all local programmes are financed with local revenues. In such an ideal case, decentralisation would reduce the problem of the commons to a smaller local game, since there are no programmes with local benefits financed with national resources. Local authorities would not have incentives to over-expand the budget, since they cannot shift the costs of government programmes onto others outside their jurisdiction.

However, the ideal case depicted above is quite far from the reality of most countries: decentralisation is typically much higher in the expenditure dimension than in the revenue dimension. Inherent to the decentralisation process is the following asymmetry: on the expenditure side, there are a large number of important "local" public goods and services which are in principle better provided by lower level governments. On the revenue side, however, finding good tax bases for state and local governments is a difficult task. Taxes that are perfectly suitable to be applied at the national level can, because of mobility, introduce serious distortions and locational inefficiencies when applied in a decentralised fashion. Equity considerations and economies of scale in tax administration further limit the set of "good" tax bases to be assigned to lower level governments[12]. This asymmetry between expenditure responsibilities and revenue capacity at the sub-national level generates a gap, known as vertical fiscal imbalance, which is typically bridged through the use of transfers from the central government.

The problem is that heavy reliance on transfers, unless these are very clearly defined, with resources allocated according to objective criteria which cannot be easily manipulated by recipient governments, and with little room for discretion and bargaining between the different levels of government, may weaken the budget constraints of the sub-national governments. When this happens, there is scope for lower level governments to shift the cost of local programmes onto others outside the jurisdiction, which constitutes the basis of the commons problem. This problem may become even more serious in cases where sub-national governments have a large degree of borrowing autonomy, in particular if the central government finds it difficult to commit not to bail them out in case of financial trouble. In this case, sub-national governments may over-borrow and overspend, and then shift the burden onto the central government.

The problem of the commons for the fiscal federalism case, where there are multiple layers of government, and the related problem of bailouts of lower level governments has been receiving increased attention in recent years, in part as a result of the advance toward monetary integration in the European Union. In fact, one of the most important arguments in favour of the controversial fiscal constraints included in the Maastricht criteria is the potential for bailouts (or inflationary financing of deficits) by the European Central Bank.

There are several versions of the problem, which introduce different forms of interaction between the central government and the lower level jurisdictions, or among these jurisdictions, which result in different sources of co-ordination problems. For example, Canzoneri and Diba (1991), who study the effects of financial integration in the European Union and explore the rationale for fiscal constraints, assume that countries decide on their expenditures independently, and do not take into account the effect of their own spending on the common interest rate. This leads to overspending. Under certain conditions, they show that governments may also compete for Central Bank seignorage, which exacerbates the incentives to overspend. Sanguinetti (1994), who studied the problem of the commons associated to decentralisation in Argentina, compares the unco-operative (decentralised) solution with the co-operative (centralised) solution, where all externalities are internalised. In his unco-operative case, he assumes that each jurisdiction can in effect decide over the size of the transfer they receive from the central government. This assumption, which at first sight may seem somewhat unrealistic, is similar to the one made by Weingast, Shepsle and Johnsen (1981) in their influential paper about pork barrel projects. In their work, each jurisdiction defines the size of their project, and then Congress validates these demands. This feature of the model is justified by the authors on the basis of evidence on the prevailing practices of universalism (by which every jurisdiction receives a project) and reciprocity (by which even those who do not benefit from a programme support it in exchange for reciprocal support by other districts).

Persson and Tabellini (1994) present a different kind of model, but with similar results[13]. They assume, following work on political economy of trade policy by Grossman and Helpman (1994), that instead of being able to completely control transfers sent to them, the jurisdictions will bribe the federal decision-makers to obtain a larger amount of common resources. As a result, the size of government ends up being too large[14].

As we discuss the different variables that characterise the nature of intergovernmental relations in Latin America, including the nature of transfers, the degree of borrowing autonomy enjoyed by the lower level governments, and the commitment capacity of the federal government in terms of a no-bailout rule, we will see that while the Persson and Tabellini (1994) story seems more appropriate for some intergovernmental arrangements, the Sanguinetti (1994) story seems more appropriate for others.

Decentralisation in Latin America[15]

In this section, we will characterise the extent and nature of decentralisation in Latin American countries, based on the following four variables:

i)   the degree of expenditure decentralisation

ii) the degree of vertical fiscal imbalance

iii) the degree of discretionarity in the transfer system

iv) the degree of borrowing autonomy of state and local governments

Most of the data was obtained from a decentralisation survey conducted at the IADB, which was responded by government officials in 20 countries in the region. Where data needed to calculate expenditure decentralisation or vertical imbalance was missing from the survey, we relied on a variety of country studies to fill in the blanks.

The Degree of Expenditure Decentralisation

In spite of recent trends toward decentralisation in several countries, Latin America is still characterised by a high degree of centralisation. Figure 4 shows the degree of decentralisation, measured as the percentage of total government spending executed by state and local governments, in countries in Latin America and the Caribbean. For the sake of comparability, we included in the figure the average degree of decentralisation for the countries in the OECD. As we mentioned in the introduction, the difference between the two sets of countries is substantial. Perhaps more important for the purposes of our paper, the Figure 4 also shows the wide variety of experiences in the region regarding the degree of decentralisation. While in most countries less than one government dollar out of ten is spent by sub-national governments, there are others, particularly Argentina, Brazil and Colombia, that are quite decentralised[16].

The Degree of Vertical Fiscal Imbalance

The problem of decentralisation goes beyond assigning expenditure responsibilities among the different levels of government, depending on which level will be best positioned to provide each particular public good or service efficiently. How the provision of these services by each level is financed is a crucial dimension of decentralisation. The literature on fiscal federalism offers important guidance on the issue of tax assignment. In a nutshell, sub-national governments should avoid collecting taxes on mobile tax bases, redistributive taxes, taxes which are liable to be exported to other jurisdictions, taxes on unevenly distributed tax bases, those subject to large cyclical fluctuations, and those that involve significant economies of scale in tax administration, or that require information at the national level. All these taxes, for efficiency or equity considerations, should ideally be left to the central government.

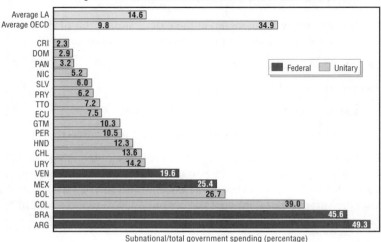

Figure 4. **Decentralisation Latin American Countries, 1995**

Subnational/total government spending (percentage)

It should be clear from the above list that the conditions for a tax to be a "good" local tax are rather restrictive. As a result, the potential revenue from the tax bases that can efficiently be exploited locally, which include property taxes, vehicle taxes and user charges, is more limited than the spending obligations typically assigned to subnational governments in decentralised economies. For this reason, decentralised countries often end up having a large degree of vertical imbalance, which is generally bridged through the use of central government transfers. The degree of vertical imbalance for each country in Latin America is presented in Figure 5. For comparison, we included in the figure the average for the OECD countries[17].

Figure 5. **Vertical Fiscal Imbalance**

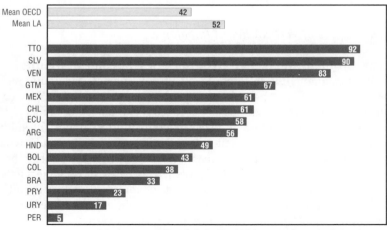

Inter-governmental transfer/subnational total revenues (percentage)

Two things can be concluded from the figure. The first is that vertical imbalance in the region is higher than that in industrialised countries. While the average fiscal imbalance for countries in Latin America is 52 per cent, that in OECD countries is 42 per cent. The second is that, within our region, the degree of vertical imbalance varies substantially from country to country. Among decentralised countries, the difference in vertical imbalance between Latin America and the OECD seems to be even greater. This suggests that finding good tax bases to assign to sub-national governments is more difficult in the case of developing countries[18].

The high degree of vertical imbalance in decentralised countries in the region creates potential for a commons type problem to develop, in particular when combined with highly discretionary transfer systems, or a large degree of borrowing autonomy at the sub-national level.

A Discretionary Transfer System

Vertical imbalances are mostly covered through transfers from the central government. There are many important angles to the design of intergovernmental transfers. Given the scope of our paper, here we concentrate on just one which, we believe, may have an important impact on aggregate fiscal performance: the degree to which transfers are discretionary. The issue is potentially important, since more than a third of the transfers in Latin America are discretionary in nature[19].

Transfers can be discretionary in terms of the determination of the total amount to be transferred, or with respect to the allocation. Transfers which are discretionary in both dimensions leave the central government a lot of flexibility to determine the amount to be transferred, and to direct resources to the jurisdictions with the greatest needs. But for the same reason, unless the central government is very strong *vis-à-vis* the sub-national governments, discretionary transfers are more likely to result in soft budget constraints for the sub-national governments, and thus do not provide adequate incentives for fiscal responsibility. Our view is based on the belief that, under discretion, transfers will tend to be allocated to those jurisdictions that are in financial strain, or simply have a gap between their expenditures and their available resources.

A sub-national government could spend excessively, declare that it has no money to pay salaries of public employees, and ask the central government for a bailout. They could cast the blame on the central government, claiming that they did not get their fair share to begin with. It may be more difficult for the central government to commit not to extend a supplementary transfer to sub-national governments when they have the discretion to do so, compared to a rules-based approach given by predetermined formulas. If commitment on the part of the central government is weak, the different jurisdictions will feel that they can shift part of the costs of the programmes they undertake onto the rest of the country. In this case, sub-national governments may spend beyond their means, and then receive ex-post transfers from the central government. This can lead to excessive spending.

Alternatively, discretionary transfers could be allocated according to political considerations. For example, they could be used as retribution for favourable votes by the district's representatives in Congress. In this case, a system with discretionary transfers would correspond quite well to what Persson and Tabellini consider the "centralised" case, where districts have to bribe the federal authorities in order to obtain a larger transfer.

In some cases, the total pool of the transfer is defined in an ad-hoc way, but the allocation follows a pre-specified formula. In such cases, the different jurisdictions will probably bargain with the central government for an increased pool, but the expected returns from this process are smaller than under full discretion, as they will only receive a small part of any increase in the total transfer. In very few cases, discretion applies to the allocation, but not to the total amount. If these transfers are small, the consequences for aggregate fiscal performance will not be too large. However, they may not generate the right incentives for fiscal discipline, at least in the smaller jurisdictions, as the transfer may still be large compared to the budgets of some of them[20].

Figure 6 shows the extent to which the transfer systems in each country is characterised by discretion, both in the determination of the total pool, and its allocation. The source for this information is our survey, which provided us with data on the most important transfers, including the method of determination of the total pool, of the allocation among the different jurisdictions, and the total amount corresponding to each transfer in 1995[21].

While there are many countries where discretion does not play a role, there are several where discretionary transfers represent a significant part of total transfers, and a few, in particular Trinidad and Tobago and Peru, where all transfers are discretionary. An index of discretionary transfers will be later used in the regressions for the size of government, as part of a measure of soft budget constraints.

Sub-national Government Borrowing Autonomy

The rules regarding borrowing by sub-national governments in Latin America vary considerably from country to country. Borrowing autonomy, like discretionary transfers, can potentially lead to soft budget constraints for the sub-national governments. At the heart of the issue is a commitment problem: it is often very difficult for central governments to commit not to bail out state and local governments when they are in financial trouble.

A case can be made for state and local governments to have some capacity to borrow. Because the benefits of public investments, such as schools or roads, are spread over time, it makes sense to borrow (at least to some extent) so that payments are spread over time as well, rather than have the current taxpayers foot the whole bill today. However, state and local governments should not borrow past the point where the rate of return (economic and social) on the marginal investment project to be

Figure 6. **Discretionality in the Transfer System**

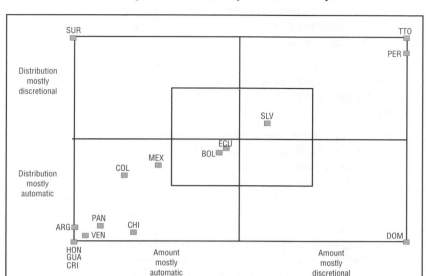

undertaken with the borrowed funds is equal to the interest rate. These governments, however, might want to borrow beyond this point if they think they can shift part of the cost of repayment onto others outside the jurisdiction. Moreover, when the risk of bailouts exists, markets are clearly not an adequate disciplining device. If a lender expects the central government to bailout the local governments in the case of default, they will gladly accommodate the borrower[22]. In this case, constraints on sub-national government borrowing may be the right policy[23].

What determines the ability of central governments to commit not to bailout local governments? Eichengreen and von Hagen (1996) have argued that an important factor is the degree of vertical imbalance. If the sub-national governments have robust tax bases available to them, and generate a large part of their revenues themselves, central governments will find it easier to ask them to bear the cost of adjustment in case of financial difficulties. If, in contrast, sub-national governments have weak tax bases, and most of their resources are transfers from the central government, it will be very costly for the sub-national government to resolve the crisis by itself, and therefore it will become difficult for the central government not to extend a bailout. This idea has been used by these authors to argue against the need for numerical fiscal constraints in the European Union[24].

Another factor that affects the degree of commitment of the central government is the existence of public banks owned by sub-national governments. In cases where the sub-national governments own banks, these banks are often the primary source of government debt. Particularly in the case of large jurisdictions, it might be difficult for the Central Bank not to rescue a financially troubled state bank, since failure to do so might result in a widespread bank run. Knowing this, state banks and governments may not be facing hard budget constraints. Central bank bailouts to state banks that are "too big to fail" have been important in some of the larger Brazilian states, such as Sao Paulo and Rio de Janeiro[25].

In cases where sub-national governments have a large degree of borrowing autonomy and the federal government cannot commit to a no-bailout rule, the assumption in Sanguinetti (1994) that sub-national governments get to choose their own transfers may not be that unrealistic.

The previous discussion has focused on the conditions for borrowing autonomy to be problematic. We will now focus on the extent to which there is borrowing autonomy at the sub-national level in Latin American countries. For this purpose, we obtained through our survey detailed information on a variety of aspects that can affect the degree of borrowing autonomy. The first four aspects relate to constraints on sub-national borrowing. Are sub-national governments allowed to borrow at all? To what degree is the borrowing decision autonomous, and which level of government has to authorise borrowing operations? Are there numerical constraints on borrowing by sub-national governments, and of what do they consist? Are there limitations on the use of debt by these governments? (For example, limits such as the "golden rule", which limits borrowing to investment purposes). The last two aspects relate to borrowing practices which might weaken these constraints: Do sub-national governments own banks, and are these important? Do they own public enterprises with liberal borrowing procedures? Table 1 summarises the information gathered for each country[26].

Table 1. **Borrowing Autonomy in Latin America**

	Borrowing by SNGs not allowed	CG approval required on all SNG debt	Debt cannot be used for current expenditures	Numerical debt limits in all or most SNGs	SNGs own banks	There are important SNG-owned firms with liberal borrowing practices	Tax-sharing used to guarantee SNG debt
Argentina (ARG)			✓	✓	✓	✓	✓
Bahamas (BHS)	✓						
Bolivia (BOL)		✓	✓				✓
Brazil (BRA)		✓			✓	✓	✓
Chile (CHL)	✓						
Colombia (COL)			✓	✓	✓		✓
Costa Rica (CRI)			✓	✓			
Ecuador (ECU)			✓			✓	
El Salvador (SLV)							
Guatemala (GTM)		✓					
Honduras (HND)		✓					
Mexico (MEX)			✓			✓	✓
Panama (PAN)		✓	✓				
Paraguay (PRY)							
Peru (PER)			✓				
Dominican Republic (DOM)		✓					
Trinidad & Tobago (TTO)		✓					
Uruguay (URY)							
Venezuela (VEN)		✓					

Taking into account all the aspects mentioned above, we built an index of borrowing autonomy at the sub-national government level for the countries in Latin America and the Caribbean. Obviously, countries where sub-national governments cannot borrow have 0 autonomy. Out of the other criteria, higher weights were given to the issue of bank ownership by sub-national governments, and the issue of government authorisation. The values of the index (which has a maximum of 4 points) for each of the countries are presented in Figure 7[27].

Figure 7. **Borrowing Autonomy**

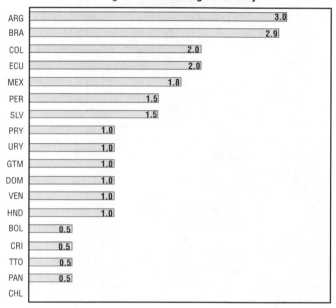

These four variables, expenditure decentralisation, vertical imbalance, discretion in the transfer system and borrowing autonomy characterise the extent and nature of decentralisation in the region. In the next section, we will explore the impact that combinations of these variables have on the size of government.

Decentralisation and the Size of Government

Most of the empirical work linking decentralisation and government size, starting with Oates (1985) attempts to examine Brennan and Buchanan's Leviathan hypothesis. Instead, the main channel that we have in mind when exploring the relationship between these variables is the potential of decentralisation to aggravate the commons problem. We should note, however, that our purpose is not that of testing a well-specified theory of decentralisation and government size, but rather to uncover some interesting stylised facts regarding the relationship between these variables.

What impact would we expect our variables to have on the size of government? Let us begin with expenditure decentralisation. Our discussion suggests that decentralisation could reduce government size if the degree of vertical imbalance is low, but increase it if the degree of vertical imbalance is large. So the theory behind the commons problem does not give us a clear prior of what to expect in terms of the pure effect of the degree of expenditure decentralisation on government size.

The expected effects of vertical imbalance are more clear-cut. The larger the degree of vertical imbalance, the larger the potential for a commons problem, since a large vertical imbalance increases the incongruence between those who benefit and those who pay for government programmes. However, we do not expect this effect to be the same for countries with different degrees of decentralisation. For example, in a country where 95 per cent of government spending corresponds to the central government, we would not expect large differences in government size, whether the remaining 5 per cent spent at the local level is financed with own revenues, or through central government transfers. In contrast, vertical imbalance is expected to have a larger impact in cases where the extent of expenditure decentralisation is larger. For this reason, rather than exploring the effects of vertical imbalance alone, we will instead consider the product of decentralisation and vertical imbalance as an explanatory variable. This product represents the extent to which there are government programmes characterised by local benefits (and provided by the local governments) which are financed out of national taxation.

Finally, we also want to capture in some way the effect of having hard or soft budget constraints at the sub-national level. Following the arguments in Eichengreen and von Hagen (1996), we use the product of vertical imbalance and borrowing autonomy as an indicator of soft budget constraints. We expect, then, that the product of vertical imbalance and borrowing autonomy will have a positive impact on government size. This impact, however, should be larger the larger the degree of decentralisation. For this reason, we will explore the impact of the product of these three variables on government size. This triple product, we believe, is the variable which captures more fully the likelihood that decentralisation will result in a commons problem. As an alternative, we used the degree of discretionarity in transfers in place of borrowing autonomy, to capture the stringency of the budget constraints. One drawback of this variable is that data is available for a smaller set of countries, because a few of them did not report the value of each of its transfers, a necessary ingredient to calculate this variable.

Since we only had cross-sectional data for 20 countries in Latin America and the Caribbean, we obviously face a problem of lack of degrees of freedom. For this reason, we added to the sample the countries in the OECD[28]. Table 2 presents the results of our regressions for our sample of Latin America and OECD countries. The dependent variable is the size of the public sector, averaged between 1990 and 1995. As control variables, we used the level of public debt in 1989, the degree of openness of the economy, measured as the share of exports plus imports over GDP, and the share of the population over 65 years of age[29]. Initial public debt is expected to have positive effects on total public expenditures through its effect on interest payments. Openness is expected to have positive effects on the size of government, following recent findings by Rodrik (1996)[30]. The age variable is expected to have positive effects as well, through its effect on the social security sector. All control variables have the expected sign, and are significant in most regressions.

Table 2. **Decentralisation and Government Size**
(Cross section regressions, average 1990-95)
Latin America and OECD

Size	(1)	(2)	(3)	(4)	(5)	(6)	(7)	(8)
Institutional variables								
Decentralisation		0.21					0.13	0.12
(t-stat)		2.71					1.20	1.15
Decentralisation*vertical imbalance			0.25					
(t-stat)			2.06					
LA decentralisation*borrowing autonomy				0.09				
(t-stat)				2.67				
OECD decentralisation*borrowing autonomy				0.03				
(t-stat)				1.80				
LA Dec*VI*BA					0.28		0.21	
(t-stat)					3.36		2.06	
LA Dec *VI*discretionality in transfers						0.47		0.38
(t-stat)						2.65		2.00
OECD Dec*VI*BA					0.05	0.04	0.02	0.01
(t-stat)					1.61	1.19	0.50	0.31
Controls								
Constant	0.10	0.05	0.08	0.02	0.00	0.00	-0.01	-0.01
(t-stat)	3.48	1.67	2.69	0.53	0.01	0.01	-0.22	-0.23
Debt 1989	1.79	2.02	2.09	7.04	8.18	7.72	8.13	7.78
(t-stat)	2.66	3.44	3.40	1.73	2.09	1.85	2.09	1.87
Openness	0.10	0.11	0.07	0.08	0.06	0.05	0.08	0.07
(t-stat)	3.01	2.65	1.83	1.69	1.41	1.12	1.73	1.45
Population > 65 ans	2.21	2.01	2.22	2.34	2.60	2.74	2.42	2.57
(t-stat)	10.36	8.15	9.92	7.98	9.52	8.98	7.83	7.59
R2	0.74	0.84	0.83	0.85	0.86	0.87	0.87	0.87
DF	39	32	32	28	28	26	27	24
N	43	37	37	34	34	31	34	31

Table 3. **Decentralisation and Government Size**
(Cross section regressions, average, 1990-95)
Latin America only

Size	(1)	(2)	(3)	(4)	(5)	(6)	(7)	(8)
Institutional Variables								
Decentralisation		0.45					0.20	0.24
(t-stat)		4.24					1.43	2.57
OECD decentralisation*vertical imbalance			0.63					
(t-stat)			3.14					
Decentralisation*borrowing autonomy				0.13				
(t-stat)				3.97				
Dec*VI*BA					0.39		0.27	
(t-stat)					7.44		2.79	
Dec*VI*discretionality in transfers						0.65		0.45
						6.60		4.09
Controls								
Constant	0.14	-0.00	0.06	-0.04	-0.10	-0.04	-0.11	-0.07
(t-stat)	2.77	-0.06	1.14	-0.58	-2.25	-0.76	-2.56	-1.72
Debt at 1989	1.63	1.76	2.02	10.27	13.97	12.19	13.26	12.57
(t-stat)	2.13	3.85	3.85	2.51	5.16	4.09	5.01	4.92
Openness	0.11	0.25	0.15	0.20	0.19	0.20	0.22	0.24
(t-stat)	2.29	3.23	1.95	2.47	4.00	3.75	4.41	5.39
Population>65 years	1.24	0.89	1.05	1.45	2.02	0.42	1.83	0.48
(t-stat)	1.54	1.87	1.93	2.63	5.52	0.43	4.91	0.62
R2	0.36	0.67	0.55	0.56	0.82	0.82	0.84	0.89
DF	19	14	14	12	12	9	11	8
N	23	19	19	17	17	14	17	14

The degree of expenditure decentralisation has a positive effect on the size of government. These effects appear to be quite large: if the difference between two countries in terms of the degree of decentralisation is 20 percentage points, the more decentralised one is expected to have, on average, a government sector which is four percentage points of GDP larger than in the less decentralised country[31]. As we expected, the product of decentralisation and vertical imbalance has positive and significant effects on government size. This means that decentralised countries with a high degree of vertical imbalance have, on average, larger governments.

The interaction between decentralisation, vertical imbalance and borrowing autonomy also has the expected sign, and is highly significant for the case of Latin America[32]. We should note that, for this variable, we allowed different coefficients for Latin America and the OECD. The reason is that the measure of borrowing autonomy is not perfectly comparable across regions. In contrast to the Latin America results, the effects are positive but not significant in the case of the OECD countries. If we include in the analysis both expenditure decentralisation and the triple interaction term, decentralisation loses significance. This suggests that, although decentralisation matters, whether intergovernmental fiscal relations are structured in a way which promotes fiscal responsibility matters even more. Results are similar when discretionarity in transfers is used instead of borrowing autonomy as an indicator of soft budget constraints, for the case of Latin American countries[33].

It could be argued that these results could be due in part to differences across regions, rather than differences across countries in Latin America. In fact, OECD countries have larger public sectors, and they also tend to be more decentralised. In order to check this, in Table 3 we present the results of our regressions when only Latin American countries are included, even though we realise that we are seriously lacking in terms of degrees of freedom. The results are even stronger, with most decentralisation variables significant at the 1 per cent level, whether the age variable or per capita income are used as controls[34].

Concluding Remarks

Decentralisation has the potential to improve on resource allocation by bringing fiscal decisions closer to voter preferences. It can also improve on the agency problem by making governments more accountable. However, by creating the possibility of interaction between different jurisdictions, decentralisation may give rise to potential co-ordination problems which may manifest themselves in soft budget constraints. In this paper, we have analysed the impact of decentralisation and the nature of intergovernmental relations on government size, for the case of Latin America. We have found that decentralised governments tend to be larger. This result is consistent with different interpretations. One of them is that because local governments can be trusted to deliver public goods that are more in line with voter preferences, they are given more resources to manage. Hence, this result per se is no indication of inefficiency.

However, we have also found that the form that decentralisation takes also affects size. In particular, arrangements that are more likely to lead to soft budget constraints seem to be associated with larger size. This evidence is a clearer indication of political distortions at work. Our findings suggest that countries that want to advance in the process of decentralisation should make sure that the form that decentralisation takes is not inconsistent with the objective of imposing hard budget constraints on lower-level jurisdictions. This may be done by limiting the degree of vertical fiscal imbalance, assigning to the lower levels all the revenue bases they can efficiently collect, by reducing the degree of discretionarity in the intergovernmental transfer system, and by limiting the degree of borrowing autonomy of sub-national governments.

Notes

1. This paper draws from work on decentralisation for the Report on Economic and Social Progress in Latin America (IADB, 1997), in which I participated together with Alejandro Grisanti, Moritz Kraemer, Claudia Piras, Arnaldo Posadas and Ernesto Talvi. I am grateful for their input into this paper. All errors, of course, are mine.

2. In six other countries, mayors are elected by the municipal councils, which in turn are elected by the population.

3. We could have focused, instead, on the effects of decentralisation on government deficits, rather than the size of government. As we will see, however, the main channels we identify below through which decentralisation can affect fiscal performance variables are more naturally linked to the size of government than to deficits. Nonetheless, we also tested for the effects of decentralisation on deficits, but failed to find any significant effects.

4. Given the lack of coverage of existing sources for public sector data, we use a database which was constructed based on the Recent Economic Development reports of the IMF, for 26 countries in Latin America and the Caribbean [See Stein, Talvi and Grisanti (1997) and IADB (1997)].

5. See Oates (1972) for a very comprehensive treatment of the case for decentralisation.

6. If local democracies do not work well, however, decentralisation could lead to capture of the local governments by special interest groups, clientelistic relationships between elected officials and powerful minorities, and other forms of corruption [See Prud'homme (1995) and Tanzi (1995)].

7. Oates actually attributes this argument to John Wallis.

8. Forbes and Zampelli (1989) and Zax (1989) studied the Leviathan hypothesis at the county level in the United States. Here, again, the evidence is mixed.

9. See Brennan and Buchanan (1980, p. 185)

10. As we mentioned in the introduction, neither of these channels should be expected to affect deficits.

11. For models of the commons problem at the level of the cabinet, see Velasco (1994) and von Hagen and Harden (1995).

12. On the problem of tax assignment among levels of government, see for example Musgrave (1983), Shah (1994), Oates (1994) and Norregaard (1997).

13. For other formalisations of co-ordination or bailout problems applied to decentralisation see Gamboa (1995), Wildasin (1997) and Barrow (1986).

14. Different authors endow different meanings to the centralisation and decentralisation labels. Persson and Tabellini (1994) use the term "centralisation" to depict the situation where revenues are centralised, and local programmes for each jurisdiction (which one could also interpret as transfers) are chosen by the federal government, as a function of the "compensation" schedule offered by the different jurisdictions. In their "decentralised" case, all expenditures are decentralised, and are financed with local revenues. The main difference among these two situations is given by the centralisation or decentralisation of the revenue sources. In Sanguinetti (1994), in contrast, the revenue sources in his co-operative and unco-operative regimes are national, and the difference pertains to which level of government determines local expenditure.

15. This section draws heavily on Stein, Talvi and Grisanti (1997).

16. Probably the most important determinant of decentralisation is country size. The political organisation of government (unitary or federal) is also important. Federal countries, indicated in the figure by grey bars, are typically more decentralised than unitary ones.

17. The measure of vertical imbalance is defined as the ratio of intergovernmental transfers from the central government, including tax sharing, over total revenues (own plus transferred) of the sub-national level.

18. While we do not find a clear association between decentralisation and vertical imbalance in our sample of Latin American countries, other authors report finding a positive association for developing countries. Using a larger database Kim (1995) finds that, in developing countries, vertical imbalance increases with decentralisation, and Bahl and Linn (1992) find a similar pattern in a sample of city governments. Their evidence suggests that, in the developing world, countries that go through a process of decentralisation will tend to worsen the vertical imbalance.

19. See IADB (1997), Table 3.4.

20. An example of these are the Aportes del Tesoro Nacional in Argentina. They are a small portion of total transfers, but represent a large share of the revenue sources of some of the smaller provinces.

21. The figure excludes those countries for which we did not have complete information on the amounts transferred, such as Brazil, Paraguay and Uruguay.

22. Lane (1993) and Ter-Minassian and Craig (1997) discuss the conditions under which market discipline can be effective.

23. Lane (1993) and Ter-Minassian (1995) for a description of different types of arrangements regarding sub-national government borrowing, and their effectiveness.

24. Probably what matters is not just vertical imbalance, but also the capacity of sub-national governments to decide on issues of tax policy. There are several countries where sub-national governments collect important taxes, but do not control tax rates or the tax base. An example is Colombia.

25. See Wildasin (1997) for a model of bailouts that delivers the "too big to fail" result, in the presence of important inter-jurisdictional externalities.

26. More detailed and complete information is available upon request.

27. For a detailed explanation of the formula used to construct the index, see IADB (1997).

28. Data on decentralisation and vertical imbalance for the OECD countries was obtained from the IMF Government Financial Statistics (1996). Data on the size of the public sector comes from OECD National Accounts (1996). Data on borrowing autonomy was kindly provided by Jurgen von Hagen.

29. As an alternative to the age variable, we also performed another set of regressions using per capita GDP as a control variable. These two variables are highly correlated, as countries with higher per capita income are those with a larger share of older population. The reason we use the age variable in our main regressions is that when both variables were included together, in most regressions the per capita income variable loses significance, while the age variable remains significant at the 1 per cent level.

30. Rodrik argues that the explanation for this empirical regularity is that open economies are exposed to significant external risk, and that a large government sector reduces the exposure to this risk.

31. Similar results were obtained when GDP per capita was used as a control variable, instead of the age variable.

32. Argentina is an outlier in regressions (5) through (8), and was excluded from the sample. In this country, the size of government is much smaller than would be predicted according to variables in the regression. A possible interpretation for this is that the 1991 Convertibility Law increased the commitment of the central government not to bail out provinces in financial trouble, as it restricts the ability of the Central Bank to increase the monetary base without backing of international reserves. In fact, the central government extended extraordinary transfers to provincial governments in 1989 and 1990, but has not done so since 1991. In this case, then, the product of vertical imbalance and borrowing autonomy may be underestimating the stringency of the budget constraint.

33. Our budget constraint variables kept the correct sign, but lost significance when GDP per capita was used instead of the age variable.

34. We also performed our regressions using a different definition of government size, one that excludes interest payments and the social security sector. In this case, the age variable and the initial debt variable were dropped as controls, and we obtained qualitatively similar results.

Bibliography

BAHL, R. AND J. LINN. (1992), *Urban Public Finance in Developing Countries,* World Bank, Washington, D.C.

BARROW, M (1986), "Central Grants to Local Governments: A Game Theoretic Approach", *Environment and Planning C: Government and Policy*, Vol. 4.

BRENNAN, J.AND J. BUCHANAN (1980), *The Power to Tax: Analytical Foundations of a Fiscal Constitution,* Cambridge University Press, New York.

CANZONERI, M. AND B. DIBA (1991), "Fiscal Deficits, Fiscal Integration, and a Central Bank for Europe", *Journal of the Japanese and International Economics*, 5.

EHADIE, J. (1994), "Fiscal Decentralization and the Size of Government", *Policy Research Working Paper* No. 1387, World Bank, Washington, D.C.

EICHENGREEN, B. AND J VON HAGEN (1996), "Federalism, Fiscal Restraints and European Monetary Union", *American Economic Review*, 86 (2), May.

FORBES, K. AND E. ZAMPELLI (1989), "Is Leviathan a Mythical Beast?", *American Economic Review*, 79.

GAMBOA, R. (1995), "Fiscal Federalism in Mexico", Ph.D. Thesis, University of California, Berkeley.

GROSSMAN, G. AND E. HELPMAN (1994), "Protection for Sale", *American Economic Review*, Vol. 84, No. 4, September.

GROSSMAN, P. (1989), "Fiscal Decentralization and Government Size: An Extension", *Public Choice*, 62.

IMF (1996), *Government Financial Statistics*.

INTER-AMERICAN DEVELOPMENT BANK (1997), "Fiscal Stability with Democracy and Decentralization", Part 3 of Report on Economic and Social Progress in Latin America, Johns Hopkins University Press for the Inter-American Development Bank, Washington, D.C.

KIM, S.-L. (1995), "Fiscal Decentralization, Fiscal Structure and Economic Performance: Three Empirical Studies", Ph.D dissertation, University of Maryland.

LANE, T. (1993), "Market Discipline", International Monetary Fund, *Staff Papers*, 40 (1).

MARLOW, M. (1988), "Fiscal Decentralization and Government size", *Public Choice*, 56.

MUSGRAVE, R. (1983), "Who Should Tax, Where, and What?", in C. McLURE JR. (ed.) *Tax Assignment in Federal Countries,* Australian National University Press, Canberra.

NORREGAARD, J. (1997), "Tax Assignment" in T. TER-MINASSIAN (ed.), *Fiscal Federalism in Theory and Practice,* International Monetary Fund, forthcoming.

OATES, W. (1972), *Fiscal Federalism*, Harcourt Brace Jovanovich, New York.

OATES, W. (1985), "Searching for Leviathan: An Empirical Study", *American Economic Review*, 75.

OATES, W. (1989), "Searching for Leviathan: A Reply and Some Further Reflections", *American Economic Review*, 79.

OATES, W. (1994), "Federalism and Government Finance", in J. QUIGLEY AND E. SMOLENSKY (eds.), *Modern Public Finance*, Harvard University Press, Cambridge, Mass.

OECD (1996), *National Accounts.*

PERSSON, T. AND G. TABELLINI. (1994), "Does Centralization Increase the Size of Government?", *European Economic Review*, 38.

POMMERHENE, W. AND F. SCHNEIDER (1983), "Does Government in a Representative Democracy Follow a Majority of Voter's Preferences? An Empirical Examination in H. HANUSCH, (ed.). *Anatomy of Government Deficiencies,* Springer, Berlin.

PRUD'HOMME, R. (1995), "On the Dangers of Decentralization", *The World Bank Research Observer*, Vol. 10, No. 2.

RODRIK, D. (1996), "Why do More Open Economies Have Bigger Governments?", *NBER Working Paper* No. 5537, April.

SANGUINETTI, P. (1994), "Intergovernmental Transfers and Public Sector Expenditures: A Game Theoretic Approach", *Estudios de Economía*, Vol. 21, No. 2, December.

SHAH, A. (1994), "The Reform of Intergovernmental Fiscal Relations in Developing and Emerging Market Economies", Policy and Research Series, 23, World Bank, Washington, D.C.

STEIN, E., E. TALVI AND A. GRISANTI (1997), "Institutional Arrangements and Fiscal Performance: The Latin American Experience", unpublished.

TANZI, V. (1995), "Fiscal Federalism and Decentralization: A Review of Some Efficiency and Macroeconomic Aspects", in World Bank Annual Conference on Development Economics, Washington, D.C.

TER-MINASSIAN, T. AND J. CRAIG (1997), "Control of Sub-national Government Borrowing", in T. TER-MINASSIAN (ed.), *Fiscal Federalism in Theory and Practice,* International Monetary Fund, forthcoming.

TER-MINASSIAN, T. (1995), "Borrowing by Sub-national Governments: Issues and Selected International Experience", mimeo, International Monetary Fund.

VELASCO, A. (1994), "A Model of Endogenous Fiscal Deficits and Delayed Fiscal Reforms", unpublished.

VON HAGEN, J. AND I. HARDEN (1995), "Budget Processes and Commitment to Fiscal Discipline", *European Economic Review*, 39.

WEINGAST, B., K SHEPSLE AND C. JOHNSEN (1981), "The Political Economy of Benefits and Costs: A Neoclassical Approach to Distributive Politics", *Journal of Political Economy*, 89, August.

WILDASIN, D. (1997), "Externalities and Bailouts: Hard and Soft Budget Constraints in Intergovernmental Fiscal Relations", unpublished.

ZAX, J. (1989), "Is there a Leviathan in Your Neighborhood?", *American Economic Review*, 79.

Fiscal Decentralisation and Macroeconomic Stability: The Experience of Large Developing and Transition Economies

Kiichiro Fukasaku and Luiz R. de Mello Jr.

Introduction

The recent years have witnessed attempts of varying degrees of success to implement programmes of fiscal decentralisation and devolution of fiscal powers to lower levels of government in both OECD and non-OECD countries [see Blondal (1997) and World Bank (1997), for further details]. Fiscal decentralisation has been motivated by different reasons in different countries and the ensuing consequences in terms of macroeconomic stability and growth have also varied significantly from one country to another.

In the case of the OECD countries, fiscal decentralisation has been advocated on the grounds that central governments have been unable to meet adequately the increasing demand for public goods and services [Tanzi (1997)]. The argument is based on the principle of subsidiarity, in so far as the performance of the public sector can be enhanced by taking account of local differences in culture, environment, endowment of natural resources, and economic and social factors. In addition, local preferences and needs are believed to be best met by local, rather than national, governments, and accountability and allocative efficiency can be enhanced by bringing expenditure assignments closer to revenue sources and hence to the median voter.

Social choice arguments for fiscal decentralisation also find support in public finance. The aggravation of fiscal imbalances and debt-overhang problems have been associated with poor macroeconomic performance, high unemployment and sluggish output growth in a number of OECD countries in recent years. By diverting resources away from growth-enhancing activities to finance current fiscal imbalances and to service the national debt, the management of fiscal policy tends to depress private investment. As a result, fiscal decentralisation is expected to promote sound macroeconomic management through efforts towards streamlining public sector activities, reducing operational and informational costs in service delivery, and stimulating private sector development.

In the developing countries, the reform of the fiscal system, including inter-governmental fiscal relations, has also become a crucial policy issue. The key policy challenge is to design and develop an appropriate system of public finance in order to provide local public services effectively and efficiently, while at the same time, maintaining macroeconomic stability[1]. The endeavour consists of giving new budgetary rights and responsibilities to sub-national governments and simultaneously promoting institutional clarity and transparency in budgeting so that spending matches resources at the sub-national level. How much fiscal decentralisation should there be? How should inter-governmental fiscal relations be managed to take into account, on the one hand, the growing need for local public goods and services and, on the other, the importance of preserving fiscal discipline[2].

The interrelationship between fiscal decentralisation and macroeconomic governance is a very complex issue and deserves special attention in the context of developing countries[3]. There is growing recognition on the part of policy makers and experts that fiscal decentralisation may aggravate fiscal imbalances and consequently endanger overall macroeconomic stability [Prud'homme (1995), Huther and Shah (1996), Ter-Minassian (1997)], unless sub-national governments are committed to fiscal discipline, and the decentralisation package includes incentives for prudence in debt and expenditure management. The imposition of stringent constraints on sub-national indebtedness and effective monitoring of sub-national fiscal positions are additional important elements in fiscal decentralisation. Successful fiscal decentralisation also depends to a large extent on the availability of expertise at the sub-national level and on the ability of sub-national governments to handle an increased volume of resources and to ensure effective expenditure management. Moreover, the devolution of revenue sources has to be matched by a proportional re-assignment of expenditure functions to sub-national governments and efforts to encourage revenue mobilisation at lower levels of government.

Given this background, the objective of this paper is to shed more light on the relationship between fiscal decentralisation and macroeconomic stability in selected developing countries, notably several large developing countries, such as the "Big Five" (Brazil, China, India, Indonesia, and Russia). By focusing on macroeconomic, rather than social choice or microeconomic, aspects of the issue, the paper highlights a number of pitfalls of fiscal decentralisation, as well as the relationship between fiscal decentralisation and output growth, on the one hand, and fiscal and monetary policies, on the other.

Public Finance Indicators: The Extent of Decentralisation

Government Size

It is not an easy task to make a cross-country comparison of the size and structure of government expenditures, given the limited availability of comparable financial data on the public sector, including all levels of government[4] and decentralised agencies under government control. This is particularly true in the case of developing and transition economies in which government-directed expenditures of public enterprises play an important role in economic activity. In the case of developing countries, it is even more difficult to grapple with the idea of an optimum size of government expenditures, since the provision of local public goods and services are in chronic shortage in most developing countries.

Some basic fiscal indicators are presented in Table 1 for a sample of 31 developing and OECD economies. A summary of data availability is provided in the Appendix (Table A). With respect to government relative size, in a number of Latin American countries, Table 1 reveals a trend since the 1980s in favour of fiscal decentralisation, measured as a reduction in the GDP share of central government spending and a corresponding increase in that of sub-national governments. This is particularly true in the cases of Argentina after 1986, Chile after 1981, and Brazil after 1989. The Brazilian experience with decentralisation is impressive, with a threefold increase in the average size of sub-national governments after 1989. In these three Latin American countries (Argentina, Brazil, and Chile), there was an improvement in the fiscal position of the central government, except for Brazil, where the deterioration of sub-national finances has put additional strain on the position of the central government [see Shah (1990, 1994) and de Mello (1997), for further details]. Although the size of its sub-national governments is considerably smaller than that of the other two countries, the Chilean experience stands out in controlling sub-national fiscal imbalances in the process of fiscal decentralisation. Moreover, unlike Argentina and Brazil, the Chilean experience was accompanied by an increase in the variance of the average government size, both nationally and sub-nationally, which suggests that the search for an optimum size of sub-national governments is far from complete.

Perhaps most striking from the international perspective is the fact that the average size of central government expenditures tends to be smaller in Asia than in Latin America and in several European OECD Member countries. The variance in government size over time also tends to be lower in Asia than in Latin America and in OECD member countries, particularly at the sub-national level. Among the latter group, the average size of central government expenditures in Belgium, Italy and the Netherlands is well above 40 per cent of GDP. Higher government expenditures in these European countries reflect a substantial expansion, notably in the 1960s and

Table 1. **Public Finance Indicators**

Country	Consolidated Central Government				Sub-national Governments			
	Government Size		Overall Balance		Government Size		Overall Balance	
	Average	St. Dev.	Average	St. Dev.	Average	St. Dev.	Average	St. Dev.
Argentina 1 (1974-85)	**16.1**	2.7	**-5.3**	2.5	**8.1**	1.5	**-2.9**	1.5
Argentina 2 (1986-92)	**12.2**	2.5	**-1.0**	1.3	**9.0**	0.6	**-2.8**	2.1
Bolivia	**16.0**	5.7	**-4.4**	8.1	**3.4**	1.5	**-0.1**	0.3
Brazil 1 (1983-89)	**36.3**	15.1	**-3.8**	2.4	**5.7**	3.5	**-0.7**	0.5
Brazil 2 (1990-93)	**32.5**	5.6	**-5.0**	3.7	**19.0**	0.5	**-2.5**	0.5
Chile 1 (1974-80)	**32.8**	4.4	**-1.6**	5.8	**1.0**	0.2	**0.0**	0.1
Chile 2 (1981-88)	**25.2**	5.3	**0.5**	2.2	**2.6**	0.6	**-0.2**	0.4
Colombia	**13.2**	1.5	**-1.2**	2.1	**5.2**	0.9	**0.1**	0.3
Mexico	**19.4**	5.8	**-5.0**	2.3	**3.3**	0.7	**-0.3**	1.3
Peru	**16.9**	2.1	**-3.2**	2.2	**3.5**	0.9	**0.0**	0.1
India	**15.0**	2.3	**-6.3**	1.7	**12.4**	1.8	**-2.7**	0.6
Indonesia	**20.1**	2.5	**-1.7**	1.6	**2.8**	0.4	**0.0**	0.1
Malaysia	**28.1**	4.0	**-5.3**	5.0	**6.2**	0.9	**-0.8**	0.9
Philippines	**13.8**	4.2	**-1.9**	1.4	**1.6**	0.2	**0.1**	0.1
Thailand 1 (1972-80)	**15.5**	1.5	**-2.9**	1.7	**3.6**	0.6	**0.1**	0.0
Thailand 2 (1981-94)	**17.2**	2.3	**-0.7**	3.8	**1.5**	0.4	**0.1**	0.1
South Africa 1 (1977-83)	**24.0**	2.7	**-4.6**	1.3	**9.9**	0.6	**-0.9**	0.2
South Africa 2 (1984-93)	**32.3**	2.6	**-5.6**	2.7	**9.9**	3.7	**-0.4**	0.3
Russia	**25.9**	n.a.	**-7.6**	n.a.	**16.2**	n.a.	**-0.1**	n.a.
Australia	**24.8**	3.1	**-1.6**	1.8	**17.1**	2.3	**-1.0**	0.8
Austria	**36.9**	3.9	**-3.8**	1.7	**16.4**	1.6	**-0.5**	0.5
Belgium	**48.5**	6.0	**-7.0**	3.2	**7.1**	0.9	**-0.6**	0.7
Canada	**22.5**	2.1	**-3.2**	2.1	**30.1**	2.7	**-2.2**	1.2
Denmark	**38.4**	4.5	**-0.7**	3.2	**31.7**	2.7	**-0.1**	0.6
Finland	**31.1**	5.9	**-2.6**	4.7	**18.2**	2.4	**-0.1**	0.4
France	**41.1**	4.6	**-2.3**	1.9	**8.3**	1.1	**-0.6**	0.3
Germany	**29.7**	3.0	**-1.4**	1.2	**22.1**	1.4	**-1.4**	0.6
Iceland	**29.5**	3.0	**-3.2**	1.3	**8.0**	2.2	**-0.1**	0.4
Italy	**42.8**	7.3	**-11.2**	1.9	**11.1**	3.4	**-1.0**	0.6
Netherlands	**52.4**	4.4	**-3.7**	2.3	**17.9**	1.3	**-0.9**	1.0
Norway 1 (1972-78)	**36.6**	2.3	**-4.1**	2.6	**22.7**	1.4	**-1.4**	0.4
Norway 2 (1979-94)	**39.8**	2.0	**-0.3**	3.0	**18.8**	1.1	**-0.9**	0.8
Spain 1 (1980-89)	**26.2**	5.9	**-3.3**	2.3	**7.9**	2.8	**-0.4**	0.3
Spain 2 (1990-93)	**28.8**	16.2	**-3.6**	2.5	**12.6**	6.9	**-1.1**	0.8
Sweden	**38.8**	7.3	**-4.6**	4.4	**24.6**	1.8	**-0.8**	0.9
Switzerland	**18.4**	2.8	**0.0**	0.5	**16.2**	8.7	**-0.6**	0.7
United Kingdom	**37.7**	3.4	**-3.2**	2.6	**13.4**	1.2	**-0.7**	1.1
United States	**22.1**	1.8	**-3.2**	1.4	**17.5**	1.0	**0.9**	0.4

Note: Government size is defined as the share of total government spending to GDP. Overall balance is the public sector balance as a share of GDP. Countries for which a sizeable discrepancy (over 5 percentage points) in the share of sub-national spending to total public sector spending was observable are presented in two sub-samples.

1970s, of the government role in providing a variety of public goods and services, including education, heath care, pensions and social security. Also, non-European Member countries of OECD (e.g., Australia, Canada, and the United States) tend to have much smaller central governments than their European counterparts. Based on historical experiences in OECD countries, Tanzi and Schuknecht (1997) argue that much of the potential social gains from government expenditures could have been realised with smaller governments, with total expenditures in the range of 30 to 40 per cent of GDP[5].

Table 1 also reveals that the fiscal system of East Asian economies are highly centralised. In spite of geographical diversity as an archipelago nation with a population of over 190 million inhabitants, Indonesia's sub-national spending share in GDP is less than 3 per cent. The ratio is less than 2 per cent in the case of the Philippines, another archipelago nation. These ratios have also changed very little over time, given that one standard deviation from the mean ratio spans a range from 2.4 to 3.2 per cent in Indonesia and 1.4 to 1.8 per cent in the Philippines. On the other hand, India is by far the most decentralised country in Asia, followed by Malaysia, and national and sub-national spending ratios have shown little variation over time. Nevertheless, even in Malaysia, which has a federal political system, the fiscal powers of the states are very limited [Asher (1989)]. The case of Thailand is particularly noteworthy: there was a remarkable improvement in the central government's fiscal position[6] after 1981, accompanied by a significant transfer of spending power away from sub-national governments to the central government. This process of centralisation goes against the general trend in the sample of countries under examination.

Fiscal Decentralisation Indicators

Turning from government size to alternative fiscal decentralisation indicators, a commonly-used measure of decentralisation is the sub-national share (net of inter-governmental transfers) of total government spending (Table 2, column 7).

In Latin America, sub-national spending shares have increased significantly in Argentina, Brazil and Chile since the 1980s, and are in the neighbourhood of 40 per cent in Brazil and Argentina. Despite decentralisation efforts, Chile remains very centralised by the region's standards, with a sub-national share of less than 10 per cent of total government spending. Also, with the exception of India, sub-national spending shares are much lower, on average, in Asia than in Latin America, given the relative centralism of the former region. Sub-national spending shares have also shown smaller variance over time for most countries in Asia. In Thailand, in particular, fiscal centralisation has led to a sizeable fall in the sub-national spending share, as mentioned above. Turning to a different continent, in South Africa, a fall in the sub-national spending share was due to an increase in spending by the centre. In the case of the OECD countries, on average, sub-national spending shares are higher than in other regions under examination, and exhibit significant variation across countries[7], ranging from over 60 per cent of total government spending in Canada, to 12 per cent in

Belgium. Canada and Spain have experienced the most drastic changes in average sub-national spending shares over time. In the case of Canada, one standard deviation from the mean spending ratio implies a range from 49 to 73 per cent. In large federations (Australia, Brazil, Germany, India, the United States), average sub-national spending shares are in the neighbourhood of 40 per cent of total government spending.

However, direct measures of fiscal decentralisation, such as sub-national spending shares, are imperfect indicators of sub-national autonomy. Relative shares highlight the composition of total spending, rather than autonomy of lower levels of government in actual fiscal policy-making and in terms of its impact on macroeconomic governance. For instance, if an increment in sub-national spending is financed through local resource mobilisation (increased local tax revenues, for instance) or met by spending cuts by the central government, no serious fiscal imbalances are expected to arise across government levels. Such imbalances tend to divert resources from the centre, which could finance the provision of goods and services. Inter-governmental imbalances are also likely to put pressure on inter-governmental fiscal relations, aggregate public finances and overall macroeconomic governance.

More importantly, a rise in sub-national spending is expected to increase sub-national dependency and put further strain on the finances of higher levels of government when it drives a wedge between resources mobilised locally and transferred from other levels of government. When additional sub-national spending is financed via inter-governmental transfers, fiscal decentralisation tends to be counter-productive. By driving a wedge between local spending and local resources, and between the costs and benefits of providing public goods and services locally, excessive reliance on inter-governmental transfers discourages resource mobilisation at the sub-national level, and reduces transparency in budget-making and accountability in expenditure management in sub-national jurisdictions. This is often called a common pool problem[8]: sub-national governments may face an incentive to over-spend in their own jurisdictions because they can internalise the benefits of public sector spending while sources of finance are mobilised elsewhere in the economy.

While it is true that reliance on local revenue mobilisation tends to reduce the common pool problem, it may create, or aggravate, an agency problem[9]. In this case, broad tax bases may be devolved to sub-national jurisdictions and the central government may be unable to monitor the use of such tax bases by local authorities. For instance, local governments may have an incentive to under-utilise their tax bases when alternative financing is likely to be obtained via, for instance, inter-governmental transfers. This is because an increase in local taxation is not without political costs and these costs may be reduced when local spending is financed from a common pool of resources mobilised elsewhere in the economy. In this case, common pool and agency problems may reinforce each other rather than being mutually exclusive[10].

In addition to common pool and agency problems, Inman and Rubinfeld (1996) highlight the scope for considerable inefficiencies in taxation in decentralised, as opposed to centralised, public economies. Such taxation failures are mainly due to the existence of mobile factors in production and inter-jurisdiction trade. For instance, by taxing locally a mobile factor or a good which is bound for export to other sub-national jurisdictions, a sub-national government may "export" the tax burden to other jurisdictions and hence rely on implicit subsidies from non-residents [Gordon (1983)]. An incentive is therefore created in decentralised federations for the under-utilisation of broad tax bases, given that sub-national governments tend to over-utilise local bases to benefit from tax exporting, when considerable taxing power is devolved to sub-national governments in the course of decentralisation.

Fiscal centralism may therefore be characterised *a priori* by the combination of low sub-national fiscal autonomy and high sub-national dependency on inter-governmental transfers. In this case, few local revenue sources are assigned to sub-national jurisdictions and the resources transferred from the centre to sub-national governments are sizeable. The centre is responsible for revenue mobilisation, both locally and nationally, and spending assignments in sub-national jurisdictions. As a result, sub-national policy-making may be limited in scope and state/local governments become agents of the centre's spending functions.

In the light of the above argument, alternative indicators of fiscal decentralisation are reported in Table 2. Fiscal autonomy of sub-national governments is measured both as the share of tax revenue in the total revenue of sub-national governments (tax, non-tax and capital revenue net of grants) and as the share of non-tax revenue in total sub-national revenue (columns 1 and 3 of Table 2, respectively). Sub-national fiscal autonomy measures the ability of sub-national governments to finance spending in their jurisdictions through local revenue mobilisation. Limited ability to collect tax and non-tax revenue in sub-national jurisdictions implies high dependency ratios, measured as the share of inter-governmental transfers[11] in total local revenue (column 5 of Table 2).

Figure 1 suggests that there is a stable relationship between sub-national fiscal autonomy and dependency. The vast majority of countries is clustered along the downward slope of the scatter diagram. As suggested above, a downward move along the diagonal line indicates an increase in fiscal decentralisation. For the countries depicted in the upper half of Figure 1, centralism may, however, be primarily administrative or, more importantly, take the form of limited policy-making autonomy at the sub-national level.

Turning to country cases, in Latin America[12], the degree of fiscal autonomy at the sub-national level, measured as the share of taxes to total local revenue, is particularly low in Peru and has fallen dramatically in Chile, after 1981, despite significant fiscal decentralisation in the period, given the increase in the sub-national spending share (Table 2), and in the size of sub-national governments (Table 1). Given that decentralisation in Chile did not generate significant sub-national imbalances, an increase in sub-national spending was made possible by raising sub-national non-tax revenue (fees, sales, fines, etc.), instead of inter-governmental transfers and/or local tax revenue. In Brazil, on the other hand, the fall in the average sub-national tax revenue share after 1989 was partly offset by an increase in inter-governmental transfers. In this case, local revenue mobilisation was hardly encouraged by the system of transfers

Table 2. **Inter-Governmental Fiscal Indicators**

	Sub-national Fiscal Autonomy				Sub-national Fiscal Dependency		Sub-national Spending Share	
	Tax Autonomy		Non-Tax Autonomy					
	Average	St. Dev.	Average	St. Dev.	Average	St. Dev.	Average	St. Dev.
Argentina 1	82.2	6.8	17.6	6.4	n.a.	n.a.	33.4	3.2
Argentina 2	83.3	12.1	15.9	11.4	n.a.	n.a.	42.7	4.0
Bolivia	52.6	13.8	35.1	12.2	6.8	4.4	17.0	4.6
Brazil 1	54.8	4.4	13.0	4.0	31.7	2.1	31.7	2.2
Brazil 2	48.3	3.8	15.9	3.6	34.4	2.1	37.3	3.8
Chile 1	40.7	8.1	15.9	3.6	43.1	9.9	3.2	0.7
Chile 2	32.1	2.7	36.7	9.0	30.1	8.2	8.0	1.0
Colombia	39.7	5.0	8.6	1.9	47.8	4.5	28.1	1.8
Mexico	78.2	5.6	15.9	5.2	6.0	4.4	16.1	5.8
Peru	8.7	2.1	17.7	3.3	72.5	3.7	17.7	4.2
India	45.8	1.3	11.6	1.3	42.5	2.0	45.4	1.3
Indonesia	15.4	3.2	5.9	1.0	78.7	3.7	11.7	1.5
Malaysia	n.a.	n.a.	n.a.	n.a.	21.7	3.9	18.0	1.8
Philippines	35.1	4.0	25.2	3.4	35.1	4.0	10.1	2.3
Thailand 1	23.3	2.8	5.1	1.1	71.5	3.2	19.1	3.2
Thailand 2	53.5	13.3	9.5	1.7	35.6	14.9	7.9	1.8
South Africa 1	16.3	1.2	30.9	2.1	49.4	1.1	28.5	1.9
South Africa 2	16.5	3.6	25.8	5.9	55.7	8.8	21.8	4.5
Russia	75.0	n.a.	7.7	n.a.	17.3	n.a.	38.4	n.a.
Australia	32.8	2.3	17.5	3.1	47.4	5.0	40.7	1.0
Austria	52.0	4.0	20.7	1.6	26.3	3.5	30.8	0.9
Belgium	33.7	2.8	7.7	1.1	58.6	3.3	12.0	1.1
Canada	56.1	4.2	14.1	0.8	28.6	2.9	61.0	12.2
Denmark	42.9	3.5	8.1	0.6	47.3	3.7	45.3	1.8
Finland	47.7	2.8	17.1	2.0	31.0	3.3	39.3	0.8
France	42.7	4.5	18.5	2.0	39.3	5.6	17.9	5.4
Germany	54.4	2.5	21.5	1.2	23.1	2.2	42.7	1.9
Iceland	82.3	12.3	13.4	7.7	6.7	0.7	21.2	5.3
Italy	13.2	7.3	8.5	1.3	77.3	6.3	20.6	2.2
Netherlands	6.7	2.4	13.4	5.2	78.5	5.4	57.2	0.4
Norway 1	46.8	0.8	n.a.	n.a.	19.6	4.7	38.7	0.4
Norway 2	48.1	4.2	11.9	3.9	39.1	1.1	32.1	0.6
Spain 1	48.4	15.1	15.5	4.3	35.1	18.3	19.5	4.7
Spain 2	31.0	1.4	8.5	0.7	51.2	18.3	38.0	17.0
Sweden	58.6	1.9	17.3	15.8	24.6	1.9	39.4	3.7
Switzerland	54.6	1.2	21.4	2.2	23.3	1.6	54.4	2.2
United Kingdom	25.5	15.7	17.3	3.1	53.1	4.4	26.0	2.6
United States	48.2	1.7	23.0	1.9	31.1	2.6	44.1	1.9

Note: Tax and non-tax autonomy indicators are defined as, respectively, the ratios of sub-national tax and non-tax revenue to total sub-national revenue (tax, non-tax, inter-governmental transfers, and capital revenue net of grants). Sub-national dependency is the share of inter-governmental transfers to sub-national governments in total revenue. Sub-national spending share is the ratio of sub-national spending to total government spending. In the case of Argentina, tax and non-tax revenue figures include inter-governmental transfers.

Figure 1. **Fiscal Decentralisation — Full Sample**

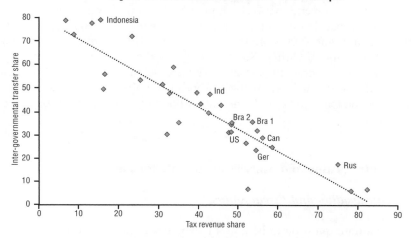

put in place, given the modest increase in the non-tax revenue share. In addition, an increase in the volume of compulsory earmarked transfers have rendered the country's inter-governmental transfer system extremely rigid, thus creating considerable budgetary pressures at the centre. The remaining countries in the sample bar Colombia (Peru, Bolivia and Mexico), with comparable sub-national spending shares, differ significantly as to how sub-national spending is financed. In the case of Peru, emphasis is placed on inter-governmental transfers and non-tax revenue, whereas local tax revenue mobilisation prevails in Bolivia and Mexico. On the other hand, Colombia's sub-national spending share is higher than in the three countries above and sub-national financing is split more evenly between inter-governmental transfers and local tax revenue mobilisation.

In Asia, fiscal dependency and autonomy ratios vary widely from country to country reflecting significant differences in the relative importance of inter-governmental transfers as a revenue source of sub-national jurisdictions. One extreme case is Indonesia. Under a unitary fiscal system, dependency is extremely high; transfers from the centre to state governments are about five times their local tax revenue. Local governments have little administrative or judicial power, and thus rely heavily on financial transfers from the central government [Hill (1996)]. Malaysia represents another extreme case in the opposite direction in which financial transfers from the central government account for roughly 22 per cent of state governments' total revenues. The federal government of Malaysia takes a much larger burden of providing public services, such as primary education and health care, than the central government of three other ASEAN countries, Indonesia, the Philippines and Thailand. Finally, in the case of Thailand, the country's fiscal consolidation effort of the 1980s involved a significant reduction in the sub-national spending share in favour of the central government, as mentioned above. This process of fiscal centralisation also led to a drastic change in the composition of sub-national revenues from inter-governmental transfers towards local taxes, which reflected a move in favour of local revenue mobilisation.

In the OECD area, two basic groups of countries can be identified. In the first group, sub-national governments rely more heavily on tax revenue, while the second group depends primarily on inter-governmental transfers, as a source of income. The first group congregates most federations in the OECD area (Austria, Canada, Switzerland, Germany, United States), whereas the second group, where inter-governmental transfers predominate as a revenue source for sub-national governments, is made up almost exclusively of the European Member countries and Australia[13]. Local tax revenue tends to be in the neighbourhood of 50 per cent of total revenue in the first group.

Fiscal Decentralisation and Macroeconomic Performance

Decentralisation and Fiscal Stance

An important question to be asked is whether fiscal decentralisation leads to a deterioration of sub-national finances and whether such deterioration affects negatively the fiscal position of the central government. Figure 2 shows a negative relationship between government size and fiscal stance, both at the central and at the sub-national levels. The figure supports the intuition that bigger governments tend to be less efficient and hence more prone to fiscal imbalances. On the other hand, as suggested by Figure 3 (Panel A), sub-national government size does not seem to contribute to the deterioration of central government fiscal imbalances. However, such conclusion cannot be inferred if attention is restricted to the sub-sample of developing countries, in which there is a strong negative correlation between sub-national government spending as a share of GDP and the fiscal position of the central government (Panel B)[14].

This negative correlation may be due to the fact that the transfer of spending assignments to sub-national governments has not been matched by a proportional reduction in the spending share of the centre in most countries in the sample. Alternatively, the transfer of revenue sources to sub-national governments, following the devolution of expenditure functions, may have deprived the centre of important income sources. In this respect, the revenue sources that are most efficiently used by the centre may have been transferred to lower tiers of government [Tanzi (1995)], thus generating imbalances at the centre[15]. Because fiscal devolution was carried out rather hastily in a number of countries in Latin America[16], sub-national fiscal imbalances may also be attributed to insufficient expertise building in local and state governments to handle larger resources and to deal effectively with expenditure management. OECD countries, on the other hand, tend to have larger average sub-national spending shares and lower fiscal imbalances than most countries in the developing country sample. This may result from more stringent control over sub-national finances or more efficient sharing of revenue sources and expenditure assignments.

Figure 2.

Panel A. **Central Government Size and Fiscal Position — Full Sample**

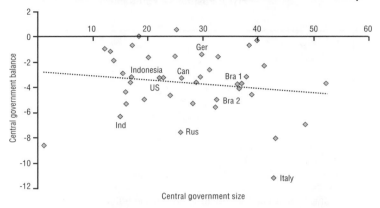

Panel B. **Sub-national Government Size and Fiscal Position — Full Sample**

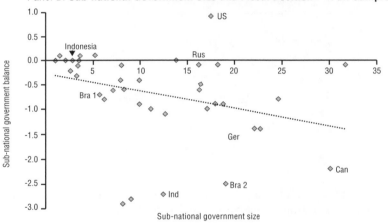

Additional evidence of a negative relationship between fiscal decentralisation and the fiscal position of the public sector is provided in Table 3. The simple correlations reported in this table support the arguments above. In particular, a negative correlation was found between the central government's fiscal balance and the share of inter-governmental transfers in total local revenue in the sample of OECD countries. In the case of the relationship between sub-national spending shares and the central government's fiscal position, a negative correlation was found for the OECD sample and a positive correlation was found for the sample of developing countries. In the former, an increase in sub-national spending is hence associated with the removal of budgetary pressures at the central government level and improvement in the central government's fiscal stance, whereas the converse seems to be the case in developing countries.

Figure 3.

Panel A. **Sub-national Government Size and Central Government Fiscal Position — Full Sample**

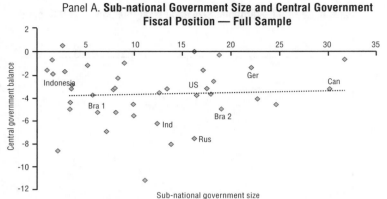

Panel B. **Sub-national Government Size and Central Government Fiscal Position — Developing Country Sample**

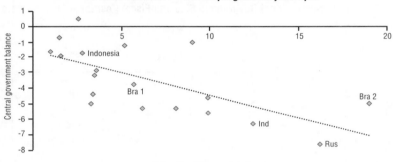

If the sample of developing countries is disaggregated between Asian and Latin American countries, a strong negative and statistically significant correlation was found between sub-national fiscal autonomy, measured as the sub-national tax revenue share, and the fiscal balance in the Latin American sample (-0.56). The correlation is considerably higher than that for the total sample of developing countries (-0.28). As for sub-national dependency, a positive and statistically significant correlation between the share of inter-governmental transfers and the government's fiscal balance was found for the Asian sample (0.47). The correlation between fiscal stance and the sub-national spending share is also positive and statistically different from zero in Latin America (0.54). The findings might indicate that the bigger the sub-national government in developing countries, the worse the fiscal imbalances at the central government level, as suggested above, unless sub-national spending is financed through local revenue mobilisation. In the case of Thailand, the policy mix of the country's successful fiscal consolidation in the 1980s involved alleviating the budgetary pressures at the centre due to the system of inter-governmental transfers, stimulating local revenue mobilisation and reducing the size of sub-national spending.

Table 3. **Macroeconomic and Fiscal Indicators: Simple Correlations**

	Central Gov. Fiscal Balance	Inflation	M2 Growth	GDP Growth
Sub-nat. tax autonomy ratio				
All	0.05	0.15	0.16	-0.13
	(0.28)	(0.93)	(0.98)	(-0.78)
OECD	-0.02	-0.48	-0.30	0.17
	(-0.10)	(-2.25)+	(-1.30)+	(0.69)
All developing	-0.28	0.22	0.24	-0.23
	(-1.21)	(0.95)	(1.01)	(-0.99)
Latin	-0.56	-0.03	-0.02	-0.21
	(-1.91)+	(-0.10)	(-0.15)	(-0.60)
Asia	-0.24	-0.61	-0.76	-0.13
	(-1.51)	(-4.76)**	(-3.35)+	(-0.81)
Sub-national dependency ratio				
All	0.17	-0.23	0.36	-0.16
	(1.03)	(-1.42)	(2.33)**	(-0.96)
OECD	-0.33	-0.56	-0.28	-0.23
	(-1.42)+	(-2.79)**	(-1.18)	(-0.96)
All developing	0.09	-0.26	0.30	-0.29
	(0.38)	(-1.09)	(1.28)	(-1.23)
Latin	-0.03	-0.50	0.13	-0.48
	(-0.08)	(-1.63)+	(0.81)	(-1.55)+
Asia	0.47	0.33	0.78	0.21
	(3.29)**	(2.19)	(3.53)**	(1.31)
Sub-national spending share				
All	0.02	-0.42	-0.19	-0.16
	(0.15)	(-2.75)*	(-1.14)	(-0.98)
OECD	-0.39	-0.25	-0.38	0.33
	(-1.75)+	(-1.07)	(-1.70)+	(1.46)+
All developing	0.40	-0.35	0.14	-0.80
	(1.82)+	(-1.56)+	(0.60)	(-5.48)*
Latin	0.54	-0.32	0.33	-0.77
	(1.80)+	(-0.96)	(2.14)+	(-3.46)*
Asia	-0.10	-0.40	-0.28	-0.91
	(-0.64)	(-2.66)+	(-0.81)	(-13.45)*

Note: Simple correlations are constructed from period averages using the indicators in Table 2. M2 growth, inflation, and GDP growth rates are available from the IFS dataset, IMF. The numbers in parentheses are two-tail *t*-statistics of the null hypothesis of zero correlation. (*), (**), and (+) denote statistical significance at the 1, 5, and 10 per cent levels, respectively.

Decentralisation and Monetary Policy

Given that fiscal decentralisation is likely to lead to a deterioration of the government's fiscal position in developing countries, it is also likely to have a bearing on monetary policy, depending on how fiscal imbalances are financed. In the case of sub-national governments, lenient market and/or institutional control over public finances may lead to insolvency problems at the sub-national level, which are frequently transferred to the Central Bank as lender of last resort. In the case of publicly-owned banks and financial institutions, for instance, dubious managerial practices[17] leads to financial distress and ultimately banking crises, the financial costs of which also tend to revert subsequently to the Central Bank. Depending on the degree of financial autonomy of sub-national governments, the same phenomenon can be observed at lower levels of government. However, Huther and Shah (1996) argue that decentralisation may foster central bank independence and ensure arm's length transactions between governments and the banking sector, by increasing transparency in the assignment of public sector functions, including that of the central bank. In this case, fiscal decentralisation may be conducive to monetary discipline.

With regard to deficit-financing alternatives, the correlation between inflation and fiscal imbalances is strong to the extent that fiscal deficits are financed through money creation. In the case of OECD countries, sub-national dependency, measured in terms of the share of inter-governmental transfers in the total revenue of sub-national governments, is negatively correlated with inflation and statistically different from zero at the 95 per cent level (Table 3). Sub-national dependency may therefore act as a constraint on sub-national spending and hence fiscal imbalances. Also, the sub-national spending share is negatively correlated with money creation in the OECD sample. By reducing budgetary pressures at the centre, a higher sub-national spending share also reduces the need for money creation to finance central government fiscal imbalances.

If the sample of developing countries is disaggregated, a rise in the sub-national spending share is likely to increase fiscal imbalances and to induce money creation in Latin America. The lack of monetary discipline is therefore likely to follow from the central government's fiscal imbalances, which are rooted in sub-national disequilibria. This is particularly true in the case of Brazil before the implementation of the stabilization plan in June 1994. For the Asian sample, Table 3 reveals that sub-national dependency is positively correlated with the fiscal balance and monetary expansion (M2 growth). Sub-national autonomy (the share of tax revenue in total sub-national revenue) has a strong negative association with money creation and inflation in Asia, where local revenue mobilisation might remove the budgetary, and hence monetary pressures created at the centre by the system of inter-governmental transfers. In Latin America, on the other hand, an increase in the sub-national spending share is likely to lead to fiscal and monetary imbalances at the centre. Overall, monetary imbalances tend to be caused by the need to finance unfunded transfers in East Asia's centralised systems of inter-governmental fiscal relations and by lack of control over sub-national spending in Latin America's relatively decentralised fiscal system. Both regions illustrate important channels through which fiscal decentralisation may translate itself into fiscal and monetary imbalances in developing countries.

Decentralisation and Growth

A positive relationship between public investment and growth has become a stylised fact in the growth literature [Ram (1986), Aschauer (1989), Barro (1990), Easterly and Rebelo (1993)][18]. However, in general, there is very little empirical research on the linkages between public finance, fiscal decentralisation and economic growth [see World Bank (1997), for further details]. Fiscal decentralisation is expected to affect growth positively by transferring spending power to the levels of government that are best equipped to meet local demands adequately, increase the efficiency of service delivery, and reduce operating costs. Accountability in expenditure management and allocative efficiency can be enhanced by bringing expenditure assignments closer to revenue sources and hence to the median voter. An overall increase in the efficiency of public sector spending is therefore expected to be growth-enhancing.

On the other hand, fiscal decentralisation may have a detrimental impact on growth, as suggested by the correlations presented in Table 3. A strong and statistically significant negative correlation between sub-national spending shares and GDP growth was found for the developing countries under examination (-0.80; and -0.77 and -0.91 for, respectively, Latin America and Asia, if the total sample of developing countries is disaggregated), when fiscal decentralisation is defined as the average ratio of sub-national spending to total government spending, while the correlation was found to be positive in the case of the OECD-country sample (0.33).

The negative correlation in the sample of developing countries can be attributed to a number of factors. First, as discussed above, tax instruments that are best used by the central government may be assigned to sub-national governments, thereby reducing the efficiency of such instruments. Second, fiscal decentralisation may be growth-reducing because sub-national governments may assign resources to expenditures that do not generate economy-wide growth-enhancing externalities. This is the case, for instance, when emphasis is placed on current rather than investment spending and when fiscal devolution is accompanied by an increase in the sub-national administrative machinery and local payroll costs [Devarajan *et al.* (1996)]. Even if emphasis is placed on capital spending, the investment component of public expenditure may turn out to be unproductive if financed by instruments that misallocate public spending. Third, growth reduction can also result from fiscal decentralisation if it increases uncertainty over tax policy[19] and leads to a mismatch between national and sub-national policy objectives.

Turning to additional empirical evidence of a negative relationship between fiscal decentralisation and growth, Davoodi and Zou (1997) analyse a sample of 46 countries over the period 1970-89 and conclude that fiscal decentralisation is growth-reducing in developing countries, but no causal link is found in the case of developed countries.

Specific evidence for China is provided by Zhang and Zou (1997), who found a negative relationship between post-reform decentralisation and economic growth in a sample of Chinese provinces. The particular case of China will be analysed in greater detail below. In the case of Brazil, de Mello (1997b) relates changes in per capita growth rates across Brazilian states to changes in their degree of fiscal dependency, after controlling for other growth determinants and initial conditions. His findings suggest a negative impact of fiscal decentralisation on output growth in the case of Brazilian middle-tier governments and show that, on the one hand, state-level public investment is a powerful growth determinant and, on the other, the dependency of sub-national governments on higher levels of government via inter-government transfers clearly has a deleterious impact on growth.

Concerning other large developing countries, there is no direct evidence as to how fiscal decentralisation affects growth performance. A casual observation of Indonesia and India, however, suggests that the difference in a country's fiscal system may have an important bearing on growth performance in the medium term. In the case of Indonesia, the government since 1966 has adopted the "balanced budget" rule as the core principle of macroeconomic management. The Indonesian central government has been running fiscal deficits in a conventional economic sense but has managed to keep them within a small range. To be sure, the "balanced budget" rule can be maintained only because the items financing budget deficits, such as aid and external borrowings, are counted as a part of revenues. Nonetheless, this rule has served effectively to keep the lid on political pressures demanding an extravagant expansion of public expenditures (Hill, 1996).

On the other hand, India's fiscal adjustment has been inadequate at both central and state levels. While the central government had managed to reduce its fiscal deficit from 8.4 per cent in 1985-89 to 6.7 per cent in 1990-94, the fiscal deficit of state governments had been slashed only marginally, despite the fact that the former can control the borrowing of the latter. In referring to the difficulty of fiscal adjustment in India, Joshi and Little (1994) states:

> … India's fiscal problem is not insoluble. The extent of soft budgets and hidden subsidies is so large that the required adjustment could be achieved quite rapidly *without compromising efficiency and equity*. Of course, the political constraints are severe. But unless they are overcome, the reform process could grind to a halt. (p. 43; *italics* are added.)

Given the discussion above, it is important to note that the relationship between public finance indicators and macroeconomic performance in terms of fiscal and monetary policies and GDP growth is more complex than is often thought. Nevertheless, despite the limitations of the methodology and data used here, the results reported above suggest that fiscal decentralisation is likely to generate fiscal and monetary imbalances that impair the growth performance of the economy in the sample of developing countries. OECD countries are, however, better equipped to reap the benefits of fiscal decentralisation, while maintaining fiscal and monetary discipline, which appears to be conducive to higher output growth. Our results also imply that the gains from fiscal decentralisation may be grossly exaggerated in the case of developing countries, given the costs involved in the process of decentralisation.

Decentralisation and Macroeconomic Governance: China and Russia

The experiences of China and Russia are analysed separately here, given the particular characteristics of reform in centrally-planned economies and the lack of sufficiently long time series for most of the variables used here. China's economic transition since the late 1970s provides a *unique* case of decentralisation experiments in which the fiscal system has fitfully evolved from one extreme of complete centralised control of fiscal powers in the 1950s to the other extreme of fiscal decentralisation until quite recently. In the case of Russia, fiscal decentralisation was promoted with a view to increasing overall allocative efficiency in the economy. It was hoped that sub-national governments would be able to trim operating costs and, as a result, generate funds to offset the unfunded spending responsibilities transferred to them by the central government [Wallich (1996)]. In fact, sub-national imbalances are lower in Russia than in most other countries with sub-national governments of comparable size. Sizeable imbalances are nevertheless evident in the case of the central government (Table 1).

In the case of China, open-door policy and decentralisation have been the two pillars of economic reform since late 1978[20]. In the Chinese context, "decentralisation" means devolving the power of decision-making from central to local governments, on the one hand, and from planning authorities to state-owned enterprises (SOEs), on the other. In the case of Russia, however, decentralisation also entailed significant public sector downsizing, through the privatisation of SOEs and the transfer of decision-making to the private sector. "Decentralisation" in China is, thus, conceptually different from "liberalisation" in Russia, since the latter implies the removal of government intervention in economic activity *at all levels*, though these two initiatives are often inter-linked in reality. What we have seen in China since the mid-1980s is the emergence of a "decentralised public-ownership economy", according to the terminology used by Fan (1996).

While decentralisation is a key to China's economic dynamism in the post-reform era, it has also brought about serious side effects, that is, making China "inflation-prone" as a result of persisting budget deficits and excessive monetary expansion at local levels[21]. Beijing was losing the control of public finance, as central budget revenue as a share of total government budgetary revenue fell from over 60 per cent in the 1970s to 37 per cent in 1993. At the same time, the total government budgetary revenue also dropped from 31 per cent of GDP in 1978 to about 12 per cent in 1994 (Fan, 1996). In the case of Russia, revenue-sharing arrangements in the post-decentralisation period also led to a fall in the centre's revenues. Revenue sources were devolved to lower levels of government as well as tax collection functions, and funds to be transferred to the centre were "shared upwards". Lack of transparency in revenue sharing encourages free-riding on the part of sub-national governments, since they seek to take advantage of fiscal powers granted to them without much helping to fund central budget revenues. As is evident from Table 2, emphasis is placed on local taxes as the main revenue source of sub-national governments in Russia, which is in sharp contrast with many developing countries in the sample and, particularly, with large decentralised federations, where inter-governmental transfers are an important revenue source for sub-national governments.

Institutional encouragement to free-riding is also found in the case of Chinese provincial/local governments [Laffont and Senik-Leygonie (1997)][22]. An additional complicating factor in the country's fiscal decentralisation policy is the central government's insufficient access to information on local SOEs. The upshot of fiscal decentralisation in China, as well as Russia, was thus a sharp decline of financial resources the central government can control and manage. In China, it has been argued that the decline of the central government in collecting taxes and allocating financial resources has seriously damaged its ability to redress regional disparity between wealthier coastal provinces and poorer interior provinces[23]. As a result, the central government has been undertaking a new step to increase its share of central budget revenue by *recentralising* resources[24]. However, doubts have been raised over the effectiveness of fiscal recentralisation because of the power struggle between the different levels of government (Laffont and Senik-Leygonie, 1997).

Finally, the movement towards fiscal recentralisation also fails to recognise the new development of local economies and the responsibility for local governments to provide public goods and services to local communities. Fan (1996) points to the increasing importance of "non-standard" revenues in local economies — he also calls them "extra-extra-budgetary revenues", since these funds are not recorded on official books. These are "funds raised from local sources by local governments and spent on local projects or used to cover local government current expenditures". While the whole scale of "non-standard" revenues has yet to be grasped, some sample surveys show that these funds account for an important share of local government revenues.[25] It has been argued that the growing demand for fiscal autonomy on the part of provinces and municipalities has much bearing on the issue of local democracy as well as on the problem of corruption [Fan (1996)].

In short, recent fiscal developments at the local level pose a fundamental question about macroeconomic governance in China. That is the apparent conflict of interests between different levels of government over the control of financial resources in an extremely decentralised economy. How to design inter-governmental fiscal transfers still remains an open question in China. In Russia, on the other hand, drastic changes in inter-governmental fiscal relations are part of a broader reform package which involves significant changes in the role of the State in the economy, divestiture of public enterprises, comprehensive deregulation and trade and investment liberalisation. In this respect, consolidating the recent improvement in the country's macroeconomic performance depends, to a large extent, on the removal of sub-national budgetary pressures, given their negative impact on public finances at the central government level. More importantly, fiscal adjustment and the alleviation of budgetary pressures at the centre cannot be achieved by simply transferring unfunded spending responsibilities to sub-national governments, and thereby changing the composition of fiscal imbalances in favour of the central government.

Concluding Remarks and Policy Implications

Many different countries, both developed and developing, have implemented public sector reform programmes with different degrees of success. An important aspect of such programmes has been the decentralisation of fiscal policy-making to lower levels of government. Fiscal decentralisation consists of re-assigning expenditure functions and revenue sources to lower tiers of government with a view to decentralising fiscal policy-making and implementation across government levels. Efficiency gains, reduction in operating costs, increased public sector performance in service delivery, and growth enhancement are the expected positive consequences of fiscal decentralisation. Loss of control over sub-national finances, and ensuing fiscal and monetary disarray at the centre are among its pitfalls.

By focusing on the three broad groups of countries examined above, this paper highlights a few glaring contrasts. First, in the case of developing countries, fiscal decentralisation is likely to generate imbalances at the sub-national level which may lead to a deterioration of the fiscal position of the central government. As a result, the growth performance of these economies may be negatively affected. Second, the OECD countries have nevertheless had higher sub-national spending shares for a much longer span of time than most developing countries examined here, without significant fiscal imbalances at the centre. In these countries, more stringent control of sub-national finances is believed to have prevented the deterioration of national and sub-national fiscal positions due to decentralisation. OECD countries are therefore believed to be better equipped to reap the benefits of fiscal decentralisation in terms of growth, while at the same time maintaining fiscal and monetary discipline.

Third, in the particular case of large developing and transition economies, Brazil has gone a long way in fiscal decentralisation, by raising sub-national spending ratios substantially, devolving revenue sources and expenditure functions to sub-national jurisdictions and granting significant autonomy in policy-making at the sub-national level. On the other hand, local revenue mobilisation has hardly been encouraged by the country's system of inter-governmental transfers. India has a long tradition of fiscal decentralisation, unlike most other Asian countries, which have in general been more centralist in fiscal policy-making and implementation. Fiscal centralism is exercised in Indonesia by concentrating revenue mobilisation under the control of the central government and financing sub-national expenditure functions via inter-governmental transfers. The recent experiences with decentralisation in China and Russia suggest that inflation follows from lax monetary policy in the case where fiscal imbalances are financed via money creation.

Overall, evidence reported here provides empirical support for the basic theoretical predictions of the fiscal federalism literature and indicates that the merits of fiscal decentralisation have to be weighed against the risks involved in increasing sub-national spending power at the expense of higher levels of government. This is likely to increase the dependency of sub-national jurisdictions, to reduce their fiscal autonomy, to increase their indebtedness, and to put pressure on sub-national finances and ultimately on good governance at the national level. As a corollary, our results also suggest that imposing fiscal discipline at sub-national levels of government, by market forces or institutional design, is a crucial pre-requisite for successful decentralisation.

Policy implications can be summarised as follows. First, the devolution of expenditure functions should be matched by sensible re-assignment of revenue sources across government levels, without depriving the centre of income sources and the tax instruments which it is best equipped to use more efficiently. Transferring taxes with broad tax bases to sub-national governments severely reduces their efficiency and deprives the centre of important short-run demand management instruments. Second, inter-governmental transfer systems should be designed to impose some control of the centre over sub-national spending and to encourage revenue mobilisation at the local level, without creating extra budgetary pressures at the centre. Monetary imbalances and macroeconomic governance problems are expected to follow, if fiscal decentralisation starves the centre of revenue sources and imposes a rigid system of inter-governmental transfers. Third, avoiding monetary laxity in the presence of sub-national fiscal imbalances helps to insulate the central government from disarray in sub-national finances, thereby preserving overall macroeconomic stability.

Notes

1. See, for example, Wildasin (1996) for a concise overview of problems of fiscal decentralisation and macroeconomic governance in a broader context.

2. There is a large body of literature on this topic in the context of developing countries. As regards Asian developing countries, see, *inter alia*, Agarwala (1992), Asher (1989, 1992), Boadway, Roberts and Shah (1994), Crane (1995), ESACP(1991), Kohli (1991), Laffont and Senik-Leygonie (1997), Ma (1995), Manasan (1990), Roy (1995), Shah and Qureshi (1994),Tanzi (1987, 1995), Tanzi and Shome (1992) and Xavier (1996). In the case of Latin America, useful references include Afonso (1996), de Mello (1997), Rezk (1997), Shah (1990, 1994).

3. See Boadway, Roberts and Shah (1994) and Tanzi (1995).

4. The government can also affect private economic activities through non-financial measures, such as formal and informal regulations, including so-called administrative guidance. This makes international comparison even more difficult.

5. This measure refers to the size of the consolidated public sector.

6. More recently, fiscal consolidation at the centre was certainly facilitated by buoyant tax revenues associated with strong economic growth since the mid-1980s, but it also reflected the government efforts to curb both operational and development expenditures. (Robinson *et al.*, 1991).

7. An increase in sub-national spending shares was particularly noticeable in Spain.

8. For further details, see Weingast *et al.* (1981), and von Hagen and Harden (1995).

9. For further details, see Hart and Holmstrom (1987).

10. The case of Brazilian municipal finances is illustrative here. Taxation theory dictates that property taxes should be collected by local governments. However, in Brazil, such tax base is grossly underutilised by municipal governments given that excessive reliance on inter-governmental transfers from state and federal funds creates little incentive for municipal governments to mobilise resources in their own jurisdictions

11. Inter-governmental transfers may be of different types (compulsory, negotiated, matching grants, etc.) and the qualitative distinction between those types of transfers is likely to shed more light on the various channels through which sub-national dependency affects macroeconomic governance and inter-governmental relations at large. Nevertheless, it was not possible, due to data limitations, to disaggregate inter-governmental transfers according to type.

12. In the case of Argentina, it was not possible to distinguish between local taxes and inter-governmental transfers.

13. Despite being part of a federation, Australian sub-national governments have low taxing power and receive most of their revenue through inter-governmental transfers.

14. The negative relationship prevails even if the outliers are removed from the sample.

15. This is precisely the case of VAT taxes in Brazil, which were devolved to middle-tier governments in the late 1980s [Afonso (1996), McLure (1997), de Mello (1997a)].

16. To a large extent, fiscal decentralisation in a number of Latin American countries was prompted by the return to democracy. Authoritarian governments had promoted fiscal centralisation and concentrated overall economic policy-making power in the central government. The gain in political power of sub-national jurisdictions represented in a freer legislature induced a process of fiscal devolution to lower levels of government.

17. Financial imprudence may be attributed to factors ranging from weak management and careless lending practices (accumulation of sizeable portfolios of non-performing loans, inadequate collaterisation, loan recovery difficulties, poor credit worthiness assessment, etc.) to the use of such institutions as agents of fiscal policy, and pernicious political interference with lending criteria.

18. See also Nagaraj, Varoudakis and Véganzonès (1997) for an interesting case study of India. Their panel-data analysis suggests that targeting public investment towards specific infrastructures — physical, economic and social — might improve regional, as well as nation-wide, growth prospects in India.

19. See Aizenman and Marion (1993), for further details. Uncertainty also affects the government size. Rodrik (1996) suggests that government size increases with exposure to external risk, given the need to stabilise income fluctuations arising from outward orientation.

20. See Fukasaku and Wall (1994) for a detailed account of China's open-economy reform.

21. The past two years have seen a successful 'soft-landing' of the Chinese economy with a substantial fall in inflation without disrupting growth. Whether China can sustain stable — but high — rates of growth with low inflation is, however, a matter of debate. This depends crucially on reforms of SOEs and the banking sector in the future.

22. The "free-rider" behaviour of provincial/local governments is often referred to as "whipping the fast buffaloes" in Chinese: the fast buffaloes (the fast-growing provinces) tend to be whipped (taxed) most, in other words, the better they perform, the worse they are treated (Laffont and Senik-Leygonie 1997).

23. For example, a recent paper by Jian, Sachs and Warner (1996) shows that regional incomes in China have begun to diverge since 1990 following the convergent trend which was observed between 1978 and 1989. They argue that regional convergence in the 1980s was associated with rural reforms and was particularly strong within the coastal regions as a result of foreign trade and investment liberalisation. However, they also argue that the tendency for divergence since 1990 will probably continue between fast-growing coastal provinces and poorer interior provinces if current policies remain unchanged.

24. Under the new revenue-sharing system announced in 1994, the central government is taking over the administrative function of collecting shared taxes and obtaining a larger share of tax revenues; for example, 75 per cent of value-added tax now goes to the central government, which can decide how much should be transferred to local governments. Ma (1995) also argues that the 1994 revenue-sharing system still suffers from weak institutional arrangements regarding the division of tax bases between central and local governments, which is based on the ownership of SOEs.

25. According to Fan (1995), the relative importance of "non-standard" revenues varies widely across provinces and townships, for example, from more than 90 per cent of total revenue in some township of Guangdong to about 40 per cent of that of Hunan province.

Appendix

Table 1.A. **Sample Summary**

	Central Gov. Size	Central Gov. Balance	Sub-nat. Gov. Size	Sub-nat. Gov. Balance	Sub-national Fiscal Autonomy		Sub-national Fiscal Dep.	Sub-national Spend. Share
					Tax Autonomy	Non-Tax Autonomy		
Argentina	1974-92	1974-92	1974-92	1974-92	1976-92	1975-92	n.a.	1974-92
Bolivia	1973-84	1973-84	1984-95	1985-95	1985-95	1985-95	1985-96	1984-95
Brazil	1980-93	1975-93	1983-93	1983-93	1983-93	1983-93	1983-93	1983-93
Chile	1971-88	1972-95	1974-88	1975-88	1974-88	1974-88	1974-88	1974-88
Colombia	1971-93	1971-93	1974-86	1974-86	1975-86	1974-86	1974-86	1974-86
Mexico	1972-94	1972-94	1970-94	1971-94	1972-93	1972-93	1973-93	1972-94
Peru	1973-95	1973-95	1990-95	1990-95	1990-95	1990-95	1990-95	1990-95
India	1974-95	1974-95	1974-93	1974-93	1974-93	1974-93	1974-93	1974-93
Indonesia	1972-94	1972-94	1975-93	1975-93	1975-93	1975-93	1975-93	1975-93
Malaysia	1972-94	1972-94	1972-94	1972-94	n.a.	n.a.	1972-96	1972-96
Philippines	1972-93	1972-94	1978-92	1978-92	1978-92	1978-92	1978-92	1978-92
Thailand	1972-94	1972-95	1971-95	1972-95	1972-95	1972-95	1972-96	1972-95
South Africa	1972-95	1972-95	1977-95	1977-95	1977-95	1977-95	1977-95	1977-94
Russia	1994-95	1994-95	1994-95	1994-95	1994-95	1994-95	1994-95	1994-95
Australia	1970-95	1970-95	1970-95	1970-95	1970-95	1970-95	1970-95	1970-95
Austria	1970-94	1970-94	1970-94	1970-94	1970-94	1970-94	1970-94	1970-94
Belgium	1970-94	1970-94	1978-94	1978-94	1978-94	1978-94	1978-94	1978-94
Canada	1974-94	1974-95	1971-94	1971-83	1971-94	1979-94	1971-94	1971-94
Denmark	1970-95	1970-95	1970-95	1977-95	1970-95	1970-95	1970-95	1970-95
Finland	1972-94	1972-94	1970-90	1970-90	1970-90	1970-90	1970-90	1972-90
France	1972-95	1972-95	1972-95	1972-95	1972-95	1978-95	1972-96	1972-96
Germany	1970-95	1970-95	1970-95	1970-95	1970-95	1974-95	1970-95	1970-95
Iceland	1972-95	1972-95	1972-93	1972-85	1972-85	1972-85	1983-85	1972-93
Italy	1973-94	1973-94	1973-85	1973-85	1973-75	1985-89	1973-75	1973-75
Netherlands	1975-95	1975-95	1975-95	1975-95	1975-95	1975-95	1975-95	1975-95
Norway	1972-94	1972-94	1970-94	1970-94	1970-77	1980-94	1970-94	1972-94
Spain	1970-93	1970-94	1980-94	1980-94	1980-93	1980-93	1980-94	1980-94
Sweden	1970-95	1970-95	1970-94	1970-95	1970-94	1970-94	1970-94	1970-94
Switzerland	1970-84	1970-84	1970-94	1970-84	1970-84	1970-84	1970-84	1970-84
UnitedKingdom	1970-95	1970-95	1973-95	1970-96	1970-95	1973-95	1970-95	1970-95
United States	1972-96	1972-96	1972-94	1972-95	1972-94	1980-94	1972-94	1972-94

Note: Data source is the IMF's GFS dataset.

144

Bibliography

AFONSO, J.R.R. (1996), "Descentralização Fiscal, Efeitos Macroeconômicos e Função de Estabilização: o Caso (Peculiar) do Brasil". Paper presented at the VII Regional Seminar of Fiscal Policy, ECLAC, Santiago, Chile.

AGARWALA R. (1992), "China, Reforming Intergovernmental Fiscal Relations", *World Bank Discussion Papers*, No. 178, World Bank, Washington D.C.

AIZENMAN, J. AND N.P. MARION (1993), "Policy Uncertainty, Persistence and Growth", *Review of International Economics*, 1.

ASCHAUER, D. (1989), "Is Government Spending Productive?", *Journal of Monetary Economics*, 23.

ASHER, M.G. (1989), "A Comparative Overview of ASEAN Fiscal Systems and Practices", in ASHER, M.G. (ed.), *Fiscal Systems and Practices in ASEAN: Trends, Impact and Evaluation* (Singapore: Institute of Southeast Asian Studies), 1-18.

ASHER, M.G. (1992), "Lessons from Tax Reforms in the Asia-Pacific Region", *Asian Development Review*, 10.

BARRO, R.J. (1990), "Government Spending in a Simple Model of Endogenous Growth", *Journal of Political Economy*, 98.

BLONDAL, J. (1997), "Fiscal Federalism in OECD Member Countries". Presented at the OECD-ESAF Seminar on Decentralisation, Intergovernmental Fiscal Relations and Macroeconomic Governance, Brasília.

BOADWAY, R., S. ROBERTS AND A. SHAH (1994), "The Reform of Fiscal Systems in Developing and Emerging Market Economies: A Federalism Perspective", *Policy Research Working Paper*, No.1259, World Bank, Washington, D.C.

CRANE, R. (1995), "The Practice of Regional Development in Indonesia: Resolving Central-Local Co-ordination Issues in Planning and Finance", *Public Administration and Development*, 15.

DAVOODI, H. AND H.-F. ZOU (1997), "Fiscal Decentralisation and Economic Growth: A Cross-Country Study", *Journal of Urban Economics*.

DEVARAJAN, S., V. SWAROOP AND H.-F. ZOU (1996), "The Composition of Public Expenditure and Economic Growth", *Journal of Monetary Economics*, 37.

DORNBUSCH, R. AND S. FISCHER (1993), "Moderate Inflation", *World Bank Economic Review*, 7.

EASTERLY, W.R. AND S. REBELO (1993), "Fiscal Policy and Economic Growth: An Empirical Investigation", *NBER Working Paper*, No. 4499.

ESCAP (1991), "Fiscal Decentralisation and the mobilization and use of national resources for development: issues, experience and policies in the ESCAP region", *Development Papers,* No. 11, Bangkok.

FAN, G. (1995), "On New Rules of Public Finance" (in Chinese), mimeo.

FAN, G. (1996), "Growth of 'Off-budget Revenue' and Evolution of Local Governance in China", mimeo, China Reform Foundation, National Economic Research Institute, Beijing.

FUKASAKU, K. (1997), "Fiscal Decentralisation and Macroeconomic Governance: Asian Perspectives", presented at the OECD-ESAF Seminar on Decentralisation, Intergovernmental Fiscal Relations and Macroeconomic Governance, Brasília.

FUKASAKU K. AND D. WALL (1994), *China's Long March to an Open Economy*, OECD Development Centre, Paris.

GORDON, R. (1983), "An Optimal Taxation Approach to Fiscal Federalism", *Quarterly Journal of Economics*, 95.

VON HAGEN, J. AND I. HARDEN(1955), "Budget Processes and Commitment to Fiscal Discipline", European Economic Review, 39.

HART, O. AND B. HOLMSTROM (1987), "The Theory of Contracts", in T. BEWLEY (ed.) *Advances inh Economic Theory,* Cambridge University Press, Cambridge.

HILL, H. (1996), *The Indonesian Economy since 1966,* Cambridge University Press, Cambridge.

HUTHER, J. AND A. SHAH (1996), "A Simple Measure of Good Governance and its Application to the Debate on the Appropriate Level of Fiscal Decentralisation", mimeo, World Bank, Washington, D.C.

INMAN, R.P. AND D.L. RUBINFELD (1996), "Designing Tax Policy in Federalist Economies: an Overview", Journal of Public Economics, 60.

JIAN, T., J. SACHS AND A. WARNER (1996), "Trends in Regional Inequality in China", *China Economic Review*, 7.

JOSHI, V. AND I.M.D. LITTLE (1994), *India, Macroeconomics and Political Economy, 1964-1991*, Oxford University Press, Oxford.

KOHLI, K.N. (1991), "The Role of Fiscal Policy in Asian Economic Development", *Asian Development Review*, 9.

LAFFONT, J.-J. AND C. SENIK-LEYGONIE (1997), *Price Controls and the Economics of Institution in China*, OECD Development Centre, Paris.

MA, J. (1995), "The Reform of Intergovernmental Fiscal Relations in China", *Asian Economic Journal*, 9.

MANASAN, R.G. (1990), "A Review of Fiscal Policy Reforms in the ASEAN Countries in the 1980s", *Philippine Institute for Development Studies Working Paper,* No. 90-14, Manila.

McLure, C.E., Jr. (1997), "Topics in the Theory of Revenue Assignment" in M.I. Blejer and T. Ter-Minassian *Macroeconomic Dimensions of Public Finance: Essays in Honour of Vito Tanzi,* Routledge, New York.

de Mello, L.R. Jr. (1997*a*), "Fiscal Federalism and Macroeconomic Stability in Brazil: Background and Perspectives". Presented at the OECD-ESAF Seminar on Decentralisation, Intergovernmental Fiscal Relations and Macroeconomic Governance, Brasília.

de Mello, L.R. Jr. (1997*b*), "Fiscal Federalism, Sub-national Finances, and Economic Growth: The Case of Brazil" , mimeo, University of Kent.

Nagaraj, R., A. Varoudakis and M.-A. Véganzonès (1998), "Long-run Growth Trends and Convergence Across Indian States", *Technical Paper,* No. 131, OECD Development Centre, Paris.

Prud'homme, R. (1995), "On the Dangers of Decentralisation", *World Bank Research Observer,* August.

Ram, R. (1986), "Government Size and Economic Growth: A New Framework and Some Evidence from Cross-section and Time Series Data", *American Economic Review,* 76.

Rezk, E. (1997), "Experiences of Decentralisation and Inter-Governmental Fiscal Relations in Latin America". Presented at the OECD-ESAF Seminar on Decentralisation, Intergovernmental Fiscal Relations and Macroeconomic Governance, Brasília.

Robinson, D. *et al.* (1991), "Thailand: Adjusting to Successs – Current Policy Issues", *IMF Occasional Paper,* No.85, International Monetary Fund.

Rodrik, D. (1996), "Why Do More Open Economies Have Bigger Governments", *NBER Discussion Paper,* No. 5537, April .

Roy, J. (1995), "Macroeconomic Management and Fiscal Decentralisation", *EDI Seminar Series,* World Bank, Washington , D.C.

Salleh, I.M. and S.D. Meyanathan (1993), *The Lessons of East Asia: Malaysia - Growth, Equity and Structural Transformation,* World Bank, Washington, D.C.

Shah, A. (1990), "The New Fiscal federalism in Brazil", *World Bank Discussion Papers,* No. 124.

Shah, A. (1994), "The Reform of Intergovernmental Fiscal Relations in Developing and Emerging Market Economies", *World Bank Policy and Research Series Paper,* No. 23.

Shah A. and Z. Qureshi (1994), "Intergovernmental Fiscal Relations in Indonesia, Issues and Reform, Options", *World Bank Discussion Papers,* No. 239.

Tanzi, V. (1987), "The Public Sector in the Market Economies of Developing Asia", *Asian Development Review,* 5.

Tanzi, V. (1995), "Fiscal Federalism and Decentralisation: a Review of Some Efficiency and Macroeconomic Aspects", Annual Bank Conference on Development Economics, World Bank, Washington, D.C.

Tanzi, V. (1997), "The Changing Role of the State in the Economy: A Historical Perspective". Presented at the OECD-ESAF Seminar on Decentralisation, Intergovernmental Fiscal Relations and Macroeconomic Governance, Brasília.

TANZI, V. AND P. SHOME (1992), "The Role of Taxation in the Development of East Asian Economies", in ITO, T. AND A.O. KRUEGER (eds.) (1992), *The Political Economy of Tax Reform* , University of Chicago Press, Chicago.

TANZI, V. AND L. SCHUKNECHT (1997), "Reconsidering the Fiscal Role of Government: the International Perspective", Paper presented at AEA Session on *Reconsidering the Fiscal Role of Government*.

TER-MINASSIAN, T. (1997), "Decentralisation and Macroeconomic Management". Presented at the OECD-ESAF Seminar on Decentralisation, Intergovernmental Fiscal Relations and Macroeconomic Governance, Brasília.

XAVIER, J.A. (1996), "Budget Reform - the Malaysian Experience", *Public Administration and Development*, 16.

WALLICH, C.I. (1996), "Russia's Dilemma" in WALLICH, C.I. (ed.) *Russia and the Challenge of Fiscal Federalism,* World Bank, Washington, D.C.

WEINGAST, B.R., K.A. SHEPSLE AND C. JOHNSEN (1981), "The Political Economy of Benefits and Costs: A Neoclassical Approach to Distributive Politics", *Journal of Political Economy* 89, No. 41.

WILDASIN D. (1996), "Introduction: Fiscal Aspects of Evolving Federations", *International Tax and Public Finance*, 3.

WORLD BANK (1992), *Malaysia: Fiscal Reform for Stable Growth*, Washington, D.C.

WORLD BANK (1993), *The East Asian Miracle: Economic Growth and Public Policy,* Oxford University Press, Oxford.

WORLD BANK (1997), *The World Development Report*, Washington, D.C.

ZHANG, T., AND H.-F. ZOU (1997), "Fiscal Decentralisation, Public Spending, and Economic Growth in China", *Journal of Public Economics*.

Fiscal Federalism in OECD Member Countries

Jon Blondal

Introduction

Fiscal federalism issues in OECD Member countries represent one of their most complex public management issues. We use the term "fiscal federalism" for convenience's sake, not because we limit ourselves to federal countries in studying fiscal relations between different levels of government. In this regard, the issues faced by unitary countries and federal countries are largely the same.

Overview

Fiscal federalism arrangements in OECD Member countries reveal the wide range of possibilities available. There are countries with very strong sub-national governments and countries with very weak sub-national governments, and everything in between. There is no single "OECD model".

The methodology used to compare fiscal federalism arrangements across OECD Member countries is to look at the share of sub-national governments in total government receipts, principally taxation. Since taxes are an important financial constraint, this can be used as an indicator for the degree of autonomy of sub-national governments in individual OECD Member countries.

Specific figures are in Table 1 but if we attempt to generalise about these findings, we can say that federal countries have the strongest sub-national governments. This is as we might expect and has been the case historically. Next in line are the Nordic countries and the Netherlands. These are all unitary countries, and in many ways share similar governance traditions. What is also significant about this group is that sub-national governments have been getting stronger in these countries in recent years. The weakest sub-national governments are to be found in unitary countries with a Napoleonic or a Westminster tradition of governance. Examples include France, Greece, Italy, New Zealand and the United Kingdom.

Table1. **Sub-National Government Share of Total Government Expenditure**
(Data Refers to 1994 – percentage)

Australia	45.4
Austria	25.2
Belgium	11.3
Canada	55.3
Denmark	51.7
Finland	28.2
France	14.2
Germany	32.0
Greece	7.9
Iceland	19.4
Ireland	26.4
Italy	23.1
Japan	36.6
Netherlands	25.7
Portugal	8.3
Spain	20.4
Sweden	34.5
United Kingdom	25.3
United States	38.7

Source: OECD.

Revenue raised by sub-national governments is half the story. The other half of the story is the share of total expenditure accounted for by sub-national governments.

Table 2 contains the data. As a general rule, the share of total expenditure of sub-national governments is greater than their share of total revenue. The difference is for the most part attributable to transfer of funds from national governments to sub-national governments. There are, however, no obvious groupings that emerge from looking at these figures. Some federal countries, notably Australia, have very significant transfers to sub-national governments, whereas other federal countries, such as the United States, have a relatively low level of transfers. Similarly, some Nordic countries, for example Denmark, have very substantial transfers whereas others, such as Iceland, have relatively few. In general, there is a tendency for other unitary countries to have a more substantial transfer of funds from the national government to lower levels.

Certain caveats need to be made about the manner in which the above conclusions were reached. First, different accounting regimes for government revenues and expenditures and divergent treatment of social security funds can significantly affect the reported financial flows. Second, the figures capture, by definition, only financial flows and do not incorporate mandates from national governments to sub-national governments. Nonetheless, anecdotal evidence tends to confirm the general conclusions reached.

Table2. Sub-National Government Share of Total Government Receipt

(Data Refers to 1994 – percentage)

Australia	29.4
Austria	22.9
Belgium	7.0
Canada	50.0
Denmark	29.1
Finland	21.9
France	10.7
Germany	29.0
Greece	3.6
Iceland	19.1
Ireland	5.4
Italy	9.9
Japan	22.9
Netherlands	7.0
Portugal	7.1
Spain	12.6
Sweden	31.3
Switzerland	39.5
United Kingdom	6.0
United States	34.3

Source: OECD.

Current fiscal federalism arrangements in OECD Member countries are largely a function of each country's history and entrenched traditions. If OECD Member countries were setting up their systems today from a clean slate, they would doubtlessly look different. The definite trend in OECD Member countries is to strengthen sub-national governments, giving them more responsibility for revenues and expenditures. But the very history and entrenched traditions that are responsible for the current arrangements are acting as a check on the pace of reforms in this area. The national government will always be the dominant level of government. In countries with strong sub-national governments, such as the United States, the Federal government still accounts for about two-thirds of all activity.

Issues

OECD Member countries face five fiscal federalism issues specifically:

— Aggregate fiscal discipline;

— Economic stabilization measures;

— Allocative efficiency;

— Regional equity considerations; and

— Operating effectiveness and efficiency.

These are wide-ranging issues, but they are complementary in many ways, and essential elements for successful fiscal federalism outcomes.

Aggregate Fiscal Discipline

The overriding goal of any fiscal system is, or at least should be, to maintain aggregate fiscal discipline, i.e. to control the totals. The fear of national governments is generally that some sub-national governments will be less than responsible in this regard and accumulate excessive and unsustainable levels of debt.

There are three approaches that Member countries have adopted to impose fiscal discipline on sub-national governments. The first is simply to have the national government impose no restrictions on the borrowing activity of sub-national governments and leave it to the market to impose the necessary discipline. The United States and Canada employ this approach.

The second approach can be termed "administrative controls." This consists of sub-national governments' consulting with the national government on their borrowing plans, in aggregate or for individual loans. (These consultations commonly incorporate a discussion of other aspects of sub-national governments finances, i.e. overall levels of revenue and expenditure.) These are generally labeled "consultations," but if disagreements between national and sub-national governments take place, it is generally the national government's point of view that prevails. This is the most common approach adopted in OECD Member countries. Prime examples include the Nordic countries, Germany with its Financial Planning Council, and Australia with its National Loans Council.

The third method consists of national governments' prescribing general rules for the allowed level of borrowing by sub-national governments. A common feature of rules-based systems is to distinguish between capital expenditure and operating expenditure, and to permit borrowing only for capital expenditure. The rules-based systems are, however, often combined with administrative control systems. The clearest example of a stand-alone rules-based system, albeit different in nature, is the Maastricht criteria for European Monetary Union with its benchmark budget deficits and government debts of 3 per cent and 60 per cent of GDP, respectively.

In looking at the three approaches, it is striking that only two OECD Member countries — the United States and Canada — rely on the market to impose fiscal discipline on sub-national governments. OECD Member countries have advanced financial markets and high-quality fiscal reporting. This would seem to suggest that the market discipline approach should be effective. Indeed, it has worked very well in the United States and Canada. Sub-national governments in the United States have relatively low levels of debt. Sub-national governments in Canada accumulated heavy debts in the early 1990s, but as the result of downgradings by credit rating agencies and higher interest rate differentials, they have adopted strong fiscal consolidation programmes. (See Figure 1).

Figure 1. **Provincial Interest Rate Spreads, Debt and Credit Ratings**

A. Interest rate spreads and debt

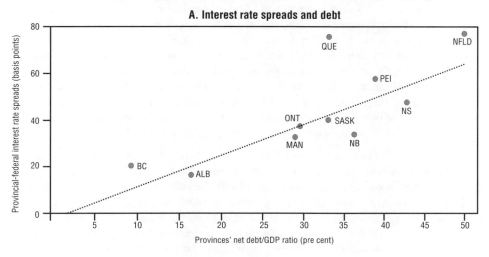

B. Interest rate spreads and credit ratings

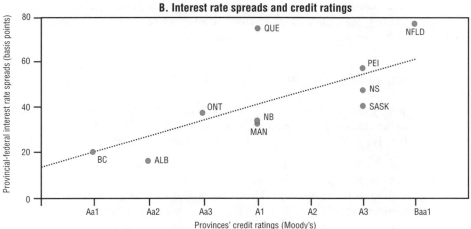

Notes: ALB = Alberta; BC = British Columbia; MAN = Manitoba; NB = New Brunswick; ONT = Ontario; SASK = Saskatchewan; NS = Nova Scotia; PEI = Prince Edward Island; QUE = Quebec; NFLD = Newfoundland.

The interest rate spread (variable "SPREAD") measures the difference, in basis points, between interest rates on provincial bonds and federal bonds in April 1995. The net debt-to-GDP ratio (variable "DEBT") are values for the financial year 1994/95. For the purpose of quantifying any relationship the variable "CREDIT" has been created and given the value of 1 for the highest provincial credit rating (Aa1), with successively lower credit ratings incremented by one. Estimated lines of best fit (with t-ratios in brackets) for all the provinces, excluding Quebec, are given by:

(1) SPREAD = 2.2 + 1.32 DEBT, R^2 = 0.792;

      (-0.2) (5.2)

(2) SPREAD = 5.4 + 7.95 CREDIT, R^2 = 0.766;

      (0.6) (4.8)

Source: Department of Finance and OECD Secretariat calculations.

So, why do more OECD Member countries not adopt this approach if it works so well in the United States and Canada? The reason lies in the fact that in the United States and Canada, it is not assumed that the national government would bail out sub-national governments if they got into financial trouble. In other OECD Member countries, there is generally the belief that the national government would come to their assistance. Of course, national governments could try to change this belief over time — primarily by not coming to the rescue of sub-national governments in financial trouble. Failing that, there is a need for more direct involvement by the national government in the borrowing operations of sub-national governments in these countries, either through rules-based approaches or administrative control approaches.

Rules-based systems have the advantage of being transparent and expeditious. They have, however, generally been regarded unfavourably. They are said to be inflexible; they are said to lose all credibility if the rules are ever breached; they are said to lend themselves to all sorts of perverse behavioural incentives in order for participants to get around the rules. There are of course elements of truth in this. But the Maastricht criteria for European Monetary Union and the impact it is having on fiscal consolidation efforts in Europe highlights the powerful role that such rules-based approaches can have. OECD Member countries will almost certainly increasingly move towards such systems and away from administrative controls which, although flexible, can often be cumbersome and tedious.

Economic Stabilization Measures

Fiscal policy is an important tool for economic stabilization measures in OECD Member countries and only the national government is in a position to run the automatic stabilizers effectively. This is acknowledged in all OECD Member countries.

The Maastricht criteria for European Monetary Union are making this an emerging issue for European Union member countries, which we can view as sub-national governments in this context. This is because countries are locking themselves into a maximum permitted fiscal deficit. This maximum does not differentiate between member countries that are enjoying robust economic growth and those suffering from economic recessions. As each country operates its own automatic stabilizers with no central European Union funds, this can lead to significant adjustment problems in individual member countries. This has been recognised with the Growth and Stability Pact, which offers some flexibility for member countries to operate with higher deficits during economic downturns; whether this flexibility is sufficient is open to debate.

The situation in the United States where the Federal government is largely responsible for the operation of the automatic stabilizers is very different. For example, when a severe recession hit California, the financial streams to the state from the federal government increased significantly (unemployment and other welfare benefits) and financial streams from the state to the federal government decreased greatly (less economic activity resulting in less taxation). This eased the adjustment process in California.

This highlights the fact that the automatic stabilizers should be located at the national government level and not at the sub-national government level. It will be interesting to see if the automatic stabilizers in European Union member countries will not evolve towards a more centralised arrangement.

Allocative Efficiency and Regional Equity Considerations

Allocative efficiency refers to the distribution of resources in an optimal manner, i.e. spending public money where it is most needed. The key benefit of strengthening sub-national governments in this respect is that they are closer to the population and thus in a better position to reflect the wishes and specific needs of each community. They can be more innovative and flexible in how they meet these wishes and needs. There is no longer a "one-size-fits-all" standard. Almost by definition, therefore, stronger sub-national governments equal greater allocative efficiency.

Regional equity considerations also need to be recognised. This refers to the disparities among individual sub-national governments, either in terms of the financial resources at their disposal or the costs of providing services. For example, should people in more affluent areas enjoy premium services while people in poorer areas struggle for basic services? Similarly, should people in urban areas enjoy better services than people in less densely populated areas? A recognition of these disparities would argue for a strong national government in order to ensure equity.

Fiscal federalism is therefore a balancing act between these poles: strong sub-national governments to achieve allocative efficiency versus strong national governments to achieve equity. One school of thought would be that regional inequity is the price you have to pay for strong sub-national governments. Another school is that regional inequity should preclude strong sub-national governments. The OECD has no member countries which illustrate these extreme poles. It could, however, be said that the United States leans towards the former and countries such as the United Kingdom to the latter. The middle ground is typically that the national government fills the gap between the revenue-raising capacities and the expenditure requirements of individual sub-national governments through transfers.

There are many types of transfer arrangements. They form a continuum in terms of the degree of discretion available to sub-national governments. Some are relatively simple while others involve complex formulas; many incorporate detailed conditions for the use of the transfers.

From the national government point of view, these conditions are necessary to ensure that the money is spent on improving the services that form the rationale for having the transfers in the first place. For example, if the national government decides to improve educational standards and supports this policy with transfers to the sub-national governments that operate the schools, it will want to ensure that the money is used for that purpose. They may go further and insist that the money is spent on improving a specific aspect of the schools, for example improving science education.

They may go further still and insist that the money is spent on buying laboratory equipment. Now, multiply this by the hundreds, or thousands, of individual transfer programmes in operation. From the national government's point of view, these conditions for individual transfer programmes are necessary in order to ensure that national initiatives are implemented in a uniform manner throughout the country.

We are, however, witnessing fundamental reforms in this area in OECD Member countries. The broad outlines of these reforms are the same across most countries: the pendulum is swinging in the other direction. Individual transfer programmes are being consolidated and the conditions attached to the transfers are being relaxed substantially. The primary motivation for this is generally to reduce national government expenditures as these reforms are usually accompanied by cuts in the total amount of transfers. This is justified in terms of the allocative efficiency argument: sub-national governments will be able to make better uses of the funds if they have increased freedom in how they are used, and will therefore require less funds.

It is too early to evaluate the impact of these reforms. OECD Member country experiences, however, seem to suggest that this may be a win-win situation. National governments win because they are reducing expenditures. Sub-national governments win because they can use the funds transferred from the national government in more appropriate ways.

Other reforms being undertaken in OECD Member countries to promote allocative efficiency include measures to clarify the roles of each level of government in specific sectors in order to avoid duplication of effort. Similarly, efforts are being made to clarify responsibility for financing expenditure programmes in order to avoid situations where the national government is responsible, either fully or on a cost-sharing basis, for the financing of expenditure programmes operated by sub-national governments. This should increase the incentive for sub-national governments to limit expenditures.

Canada has for example embarked on a major programme of change in the system of federal transfers to provinces. A complex system of separate transfers for social assistance, post-secondary education and health care, partly on a cost-sharing basis, are being combined into a single Canada Health and Social Transfer. This transfer will be a block grant, i.e. not an open-ended, cost-sharing transfer. This reform is being accompanied by a decline in total transfers to provinces, as a percentage of GDP, of one-fifth over a three year time period.

Operating Effectiveness and Efficiency

The last issue is operating effectiveness and efficiency. There are two aspects to this issue. The first is whether sub-national governments have the managerial and technical capacity to carry out the functions assigned to them. The second refers to "value for money" efficiency — Are sub-national governments carrying out their functions at least cost?

The question of managerial and technical capacity is generally related to the size of sub-national governments. There is a size threshold below which the necessary economies of scale cannot be achieved in operation. The problem of insufficiently large sub-national governments is an issue for most OECD Member countries which have tended to alleviate the problem in one of two ways. First, by merging sub-national governments to form larger units. Second, by creating special-purpose organisations operated by several sub-national governments. For example, a secondary school may be operated jointly by several small jurisdictions. OECD Member countries' experience would suggest that, although the second option is easier in political terms, the first should be preferred in terms of operating effectiveness and efficiency. This is because a plethora of specific-purpose organisations can obscure accountability and, as a result, operating effectiveness and efficiency can suffer.

Secondly, there is concern in OECD Member countries to ensure that public services are being operated at lowest cost by sub-national governments. In most cases, this is said to be a problem for the electorate in each jurisdiction. This highlights the importance of clear lines of accountability. There is, however, a notable exception to this "hands-off" approach, and that is the United Kingdom. They have set up an Audit Commission for Local Governments, established a Citizen's Charter which sets performance standards for various public services, and instituted a programme of Compulsory Competitive Tendering by local governments.

The Audit Commission is responsible for auditing the finances and performance of each local authority. The Audit Commission's primary influence is due to the respect it enjoys and that it provides the electorate with information by which to hold local authorities accountable. For example, it has established "league tables" where it compares how effectively and efficiently different local governments perform the same service. For example, why does it cost more for local government "A" to perform a certain services than it does for local government "B"?

The Citizen's Charter established a framework for "setting, monitoring and publication of explicit standards for the services that individual users can reasonably expect (and) publication of actual performance against these standards." Citizen's Charters have been established for a variety of local government services, including education and public housing. A key benefit of these Charters is that they are at the level of the individual user and they provide benchmarks for them to judge the performance of public services.

The Compulsory Competitive Tendering programme is a requirement for local governments to market-test specific activities. Conceptually, market-testing is essentially contracting out with the exception that in-house personnel can compete against an outside contractor in the bidding process. There is thus no presumption that activities that are being market-tested will be contracted out to private suppliers. The objective is to expose in-house personnel to the discipline of the market and thereby foster efficiency. This programme was first started for blue-collar activities, such as rubbish removal and cleaning services, but is now being expanded to include white-collar activities, such as legal and financial services.

All these British initiatives, the Audit Commission, the Citizen's Charter, and the Compulsory Competitive Tendering programme, appear to have been highly effective in promoting efficiency in the delivery of service by sub-national governments.

Conclusion

The overview of fiscal federalism arrangements in OECD Member countries reveals that there is no single "OECD model". The arrangements in individual OECD Member countries are very diverse. The discussion of the major fiscal federalism issues facing OECD Member countries revealed the vast array of considerations which have to be taken into account in designing successful fiscal federalism arrangements.

Institutional arrangements are of course very important, but they do not by themselves guarantee success or failure. Political will alone determines that. Institutional arrangements can make it easier to achieve successful fiscal federalism outcomes if the political will is there, but they can never achieve successful fiscal federalism outcomes if the political will is not there.

PART TWO

PRACTITIONERS' VIEWS

Argentina

Andrew Powell[1]

What follows is a discussion of the effect of the 1991 Convertibility Law on the political economy of Argentina with special reference to fiscal affairs. First, we provide some background on the effect of the convertibility regime in Argentina before describing more exactly what the Convertibility Law is and discussing the potential effects of convertibility on fiscal discipline. This regime has already weathered some "tests" and their changing nature highlights the high level of credibility that this regime has now achieved. The final section concludes by describing the current political economy of convertibility and makes a prediction for a revealing future test, namely the 1999 presidential election.

On the Effects of Convertibility on Argentina

Convertibility has had profound effects on Argentina and has been markedly different from previous attempts at stabilization. Figure 1 shows the recent history of Argentine inflation, with selected previous plans labelled, and the quite remarkable post-1991 stabilization. Convertibility brought inflation down more rapidly than previous attempts and, more important, inflation remained low. Currently Argentina has one of the lowest inflation rates in the world (0.7 per cent forecast for 1997).

Convertibility and the accompanying economic stability has also brought many other profound changes to Argentina. Perhaps the most striking changes involve real interest rates and the financial system. Figure 2, shows what would have happened if an investor had put 100 pesos into an Argentine bank in 1940. In real terms, some 90 per cent of the investment would have been lost by 1955, a further 90 per cent by 1975, another 90 per cent by 1982, although the country had not yet experienced hyperinflation! Indeed by 1990, an estimated 99.98 per cent of the original real investment would have been lost. This history explains the virtual disappearance of Argentina's financial system and the country's poor overall economic performance in the postwar period.

Figure 1. **Stabilisation Plans in Argentina**

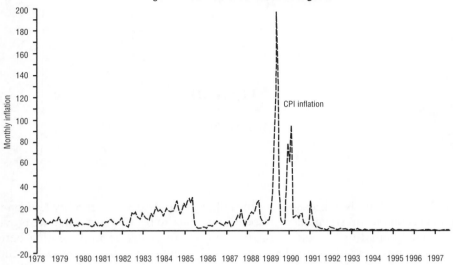

However, the figure also shows that real interest rates became positive after 1991. Although an investor would have had only about 2 centavos of the original 100 pesos in 1991, by 1997 this would have become more than 3 centavos, all in 1940 prices. This fundamental reversal reflects deep changes in the political economy of savings behaviour and debt structure in Argentina, which in turn has an impact on the Argentine people's commitment to convertibility and hence on the regime's credibility.

Figure 2. **Cumulative Return on Bank Savings**

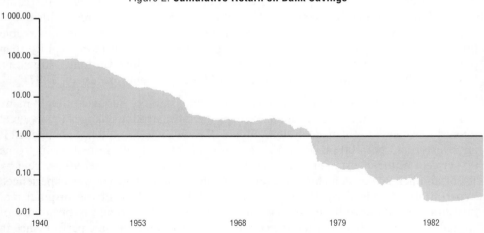

In the past, both the private and public sectors had significant peso debts. Every few years, there would be a call for a devaluation, generally promoted as a means of increasing competitiveness, but in fact serving to limit peso liabilities. Frequent devaluations fuelled inflation, and price indexation was extended. However, as inflation gathered pace, price indexation became more and more imperfect and there was an increasing use of the dollar as the numeraire. Finally, with hyperinflation virtually all significant transactions were conducted in dollars and Argentina's domestic financial system shrank, so that M3/GDP fell to just 5 per cent in 1989.

The hyperinflationary experience was extremely salutary for Argentina and it might be argued that it radically changed preferences. Price stability became the overriding policy concern and it was in this context that the 1991 Convertibility Law was passed.

Under convertibility and price stability the Argentine financial system has now grown to the point where M3/GDP was 23 per cent as of October 1997. Given that the Argentine M3/GDP was about 40-45 per cent in the 1940s and 1950s, it can be roughly estimated that about 50 per cent of the Argentine capital that left the country in the postwar period has now returned. The financial system's bank deposits are now about 55 per cent dollarised and bank loans are 62 per cent dollarised.

The significant dollar debts in both the private and public sectors have altered the "political economy" of devaluation in Argentina. rather than calling for a devaluation, big business, banking, and the public sector would now lose the most from devaluation under the current structure of debt contracts. This increases commitment to the regime and hence to its credibility.

Table 1 illustrates the tremendous economic success obtained under the convertibility plan, showing that growth, investment, productivity and trade have all increased significantly. Also note that the 1991-97 averages include the 4.6 per cent fall in GDP in 1995. Moreover, there has been a great improvement in fiscal performance between the six years of convertibility (1991 to 1997) and the preceding six years (1984-90), when the fiscal deficit fell from an average of almost 6 per cent of GDP to just 0.7 per cent of GDP for the 1991-97 period. Moreover, this improved fiscal performance was achieved despite a major reform of the pension system which added roughly one per cent of the GDP to the fiscal deficit for each year from 1995 to 1997 inclusive.

However, this does not mean that convertibility by itself was responsible for the profound fiscal reforms that have been undertaken in Argentina. It was the deep-rooted change in preferences of Argentina's population which demanded economic order that provided the political will to effect the fiscal reforms. Important fiscal reforms were begun as early as 1989, predating the convertibility plan. Nonetheless, convertibility has been important in maintaining fiscal discipline.

Table 1. **Results of the Programme**

	1984-90 (percentage)	1991-97* (percentage)
GDP	-1.4	6.0
Investment	-6.0	15.9
Labour Productivity	-2.9	4.4
Trade	4.2	18.4
Fiscal Balance/GDP	-5.7	-0.7
M3/GDP	11.8	17.1

Notes: * Estimated.
        Average annual growth rates unless specified.

Parenthetically, it seems unlikely that a currency board could impose the fiscal reforms necessary to make them sustainable. A board may help to "lock in" a fiscal reform that has already been put into effect, or at least where the "political will" for it already exists, but it would be rather risky to expect a currency board to tilt the balance towards a sustainable fiscal reform programme when the "political will" for such a programme may be lacking.

On the Convertibility Regime[2]

It is perhaps useful at this point to review what the convertibility regime actually entails. There are three aspects which are fundamental. The first cornerstone is the currency board. The central bank must back 100 per cent of the monetary base with international reserves. Actually, there is some flexibility to the extent that one-third of this backing can be held in the form of dollar-denominated Argentine government bonds valued at market prices. This means that although there is no active monetary policy in Argentina, the convertibility system allows the central bank to provide liquidity to the banking system subject this and other limits. In fact the backing with international reserves, excluding government bond holdings, covered over 99 per cent of the central bank's "financial liabilities" as of the end of November 1997[3].

Second, the convertibility regime prohibits the central bank from financing the government (except through bond holdings, as described above) and it categorically prohibits central bank lending to provincial governments, state enterprises or private non-financial enterprises. Financial institutions may be assisted under strict regulations covering lender-of-last-resort activities (repos and rediscount operations). These prohibitions and restrictions are fundamental to the regime and eliminate any possibility of government recourse to the inflation tax or to "subsidised" financing by the central bank.

Third, the system's transparency has been extremely important. The central bank has worked to increase the monetary regime's transparency to a degree that is probably unsurpassed in any other country at present. The reserves of the central bank and its financial liabilities are published daily with a lag of only two days! These statistics are regularly carried by news services such as Reuters. The total deposits of the banking system are also published daily as is total credit in the financial system. Furthermore, the central bank is now publishing a monthly summary balance sheet of the banking system, with details on how banks satisfy their regulatory requirements and a database on the financial system's non-performing loans. All of this information is now available on the central bank's web site[4]. This transparency has had an effect, not only on confidence within the financial system but also beyond, with some now calling for a "convertibility plan" for other areas of economic management[5].

It is also important to note that the monetary reform was accompanied by other fundamental reforms. This included fiscal reform, a major privatisation programme, and opening of the current and capital accounts. Indeed, Argentina adopted one of the most open trading regimes in the region, bringing the discipline of foreign competition to bear on domestic producers, not only in the non-financial goods and service sectors, but also in banking and other financial services.

On Convertibility and Fiscal Discipline

We now turn to the effect of the monetary policy regime on fiscal performance. Aizenman and Powell (forthcoming) provide a useful economic model of decentralised spending to illustrate how convertibility may affect fiscal decision making[6].

In this model there are a number of potential equilibria. In particular, there are two extreme cases, the first a non-co-operative equilibrium where individual fiscal agents make autonomous choices, whether they are spending ministries or provinces in a federation. In the extreme case, government expenditure is essentially determined by an external credit constraint with each agent spending as much as possible today because if it does not, it is unsure whether any amount saved for its future needs will not have already been spent by the other agents[7].

At the other extreme, there is a fully co-operative equilibrium where each agent of the government does the right thing and government saving is set at an optimal (much higher) level determined by a "Barro rule", depending critically on the time preference and the interest rate. The aim of our model was to show that the co-operative equilibrium was unlikely unless there was some monitoring device (for example, elections in which a misbehaving government could be voted out of office) and it was possible to switch between the non-co-operative and co-operative behaviour depending on income levels, risk aversion, etc. (similar to models of collusive behaviour in industrial economics where, for example, collusion may break down when increased demand provokes a price war). Hence, in our context, depending on parameter values, pro- or counter-cyclical fiscal policy are both theoretical possibilities.

Although in this model the external credit constraint is essentially exogenous, we do suggest that it may depend on income. However, consider the case of one government that has access to an inflation tax and another government that does not have access to such financing because of a convertibility plan. The general point is that government spending is not independent of the cost of government financing in an interesting way. An inflation tax may permit non-transparent financing and, hence, at a low "political cost". This increases spending in the non-co-operative equilibrium as the credit constraint is relaxed in some way. However, denying the government access to an inflation tax increases the "political cost" of financing. Higher deficits must be financed through borrowing, and hence this brings greater monitoring by financial markets. This has a direct effect on the non-co-operative equilibrium by reducing the "deficit buyers", in the language of Ricardo Hausmann. However, it may even make the non-co-operative equilibrium so much worse that the co-operative equilibrium gets chosen. Put differently, it could tilt the balance towards the co-operative solution.

By denying access to the inflation tax and through the interplay of government financing and spending decisions, the role of a central bank or a currency board in Argentina's case, is extremely important in determining the context in which fiscal decisions are made. In other words, with a currency board, and when the government has denied itself access to the inflation tax and deficits must be financed clearly through increased borrowing, it is possible that the non-co-operative equilibrium becomes sufficiently unattractive that the co-operative solution will be chosen. This may then help to maintain the fiscal discipline required to sustain the currency board.

On Tests of the Convertibility Regime

This regime has not been untested, and, indeed there is a trend in the tests that we have witnessed. Early tests occurred at the beginning of 1992, just nine months after its establishment, and again in November of the same year. On the latter occasion the central bank lost some $500 million of international reserves, or some 5 per cent of the stock. These tests were essentially internal in nature, not being provoked by any external event.

Perhaps the most critical test of the regime to date was that of the so-called Tequila period following the Mexican devaluation at the end of 1994. The Tequila test was a mixture of external events (the shakeout in emerging markets following the Mexican devaluation) and internal factors. Important internal factors included concerns regarding the current and fiscal accounts, the lack of an IMF programme and, perhaps most important, the approaching presidential election of 14 May 1995 under a new electoral system. This election was the first in Argentina to include two rounds in a run-off system.

Between December 1994 and May 1995, Argentina lost about $5 billion (or 27 per cent) of its international reserves and no less than 18 per cent of it bank deposits. However, these aggregates hide the full impact of the shock on certain types of institutions. The wholesale banks as a group, for example, lost some 67 per cent of their deposits, which provoked significant contagion effects through the rest of the financial system[8]. The central bank was able to offset part of the shock, by providing liquidity to the financial system by using excess reserves, as specified under the Convertibility Law, and also by using the significant reserve requirements that existed at that time[9].

There is a current view that the Argentine financial system was weak before the Tequila shock and then, thanks to the financial crises, there was significant bank restructuring which strengthened the system, but this view does not square with reality. The Argentine financial system survived Tequila as well as it did because, in general, it was very strong indeed. This was shown by the very small number of actual bank closures and the very rapid rise in deposits once an agreement was reached with the IMF (in March) and the election result known (on 15 May)[10]. The major restructuring, which further strengthened the financial system, did not occur until later in 1995 and in subsequent years when there was a significant injection of foreign capital[11]. The financial system that indeed grew very rapidly after May 1995 was basically the same one that suffered the shock in late 1994.

The financial system has also been further strengthened since the Tequila period by certain regulatory changes. In particular, the central bank has developed a "systemic liquidity" policy which consists of two main pillars[12]. First, the reserve requirements have been altered so that Argentina now has remunerated liquidity requirements equivalent to some 20 per cent of deposits, and second, an external contingent credit line has been established with 13 international banks, amounting to a further 10 per cent of the deposit base. Hence, the Argentine financial system has some 30 per cent of the deposit base in "systemically liquid" assets (i.e. assets that are liquid even if there is a systemic crisis) to confront any type of problem. Moreover, other aspects of banking oversight have been improved with the adoption of a mixed strategy incorporating traditional banking regulation and supervision with rules to enhance market discipline. These include improvements in disclosure rules, the obligation for banks to issue subordinated debt and the requirement for banks to obtain two private credit ratings from accredited rating agencies[13].

Here it might be useful to look briefly at the reaction of the real economy to the Tequila crisis. As mentioned, there were concerns regarding the current account deficit, which had reached more than 3 per cent of GDP as economic growth accelerated to 8.5 per cent in 1994. As recession hit, many were surprised by the rapid turnaround in the current account. Exports grew by an incredible 32.4 per cent between 1994 to 1995 whilst imports fell by 6.8 per cent. These figures are not just important because they implied a rapid turnabout in the current account, but also because they reflected a tremendous increase in the competitiveness and flexibility of the Argentine economy.

The next test involved the change of economy ministers in July 1997. This was important as Domingo Cavallo was no ordinary economy minister. He had been the architect of the convertibility plan and therefore, a key personality in the Argentine recovery in the eyes of many and of foreign investors in particular. Although this test was provoked by an internal event it was still classified as principally an external test. The reason is that the concern was largely concentrated in foreign investors' minds. Very few Argentines would have doubted that the convertibility plan might have been put at risk by a change in the minister, whoever might be chosen from the "short list" then in the air. As it happened, the appointment of Roque Fernandez as economy minister quickly calmed foreign investors and, as predicted, the convertibility regime remained.

In October 1997 Argentina faced a further test as fallout from currency crises in Southeast Asia hit other emerging markets. This is perhaps the clearest example to date of a purely "external shock". Again, we have seen further evidence of the increased credibility of the Convertibility regime, and although both stock and bond market prices have fallen significantly, there has been no significant loss of reserves and no fall in bank deposits[14]. Thus, there has been no flight from Argentina either by foreign or Argentine capital.

The initial tests of the convertibility regime were clearly internal in nature. However, later tests became increasingly external, with "Tequila" as a significant watershed. This trend reflects the growing credibility of the regime over time. It appears that the regime's credibility is now very high for both foreign and domestic investors.

The Next Test and the Current Political Economy of Convertibility

The final test is the presidential election due in 1999. Without trying to say who is going to win, my prediction is that whoever is the leading candidate for that election will be a supporter of the convertibility regime. The basis for that belief is that if the leading candidate were not supporting the convertibility regime, then that person would not be the leading candidate!

Thus convertibility has had a very deep effect on the political economy of Argentina which is best described as "focusing the debate". Convertibility is such a transparent rule that politicians must take their position at an early date. The first question that an analyst or journalist is likely to ask of a politician will concern convertibility. If a politician wants to say he or she is not in favour of it, then he or she must offer an alternative, for not to do so would be political suicide. Although putting forward an alternative may not sound so difficult, to make that alternative credible would be extremely difficult, if not impossible. Hence, having a credible economic policy in Argentina today is tantamount to saying that that a politician in question supports convertibility.

These remarks are not intended to suggest that Argentina has found a perfect system and that there are no problems. We all know that some significant problems remain in Argentina and that probably the most important of these is the current high level of unemployment. Opinion surveys in Argentina regularly ask how people feel about economic policy. Over time, those saying that they have a positive view of economic policy has been decreasing, with only 15.7 per cent responding in this way as of October 1997. The high level of unemployment was consistently found to be the most important concern. However, in response to the question whether Argentina should abandon convertibility, 60 per cent said no[15].

One interpretation of these results is that although Argentina has found the right institutions with respect to monetary policy, it has yet to find the right institutions for the labour market. In this domain, increased labour market flexibility, transparency and choice are long overdue in Argentina.

Conclusion

Finally, it would be wrong to say that convertibility has changed Argentina. What has changed Argentina is a change in the preferences of the people who, in part due to the experience of hyperinflation, now place a very high importance on economic stability and sound economic and fiscal management. However, an independent central bank or a strong convertibility law can help to ensure that those preferences are put into practice and that sound economic management can be maintained. It is doubtful that a monetary regime, in itself, could bring about the fiscal reforms necessary for the major macroeconomic stabilization required to make that regime sustainable. However, it can certainly help to maintain fiscal discipline once the reform has been carried out.

This is particularly important in a country such as Argentina, which has a political system of proportional representation with large electoral districts. It also has one of the most decentralised economies in the region. This implies the existence of many of the co-ordination issues considered in depth in other papers presented at this conference. The convertibility regime addresses many of the co-ordination and related issues which have been raised. The legal prohibition on using the inflation tax and the consequent increase in transparency create a very different context for Argentina's fiscal policy decisions than in the past.

Notes

1. The author is Chief Economist of the Central Bank of Argentina. Acknowledgements are due to Dr. Pedro Pou, president of the Central Bank, as parts of the presentation draw on a number of his speeches; to the members of the research department of the Central Bank, where many of the ideas have been generated; and especially to Andrea Molinari for excellent research assistance.

2. By the "convertibility regime" we are referring to the 1991 Convertibility Law plus the Central Bank's 1992 charter.

3. Financial liabilities are notes and coins in circulation plus the liquidity requirements held by the banking system in the Central Bank (actually held in the form of reverse repo. operations).

4. The Central Bank's internet site is: www.bcra.gov.ar. The information on the banking system and non-performing loans is provided by the Superintendency of banks which is a semi-autonomous unit within the Central Bank.

5. This point was made by Mariano Tommasi in the floor discussion after this panel.

6. See Aizenman and Powell (forthcoming).

7. This now appears to be known in the literature as "the dynamic commons problem", although it is also sometimes more colourfully referred to as a "voracity effect".

8. See D'Amato, Grubisic and Powell (1997) for further description and an econometric analysis of these contagion effects.

9. Following estimates presented in Powell (1996), the total loss of deposits of $7.9 billion was financed by a lowering of reserve requirements ($3.2 billion), repo and rediscount operations ($2.2 billion), foreign credit lines ($2.1 billion) and a drop in credit ($400 million).

10. During this period ten financial institutions were closed, eight of them being banks.

11. In 1997, controlling stakes in Banco Rio, Banco Frances (and hence Banco Credito Argentino) and Banco Roberts were sold to Banco Santander, Banco Bilbao Vizcaya and the Hong Kong and Shanghai Bank respectively.

12. The need for a "systemic liquidity" policy arises if a country suffers from a temporary lack of access to international credit and, at the same time, wishes to extend lender-of-last resort assistance to its banking system. Then any objective such as an exchange rate, monetary or price stability target will be extremely difficult to maintain without a significant margin of "systemic liquidity". See Pou (1997) and BCRA (1997) for further details.

13. This is referred to as BASIC banking oversight in Argentina where the acronym stands for: B, bonds; A, auditing; S, supervision; I, information; and C, credit rating. See BCRA (1997) and Powell (1997) for greater detail.

14. According to the information available at the time of writing, the international reserves of the Argentine financial system increased by 3 per cent between 23 October and 8 December 1997, while total deposits increased by 3 per cent between 23 October and 2 December 1997.

15. The opinion survey cited was conducted by the Centro de Estudios Unión Para la Nueva Mayoría. Regarding convertibility, a further 27 per cent of those polled apparently did not know whether Argentina should end Convertibility, and only 13 per cent said that Argentina should change its monetary regime.

Bibliography

AIZENMAN, J. AND A. POWELL, "The Political Economy of Saving Behaviour and the Role of Capital Mobility", *Journal of Development Economics*, forthcoming.

BCRA (1997), "Main Features of the Regulatory Framework of the Argentine Financial System", Buenos Aires.

D'AMATO, L., E. GRUBISIC AND A. POWELL (1997), "Contagion, Bank Fundamentals or Macroeconomic Panic? An Econometric Analysis of the 1995 Argentine Banking Problems", BCRA *Working Paper* No. 2, Buenos Aires.

POU, P. (1997), "Maintaining Financial Stability in the Global Economy", speech given at the Federal Reserve Bank of Kansas 1997 Annual Jackson Hole Conference, panel discussion on "Lessons from Financial Crises", to be published in conference proceedings.

POWELL, A. (1996), "On Central Banks and their Lender of Last Resort Function: 'Constructive Ambiguity' and 'Cheap Talk' ", mimeo, BCRA, Buenos Aires.

POWELL, A. (1997) "Using the Market as Regulator: Developing BASIC Banking Oversight in Argentina", mimeo, BCRA, Buenos Aires.

Brazil

Marcelo Piancastelli de Siqueira

This note discusses the recent experience of fiscal federalism in Brazil with particular reference to the Treasury administration, where I am co-ordinating fiscal policies at the State level, and its relationships with sub-national governments. To begin with, I would like to describe and comment briefly on the relative magnitude of the Brazilian federation. Second, I will describe how the Treasury is managing the debt problem facing Brazilian States. Finally, I would like to discuss a number of policy initiatives that are being undertaken to reform the Brazilian federation.

The Brazilian federation is made up of 27 States including the Federal District. The States are very powerful relative to the central government, not only economically but also politically. For instance, the State of São Paulo is the fourth largest Latin American economy with a GDP equivalent to roughly $280 billion or about a third of Brazil's total GDP. On the fiscal front, the aggregated total expenditures of all State governments amount to 73 per cent of the central government's total expenditures. Considering that each State has its own governor, its own legislature and its own budget, absolutely independent from the federal government, the State governments enjoy a lot of political and economic autonomy. The issue of political representation at the national level is thus both important and sensitive in Brazil. While in the Senate each State has equal representation — three senators per State, in the Lower House the rich southern States tend to consider themselves to be under-represented, relative to the northern or north-eastern poor States.

There are additional aspects of fiscal federalism in Brazil which deserve special attention.

First, the drastic reduction of inflation with the implementation of the Real Plan in 1994 was never imagined to cause such an important transformation in the working of the federation and public finances. In early 1995, State governments faced financial difficulties as expenditure management at the sub-national level had relied heavily on inflation-related capital gains to make ends meet every month. Also, the debt problem became a very heavy burden due to the sharp increase in real interest rates as a result of the issuing of bonds that major States had floated in the market. The federal government launched a restructuring plan to discipline and co-ordinate the State policies in this area; 22 States have already signed an agreement with the federal government. The Senate is expected to monitor State fiscal policies and to ensure compliance with the terms of the contract.

In 1995, most States were in debt with poor primary balances, but by 1997 14 States had managed to produce positive primary balances as opposed to only five in 1995. The policy has been working effectively and almost half of the States have already reorganised their financial structures. The State of São Paulo, for instance, which is one of the most important in economic terms, had a surplus of $1 billion dollars in 1997. Others, such as Rio Grande do Sul, Minas Gerais and Rio de Janeiro, are still facing financial difficulties due to high payroll costs.

Second, the primary rule of the agreement with the Treasury, stipulates that unless the level of net debt reaches a 1-to-1 ratio with respect to net revenues, the State will not be allowed to make new credit operations. This applies especially where multilateral institutions, such as the World Bank and the Inter-American Development Bank are concerned, except when the proposed operations coincide with the macroeconomic policy of the central government. In Brazil, although the States are allowed to borrow directly from international financial institutions, a guarantee from the Treasury is required for most of them, and this guarantee will only be provided when the State has the payment capacity according to a credit rating system established in 1997. The States are no longer allowed to float bonds domestically or to carry out any operations anticipating budgetary revenues above the previous years' ceilings.

Third, the agreement also involves projections for debt accumulation and repayment. On the whole, these projections show that the four major Brazilian States will have their debts to zero by the year 2017. Before that, by 2004-2005, they will have reached the 1-to-1 ratio that allows them to come back to the financial markets. Obviously, there is an implicit subsidy in this financial restructuring programme, but the programme does not allow the States to issue new debt. As for the State banks, the federal government will provide financial assistance to the troubled ones conditional upon their liquidation or privatisation. Otherwise, the States have to carry the financial burden by themselves.

A *fourth* major initiative concerns payroll costs. State governments that had misread inflation in 1995 ended up with underestimating current expenditures. A number of States still have to reduce their payroll costs by more than 30 per cent in order to abide by the constitutional provisions that prevent them from spending more than 60 per cent of their net revenues on wages and salaries. These States are now embarking on privatisation programmes and they are being persuaded to divert their privatisation proceeds to create State pension funds. State privatisation policies are now being fully implemented and a total of over $13 billion has been raised at the sub-national government level alone, particularly in the electricity and transport sectors.

A *final* aspect of the Brazilian experience is a "radical democracy implementation programme" embedded in intergovernmental fiscal transfers. An education fund has been created in such a way that 15 per cent of VAT revenues and all the constitutional transfers to the States will be transferred directly to their municipalities within each State in order to finance basic education expenditures every ten days. For 1998, for example, an amount of $13 billion will be paid into the fund on the tenth, twentieth and thirtieth of each month. Of this amount, 60 per cent must go to improving the quality of education and teaching conditions. Many States have already signed and agreed with the conditions of this fund, and this programme will start on 1 January 1998.

Chile

Carlos Ominami

Ricardo Hausmann correctly described democracy and decentralisation as major new trends which have also been accompanied by a very clear improvement in fiscal discipline. Is this fiscal discipline a direct result of democracy or a result of the new rules of game required by the economic system? This is difficult to say. Chile experienced some highly satisfying results in both democratic development and economic growth, with an average growth rate of about 7 per cent from 1990, and decreasing inflation, which declined from about 28 per cent at the end of the 1980s to about 5.5 per cent in 1997. A key factor in these developments was a public finance management which was able to maintain a surplus of about 3.5 per cent of the GDP in recent years.

The seven following points respond to the problems raised by Ricardo Hausmann earlier in this volume and also refer to the solutions he suggested.

First point. A strong government is absolutely necessary. This does not mean an authoritarian government, but a government supported by a majority coalition. A strong government is also a government whose priorities are clear. When priorities are clear it is possible to reject many things, but if aims are undefined, it is very difficult to reject anything at all. A strong government defines the budget limits and maintains them at all costs. In a strong government the finance minister and the head of the budget demonstrate firmness. It is also essential for a strong government to have the constitutional power to approve the budget. The government sends its budget to the Parliament, which has a defined period — 60 days in Chile — for approving or rejecting it. If the budget has not been approved by the Parliament in 60 days, it is put into effect under constitutional powers.

Second point. An autonomous central bank helps maintain fiscal discipline. In particular, an autonomous central bank has responsibility for controlling inflation and can point out to the government when the budget is incompatible with country's goals for controlling inflation.

Third point. Also developed by Ricardo Hausmann, this point concerns a political system created by major political forces. From a political standpoint, a highly fragmented system makes the aggregation of the society's preferences extremely difficult. Thus Hausmann is right when he says that proportional systems tend to increase deficits. It is necessary to have electoral systems which produce a majority or in any case electoral systems which can encourage the formation majority coalitions; but it should be recognised that systems which eliminate all proportionality can also lead to exclusion. For example, in the case of Chile a political group representing a quarter of population can be excluded from the Parliament, which is something serious.

Fourth point. It is necessary to have a parliament, or a congress, which is highly capable of evaluating public programmes and the budget's implementation, but, in contradiction to Hausmann, this congress should not have any power to increase the budget or reallocate expenditure. This condition is essential to stability. Indeed, the most responsible and moderate legislators would be unable to oppose, for example, theoretically reasonable proposals for increasing pensions, wages of public administration workers, etc. Thus this responsibility should be restricted. The government manages and proposes the budget, while the parliament monitors the budget's implementation.

Fifth point. In Chile, centralised formulation of the budget and equally centralised tax collection have been fundamental for assuring good management of public finances. The budgetary limits have to be drawn up *ex ante* from macroeconomic considerations and not *ex post* from needs expressed by regions or local communities. On the other hand, the most fruitful and interesting path to decentralisation is a gradually decentralised allocation of sectoral resources defined in the budget. That does not actually mean that the centralised ministries decide what will be done in the regions, but that the budget has to be defined in a completely centralised way.

Sixth point. An informed public opinion, a free press and a certain economic culture of civil society are also essential monitoring mechanisms. This domain also includes the possibility of having social participation, enabling people to be associated with the management of resources which by definition are scarce. When people are involved and are able to participate, they share much more directly and positively in the management of public resources.

Seventh point. Perhaps most fundamental is the increased political value of stability. Fiscal austerity cannot only be considered as a constraint, for it is also the foundation for achieving stability which, in turn, preserves the purchasing power of the most impoverished people. In Chile, for example, that has disciplined the political parties and activists. This increased respect for stability is especially developed in all the countries which have experienced high inflation. The political significance of stability can be witnessed in Chile, Argentina and in all countries which have experienced acute stabilization problems.

These guidelines, presented in a very oversimplified manner, have enabled Chile to ensure fiscal discipline which has been the basis of good economic results in a democracy.

Colombia

Rudolf Hommes

The issue of the economic efficiency of single-minded rules remains open. For example, Ricardo Hausmann (elsewhere in this volume) proposes that a budget authority independent of the political process should be appointed — using the autonomous central bank as a model — and this has been sharply criticised. There is a natural reluctance to concede that the budget process should be depoliticised, given that the approval of the budget is at the core of parliamentary and congressional activity in a democracy. Nevertheless, the budget authority should have a degree of independence from politicians, the minister of finance should be able to cut spending unilaterally, and single-mindedness and some fixed rules are beneficial.

Once, when discussing the central bank's role in Colombia, Professor Dornbusch of MIT was critical of a law mandating the central bank to achieve a single objective — bringing down inflation year after year without other distractions. He thought that this was a nonsensical rule. The rest of the government, however, is pro-inflationary and pro-spending and there is thus a need for at least one institution to pursue the single objective of lowering inflation to counteract the bias of the rest of the government. In the interaction between this institution and the rest of government, the policy mix will achieve a balance between development and growth objectives on one hand, and between fiscal and monetary prudence on the other. Likewise, a strong and rather single-minded minister of finance is a precondition for maintaining stable public finances and sustainable long-term growth in developing economies. The rest of the government tends to have a very strong bias towards spending, and if the minister of finance does not oppose it, the fiscal bias would be even stronger than the one observed.

Next, let us turn to Hausmann's proposed rules. One cannot take the political system as a given, as he suggests. Economists have to accept constitutions as a given but not all political practices. For example, *clientelism* and *patronage* are especially perverse for fiscal policy, and should be eradicated from our political systems, or at least there should be institutions that would significantly reduce the extent of such practices and their fiscal impact.

Second, it is necessary to have an autonomous scorekeeper but the problem is how to select one. Who decides who the scorekeeper is going to be? We have some experience in Latin America with congressionally selected scorekeepers. They end up serving the purposes of the congress, which is not what Hausmann had in mind. We also have had negative experiences with executive scorekeepers. Neutral scorekeepers, almost certainly, would have to be appointed by the private sector — by what we now call the civil society — but this raises questions about the political system, corporatism and the nature of democratic organisation. Also, questions might arise about whether the scorekeepers could be really autonomous and neutral. Noone can be completely objective and this should not be above discussion, because it is not very easy to find an institution that can keep a score autonomously. What needs to be done is to give the scorekeeper an objective, a fixed set of rules, and then the scorekeeper can exercise independence in pursuit of this objective.

Another problem is that the scorekeeper as an institution would not only calculate cyclically adjusted deficits but would also monitor them. For some reason, Hausmann is not taking into account the central bank's role. The central bank should have the role of surveillance and monitoring. If the central bank did this properly, following rules that take into account the objectives of good macroeconomic policy, then an additional scorekeeper would not be needed.

This leads to the behaviour of the central bank. Unless there is an extremely powerful finance minister, the executive is generally unable to keep expenditure at a level that would be reasonable in terms of fiscal policy. The "spending ministers", and even the president or the prime minister, generally favour and obtain higher spending, well above the expectations and desires of the finance ministry. When an independent central bank works well and the government is compelled by law or the constitution to co-ordinate macroeconomic policy with the central bank, stability would be much better served than when a member of the executive is the sole defender of fiscal prudence.

It should also be emphasized that multilateral institutions could play a role with respect to the procyclical behaviour of governments. Ideally, debt should be prepaid during a boom and resources should be obtained from the financial community when there is a recession. Of course, the private financial community wants to do just the opposite, but there is a role that multilateral institutions could play. When we had a surplus in our capital account in Colombia in the early 1990s, we wanted to prepay multilateral debt, but encountered tremendous obstacles from the bureaucracies. Well, one understands why, but multilateral institutions as public bodies should have the flexibility to allow prepayment of outstanding loans, which facilitates cyclical management. If multilateral institutions are prepared to come to the assistance of countries when no other institutions would, they should be equally flexible during booms and be willing to assist countries to deal with the negative financial impact of the upswings.

There is a need to develop a culture of economic prudence in the society. In addition to institutions regulated by laws, rules and so on, it is also necessary to have a culture that will reward well-behaved administrations and punish populism and profligacy. This is important. For example, until quite recently Colombia had a long history of reasonable fiscal behaviour. One of the reasons why that was possible is that public opinion for many years rewarded the maintenance of prudent macro policy.

Regarding the discipline of local governments, there clearly is a case for controls on debt, but the issue is not so simple. The central government may be tempted to exclude local governments from the financial market to finance its own deficits. For example, Bogotá, Colombia's capital city, has established itself as a good financial risk through admirable management of its own finances. It is the only city in Latin America that has obtained an investment-grade rating from the leading rating agencies. Nevertheless, the central government prohibits Bogotá from tapping the international financial market because it does not want to have competition from the city. In this case, an efficient administrator with good investment projects — the city of Bogotá — is officially excluded from the cheaper markets and is confined to the much more costly and limited local capital market by a poor administrator wanting to finance its current deficit. This leads to inefficiencies and distortions and is a tradeoff that has to be taken into consideration. When strict controls on local government indebtedness exist, there should be an institution to provide financing for them, a bank or an independent municipal financing agency. If well-managed local governments are excluded from sources of financing, they cannot be expected to perform efficiently, especially when the government is not doing such a good job itself. In short, when the central government monopolises credit, as it does in some countries, there should be a public, private or a mixed public-private institution that would provide the funds in an efficient manner to local governments.

Finally, it seems that too much attention is being devoted to discretionary versus non-discretionary transfers, which ignores the fact that the rest of the budget *is* discretionary. In terms of political behaviour, it would be much better if transfers were automatic and non-discretionary, but the discretionary nature of the budget at large should not be overlooked. All the problems that non-discretionary transfers are supposed to prevent appear in the rest of the budget. In Colombia, we have non-discretionary transfers that are clearly defined in the constitution, but the rest of the budget is used for purposes that the fixed rules and non-discretionary transfers are supposed to prevent. In other words, the budget has increased substantially after the rule of non-discretionary transfers has been imposed. This is because the central government tries to "buy" the loyalty of the local governments and local politicians with the rest of the budget, since the transfers give local managers a high degree of independence *vis-à-vis* the central government. The Colombian government ended up spending twice the amount that it would otherwise have spent for education and other social services as a result of the non-discretionary transfer mechanism that allowed autonomous expenditure by local governments and enhanced their political independence, and in addition to the political use of budget funds to secure the loyalty of local bosses.

Germany

Harald Rehm

An issue which deserves more attention in a discussion about fiscal decentralisation is the question of horizontal distribution of tax revenue: how taxes should be shared within one level of government, in particular between the States. Politically, this is a very contentious issue.

Germany is composed of 15 States. As a general rule, taxes accrue to the States where they are collected. This rule is superseded by a constitutional requirement that there should be a reasonable equalisation between financially fortunate and less fortunate States (each including their respective municipalities). This necessitates transfers between the States, for which an ever more complex set of rules, regulations and mathematical formulas has been developed over the years.

As a result of the equalisation process the final distribution of tax revenue among States looks entirely different from the original one. For all practical purposes, tax revenues are nowadays largely being levelled out. There are even perverse results: after equalisation, some recipient States have higher per capita tax revenue than contributing States.

In spite of all this, the aim of harmonizing living standards has not been achieved. Instead, recipient States are accumulating higher debts than contributing States. Thus it appears that the current system of equalisation leads to some degree of financial laxity; there is no genuine incentive for an efficient use of resources. Under the circumstances, criticism is rising and two contributing States have announced their intention of turning to the Constitutional Court if a political consensus for change cannot be reached.

Excessive levelling of the States' revenue and expenditure risks undermining their sense of responsibility, their individuality and thus their very Statehood. Therefore, restraint should be exercised when it comes to financial equalisation: gross differences should be mitigated but not eliminated.

Ricardo Hausmann's "ten commandments" deserve a few comments. First, it is obviously desirable to have an autonomous scorekeeper but it is extremely difficult to find one, i.e. to agree on a process of selecting one that is acceptable to all parties involved. But it can be done. Germany provides an example involving the making of tax estimates.

First we have a system in which independent economic research institutes, the Bundesbank, State representatives, local community representatives and federal government officials meet in the autumn and spring of each year to establish the tax estimates. This procedure provides reasonable assurances that there is no bias in making the tax estimates, and the results are generally accepted without dispute. This is an example of an autonomous scorekeeper functioning as it should.

Second, cyclically adjusted deficits provide a useful analytical instrument, but one which must be used with caution for actual fiscal policy. In particular, considering that there are other adjustments as well, e.g. interest adjustments, I made some calculations a while ago, applying one adjustment after the other, and determined that it is easily possible to define away a deficit. In fact, a deficit can even be turned into an apparent surplus. Although cyclical adjustments are analytically useful, the finance minister's problem is that debt service has to be paid on actual nominal deficits. Also, investors' confidence depends on real, not adjusted, information. This should be kept in mind when talking about cyclically adjusted deficits.

Third, the choice of a spending level to be delegated to the executive is obviously a very appealing concept to a civil servant. The executive in most cases probably does better than the parliament where there is a "commons problem." On the other hand, this issue goes to the heart of parliamentarianism. After all, parliaments came into being primarily to restrain the once unlimited power of absolute rulers to tax and spend. One should be careful not to exclude parliaments too much from the budget process.

Fourth, non-discretionary transfer rules are desirable, but one wonders whether one should reject the idea of revenue-sharing and have a fixed overall percentage of GDP. This may result in an inequitable distribution of tax revenue if its evolution is not in proportion to the GDP. Clearly defined shares of revenue may provide a better basis of calculation for different levels of government, so they will experience the economy's fluctuations and one level is not exempted at the cost of another from the need to react to a changing economic environment.

Finally, we could add an "eleventh commandment" to Hausmann's list, namely, to make sure governments below the national level have the institutional capacity for carrying out financial policy effectively and efficiently, and this reinforces the view which is put forward by Kiichiro Fukasaku and others elsewhere in this volume. This is also a strong message of the World Bank's *World Development Report* 1997. Indeed, weak institutions can more than offset any theoretical gain from decentralisation.

Mexico

Ariel Buira

My brief remarks will first discuss the prospects for the 1998 budget in Mexico in the new political environment and then there will be some comments on the paper by Ricardo Hausmann, trying to relate it to the Mexican situation. It goes without saying that what follows are strictly my own personal views.

During the past two decades, Mexico has undergone a major political transformation, making a transition from a single-party government to a system of diverse and competitive political parties. This has involved a passage from elections that were generally uncontested to increasingly contested ones.

Until very recently, the desires of different interest groups, projects and alliances were negotiated within the confines of one party, and elections were largely a formality that signified the culmination of prior political bargaining. However, since the elections of last July the political scene has changed dramatically. For instance, in 1979 the PRI received 70 per cent of the votes for Congress while the PAN received less than 11 per cent, the Communist party 5 per cent. Last July, the outcome was rather different. The PRI obtained 38.5 per cent of the vote and lost control of the lower house of Congress. The PAN received 27 per cent and the PRD on the left 26 per cent.

The same election renewed one-fourth of the Senate, the assembly of the federal district, six governorships and local congresses, with the result that parties other than the PRI now govern some 53 million Mexicans out of 94 million at the state and local levels. This of course poses new challenges for the administration, particularly since the elections were interpreted by many as a rejection of the so-called neo-liberal economic policies.

With respect to the 1998 budget, on the expenditure side the opposition called for a sharp increase in the decentralisation of public expenditure. Today some 80 per cent of tax revenues are allocated to the federal government, 16 per cent to the states and around 4 per cent to 2 400 municipalities. They asked for a doubling of resources to municipalities for poverty alleviation and a significant increase in social expenditure and for in expenditure for education.

On the revenue side there was a wide range of proposals, but the opposition primarily wanted a reduction in the value added tax from the present 15 per cent and the elimination of the tax on assets of firms. One party wants a reduction of the income tax rate from the present 35 per cent while another party proposes increasing income tax on higher income groups, but both agree on exempting workers earning up to four times the minimum wage from income taxes.

The opposition parties argued that the revenue losses and increased expenditure could be compensated for by a reduction in the government's current expenditure through the elimination of waste, corruption and discretionary funds. As a result of a very intense process of consultation with the opposition in the last two months, a budget has been submitted that tries to meet many of the opposition's demands.

The budget tries to broaden the tax base, simplify tax administration, promote savings, and increase equity by reducing tax evasion. It has five main thrusts. A 10 per cent increase in social expenditure in real terms represents a 10 per cent increase in expenditure for education and health services in general, although the increase is 20 per cent for health services for people not covered by social security. Twenty-five per cent of real resources are destined for combatting poverty and promoting increased participation of the population in education, use of pension resources and so forth.

A third thrust involves quantum leap in federalism and decentralisation. There is an amendment of the fiscal co-ordination law to establish federal contributions to the states and municipalities by the creation of three funds, one for basic education, a second for health and a third for social infrastructure of municipalities. The funds will not only provide increased resources but also much greater transparency and accountability of their use by allocating resources directly to state governments through some transparent formula. The states, in turn, will propose a formula for sharing these funds with municipalities. The public will know exactly the amount of transfers to state and municipal governments, and for the first time it will be able to hold the municipalities and the state governments accountable for their use.

Total public expenditure is expected to rise by less than growth of GDP to be able to accommodate the increased cost of social security reforms and perhaps there might be a little additional room to increase public investment in real terms, with particular attention to energy, transportation, hydraulic infrastructure and agricultural resources. In my view the budget responds to the opposition's demands. It increases decentralisation, it allocates increased resources for social expenditure, fighting poverty, education and so forth, and it certainly increases accountability and transparency. It is a proposal that probably allows all parties concerned to obtain part of what they wanted.

The administration proposal would limit the public sector deficit to 1.25 per cent of GDP. The opposition parties have called for deficits ranging from 1 per cent to 1.5 per cent. Some members of the opposition have even called for deficits of up to 3 per cent. But these are all relatively modest by our past historical standards, and they are certainly acceptable by the Maastricht standards. The outcome is likely to be below the deficits recorded during the Salinas administration.

Actually the size of the deficit is less of an issue than the effects of even a modest deficit on debt, inflation and crowding-out. Even the parties of the left are fully aware of the risks of instability caused by a large public sector deficit. While we anticipate considerable tension and hard bargaining in the line-by-line discussion of revenue and expenditure, the final outcome does not give much cause for concern. The fact is that the Congress cannot change economic policy in a dramatic way since some three-fourths of the expenditure corresponds to debt service and current expenditure such as salaries for civil servants and teachers. Thus the room for manoeuvre is narrower than might appear at first sight. Moreover, the recent turbulence in financial markets, has reminded all parties of the dangers to stability that could be posed by an imbalance in public finances. Furthermore, the opposition is probably also looking towards future elections, wanting to gain the confidence of the voters and of the markets as a way of improving their chances.

Now, let me turn to the question of how to ensure sound fiscal outcomes in democratic and decentralised societies. First, I want to commend the IDB and Ricardo Hausmann for an excellent and stimulating paper in which the advantages and the shortcomings of various institutional arrangements are explored very lucidly.

The analysis of institutions and procedures is a valuable exercise that has perhaps been lacking in our part of the world, and it certainly furthers understanding. However, one soon becomes aware that in some cases there are too many the factors to be evaluated and at times they have opposing effects. This is very clearly set out in Tables 2 and 4 of the paper, showing that the solution to one problem usually raises difficulties in another, i.e. delegation which facilitates co-ordination may aggravate the agency problem. Commitment problems may be addressed through rules, but at the cost of reducing the flexibility required to operate in a volatile environment.

Since there are innumerable trade-offs, much depends on the analyst's skill in attaching weights to conflicting considerations and integrating them. Theory can probably help, but cannot be a substitute for a perceptive gift for grasping the situation's total pattern and how things hang together.

The ten strong statements or commandments given by Hausmann for organising a fiscal institution should be seen as a useful check list of recommendations for public authorities. They come at an appropriate moment for us in Mexico because we are in the midst of this transition, which I have mentioned, and in a new situation of competition amongst parties where there are many people who are inexperienced in economic matters. The path for discussion of budget issues is not fully charted and these ideas can provide useful reference points and should be considered in the formulation of new rules and policies. This would certainly help to ensure that the process of democratisation and the decentralisation that is under way would not endanger fiscal discipline.

Some recommendations might appear rather obvious when they are spelled out, but nonetheless are valuable and really thoughtful. Certainly, the nature of the political and electoral system should be taken into account when adopting budgetary institutions to insure the desired outcome. Of particular interest to me was the proposal for the establishment of an autonomous scorekeeper, a sort of objective referee, presumably impartial body of independent economists, and perhaps accountants, who would assure credible fiscal transparency. Such an agency should review the projections and perhaps also calculate the underlying cyclical position. This would provide a useful signal to the markets, would help the budgetary discussion and give the markets greater credibility.

We had a recent very successful experience with an electoral scorekeeper in Mexico. The Federal Electoral Institute, which is composed of representatives of civil society, has had considerable success in establishing rules for the registration of voters and the conduct of electoral campaigns. It was able to insure for the first time in many years electoral results that were largely unchallenged. Thus something along these lines might be very useful in the economic sphere.

Establishing procedures for achieving increased transparency in fiscal accounts would itself help eliminate unnecessary controversy from the political process and would enhance the legitimacy and the credibility of government.

Uncertainty about how much is collected in taxes and how taxes are spent has probably been the single largest cause of criticism of, and of reservations, towards the public administration, justified or not. The lack of transparency has often been used by tax evaders as a moral justification for their actions. In effect, they say, "You know these people pocket some of the money so why should I pay".

Transparency will increase the accountability of government officials and the government's credibility, thereby contributing to the consolidation of a more democratic and open society. It will also help ensure that decisions represent social preferences.

Now, some other statements are more controversial. Why should Congress not be permitted to raise taxes and increase expenditure if it feels that some programmes or needs are underfunded? Why should one limit the ability of the executive to have a deficit consistent with the cyclically balanced budgetary position? This might occasionally be welcome to financial markets but it is procyclical and, as Hausmann himself points out elsewhere, it may be questionable economics.

The political sensitivity of many of the issues raised suggests a need for reaching a consensus on procedures as well as objectives. These proposals would require thorough discussion by the public and adequate consideration by the Congress. There are questions which probably have several valid answers, not just one, the answers depending on the multitude of circumstances and on the timing. Again, I recall an observation which holds that the suspicion of intellectuals towards politics largely stems from a desire to see life in some simple symmetrical fashion, putting too much faith in the application of conclusions derived from purely theoretical considerations.

In dealing with these issues there can be no substitute for a case-by-case pragmatic approach and good sense. Finally, on the issue of the political culture, the responsibility and increased economic literacy of participants in the political process may be enhanced by reforms such as those proposed. The opinion of participants in the process can provide an alternative answer to the question of how to ensure sound financial outcomes.

Public opinion in a number of countries in Latin America has become increasingly informed and prudent in fiscal and monetary matters as a result of the crisis experienced in the 1980s and the 1990s. A culture of stability and a vigilant public opinion appears to be emerging, a development which seems to parallel that which occurred in some other countries. One can recall Germany after the war and the ensuing hyperinflation. A vigilant public opinion has served that country well and will serve us well in a more democratic atmosphere, since democracy introduces this accountability and increased responsibility for political decisions.

Portugal

Jorge Braga de Macedo[1]

It seems appropriate to begin with some brief excepts from a *Financial Times* article entitled "Schadenfreude".

"As the big guns in the European Union struggle to get into the starting line-up for the single currency, the Portuguese seem to be taking quiet pleasure in re-exporting some of the condescension they have received in abundance from Europe's prosperous centre."

These unusual observations about Portugal from the *Financial Times* continues:

"As the citizens of the EU's second poorest country become comfortable with the idea that they really are in line for entry, if and when the whole thing kicks off in 1999, the Portuguese are beginning to express straight-faced sympathy for those who only a couple of years ago weren't giving Portugal more than a walk-on part in the Euro plot."

In other words, the Portuguese government's representative at international forums is saying to more skeptical colleagues: "No, you must understand, Germany will get its accounts in order and so will France, absolutely, we know..." and so on. The article ends with a proverb: "He who laughs last, we say in Lisbon, laughs longest." For our purposes, we can replace Lisbon with Latin America.

Some brief hypothetical considerations can help explain how Portugal moved towards a stability culture, and rather quickly by international standards. The perceptions of the two main observers of regime changes, namely voters and traders, were affected by so-called geographic fundamentals, as suggested in the "Schadenfreude" article.

"If you are south of the Pyrénées, you can't live without inflation." That would be one way of expressing a "geographic fundamental." Another one would be: "If you're west of the UK you cannot possibly hope to be in the single currency." Yet another example: "How does a former colony of Sweden — namely Finland — dare join the Euro when Sweden pretends it has an opt-out clause?" There are many other alleged geographic fundamentals about the rest of the world.

There are also historical myths. For example, since the stability observed in Portugal from the 1930s until the 1960s was not based on democratic rule, it was widely assumed that the Portuguese people opposed democracy and financial stability. However, that myth is belied by the democratic and financial stability during about half of the 19th century when Portugal's currency, the *real*, was on the gold standard. But since that period of stability was under a monarchy, it is ignored because of "republican myths". Here again perceptions based on the recent past discounted prior periods of convertibility[2].

Thus it is important to be aware of historical and geographic myths. If a regime has been successfully transformed — and that should be the main point of the lesson from Portugal — then it is clear that the stability culture benefits the periphery more than the centre. This is because change has been carried out and the improvement is very clear. In other words, a credit rating is more transparent and certainly more amenable to improvement than a geographical location. That is our main contention, which will now be discussed, beginning with the decision to enter the Exchange Rate Mechanism of the European Monetary System, or ERM for short.

The Portuguese government applied to join at a rate of 180 escudos, a parity in terms of the ECU rather than the German mark, on 4 April 1992, the weekend after the 1992 budget had obtained parliamentary approval. Fearing that a weaker escudo might be contagious for sterling on the eve of the British general election, the monetary committee (whose members were acting as representatives of the Council of Economic and Finance Ministers — ECOFIN — and central bank governors) finally agreed on the notional central rate of 178.735, that is, the prevailing rate since the entry of sterling in October 1990.

The social partners in Portugal had been briefed on Friday afternoon and the government called for a parliamentary debate the following week. The opposition criticised the move, claiming that Britain had presented another "ultimatum" (as in 1890!). Public opinion was surprised. A disgruntled former colleague from Nova University called the decision a "vanity move" by the prime minister, suggesting that the government was unable to explain the regime change domestically even though the outcome of the Danish referendum and a severe recession had made it impossible for the escudo to join the original ERM. This implied that the escudo was in the same boat as the Greek drachma, rather than with the peseta. The drachma, escudo and peseta are the currencies of the three recipients of the cohesion fund, the countries whose fiscal problems made them unlikely candidates for the first round of the EMU.

The novelty of combining financial discipline and political stability in a democracy may have made the timing of the entry less obvious at home than to market observers abroad. In any event, the escudo has kept a central rate of around 196 since the realignment of the peseta in March 1995, and it is more likely to become the euro on 1 January 1999 than any other currency outside the traditional DM core area (France, Benelux and Austria).

Entering the ERM left the domestic financial press largely indifferent. There are still very few newspaper or even scholarly references to the effects of a decision, which the then prime minister repeatedly stated had been one of the most important reforms implemented during his decade in office. The reason for this neglect may be due to the fact that the domestic stability culture paradoxically was recovered during a period of system instability. Alternatively, it may be attributable to the hopes of protectionist forces that there would be a withdrawal from the ERM, as with the pound sterling, forcibly ejected from the ERM in September 1992, along with the lira.

In a financial system that was highly protected from competition and facing weak supervision, central bank policy came to depend increasingly on issuing short-term domestic debt to mop up the growing capital inflows, which were attracted by the favourable investment climate and, increasingly, by the highly remunerative real interest rates that could be earned on pure arbitrage operations.

The fear that financial freedom would threaten monetary control and the soundness of the banking system was ingrained in the central bank, which had always administered the exchange controls on the escudo. The virtual grip on policy making that the bank's board enjoyed in 1990-91 made it difficult in 1992 for the institution to believe that full currency convertibility could be restored before the special dispensation negotiated with Brussels had expired in 1995. Teams from the treasury and the bank met regularly to establish a two-way dialogue. The ministry team also held meetings with all previous ministers of finance where current and several past central bank governors were able to discuss the state of the economy and the progress of convergence.

At the beginning of 1993 the central bank was publicly urged to adjust to the time of full currency convertibility. Two implications of this were not made explicit as they had been raised in the sessions with the board of the central bank: allowing greater banking competition and, if need be, letting the escudo leave the top of the 6 per cent band of the ERM. The resignation of a board member of the central bank who had become the most outspoken advocate of the hard escudo policy followed in 1990-91, gave this adjustment undertones of a crisis rather than being a natural adaptation to an enhanced financial reputation. Thus the socialist opposition, which was openly calling for a slower disinflation and an autonomous depreciation of the currency, was able to side with the independence of the central bank. The social-democratic business elite, surprised by entry into the ERM, suggested a reversal in the orientation of macroeconomic policy and pressure on the monetary authority. There were no negative international effects and the ERM partners knew the code of conduct would be upheld[3].

As there has not been any serious speculative attack against the escudo since the early 1920s, the domestic turbulence of March 1993 may be just another example of the resilience of monetary myths. In fact, the suggestion that the treasury and central bank no longer had the same aims represented a delayed reaction to the liberalisation of capital movements, which some members of the central bank board had adamantly opposed in August 1992. On the other hand, the more flexible policy of following the peseta, which had begun in September 1992, probably could not have been sustained without some change in the board.

Table 1 shows the decomposition of real interest rate differentials relative to the dollar and the mark. The peseta's difficulties allowed the escudo to realign several times during the ERM crises of 1992-93 without loss of financial reputation. This interpretation is confirmed by the declining covered interest differential against the dollar and mark and by the oscillations of the other components of the real interest differentials, the exchange risk premium and the change in the real exchange rate during the tenure of the ministers of finance and central bank governors shown in Table 2.

Table 1. **Average Real Interest Rate Differentials (%)**
(Annual average of monthly data)

	RIRD r-r*	CIRP i-i*-fd	REX e+p*-p	ERP fd-e
A: PTE/USD				
1984	-1.1	-2.9	11.9	-10.1
1985	8.8	-6.8	-25.2	40.8
1986	4.4	-4.8	-15.2	24.4
1987	3.1	-0.1	-8.2	11.8
1988	-1.5	0.0	4.0	-5.5
1989	-2.8	-0.8	1.7	-3.7
1990	1.0	1.8	-17.3	16.5
1991	6.0	4.6	-5.1	6.5
1992	7.3	0.4	-12.1	19.0
1993	6.7	0.6	15.9	-9.8
1994	4.3	0.6	1.4	2.3
1995	2.6	0.1	-10.8	13.4
1996	1.9	-0.1	3.5	-0.7
1997	0.9	-0.3	8.0	-6.9
B: PTE/DM				
1989	-2.0	-0.1	-7.5	5.5
1990	-1.5	1.7	-5.3	2.1
1991	2.0	5.0	-8.7	5.8
1992	2.3	0.3	-5.7	7.8
1993	3.3	2.1	9.9	-8.7
1994	3.6	-0.5	3.3	0.8
1995	3.1	-0.1	0.2	3.1
1996	2.2	0.5	-3.5	5.2

Source: Rocha de Sousa (1997).

The gradual convergence path was retained in the revised convergence programme (PCR) approved with the 1994 budget, but a cabinet reshuffle was announced shortly before local elections. The new cabinet had the same overall stance but with a new style and an economic policy geared towards gradually recovering growth and convergence. The PCR obtained the ECOFIN seal of approval without difficulty at the same time that a global bond issue in ECUs was received with the same success as the previous one.

Table 2. Average Real Interest Rate Differentials
(percentage per annum)

		RIRD $r-r^*$	CIRP $i-i^*-fd$	REX $e+p^*-p$	ERP $fd-e$	
A: Pte/Usd						
Ministers of Finance						
Miguel Cadilhe	m	-2.8	-0.8	1.7	-3.7	
January-December 89	c.v.	-0.6	-2.4	2.4	-1.5	
Miguel Beleza	m	3.1	3.0	-12.3	12.4	
January 90-October 91	c.v.	0.9	0.8	-0.7	0.6	
Braga de Macedo	m	7.1	0.9	1.1	5.1	cor 12 December
November 91-December 93	c.v.	0.2	3.8	14.8	3.6	
Eduardo Catroga	m	3.7	0.4	-3.4	6.6	
December 93-October 95	c.v.	0.3	1.1	-3.5	1.8	
Sousa Franco	m	1.8	-0.2	1.7	0.3	
October 95-Feb 97	c.v.	0.4	-1.7	3.0	20.2	
Central Bank Governors						
Tavares Moreira	m	2.2	2.1	-6.9	6.9	
January 89-May 92	c.v.	2.0	1.4	-1.4	1.4	
Miguel Beleza	m	6.1	-0.2	5.9	0.4	
June 92-June 94	c.v.	0.3	-16.6	2.9	48.4	
António De Sousa	m	2.6	0.1	-4.2	6.7	
July 94-September 96	c.v.	0.5	5.7	-1.9	1.3	
B: Pte/Dm						
Ministers of Finance						
Miguel Cadilhe	m	-2.0	-0.1	-7.5	5.5	
January-December 89	c.v.	-0.5	-16.6	-0.3	0.2	
Miguel Beleza	m	-0.1	3.1	-7.2	4.0	cor 12 December
January 90-October 91	c.v.	-14.9	1.0	-0.4	0.7	
Braga De Macedo	m	3.0	1.6	1.2	0.2	
November 91-December 93	c.v.	0.6	2.5	7.5	54.7	
Eduardo Catroga	m	3.4	-0.3	2.4	1.3	
December 93-October 95	c.v.	0.4	-4.7	1.8	3.9	
Sousa Franco	m	2.3	0.3	-2.5	4.6	
October 95-September 96	c.v.	0.4	4.3	-0.9	0.4	
Central Bank Governors						
Tavares Moreira	m	0.0	2.4	-7.1	4.7	
January 89-May 92	c.v.	-395.8	1.3	-0.3	0.5	
Miguel Beleza	m	2.7	0.3	5.2	-2.9	
June 92-June 94	c.v.	0.7	10.5	1.5	-3.0	
António De Sousa	m	3.1	-0.1	-1.3	4.5	
July 94-September 96	c.v.	0.3	-18.3	-1.6	0.4	

Based on Rocha de Sousa (1997) and subsequent calculations.

The minister of finance's calls for lower interest rates, directed at a domestic business audience, had foreign repercussions, especially when they were echoed by the prime minister. Then leaks to the financial press about differences between the minister and the governor on banking supervision led to the replacement of most of the board in the spring of 1994. Since then, the statutes of the central bank have been changed to make it more independent of the government, introduce some accountability in parliament and improve regulatory and supervisory procedures.

Another indication of the continuity of the 1992 multi-annual fiscal adjustment strategy (MAFAS) pegged to the ECU, was that in 1993 the PCR proposed extending the expenditure ceilings into 1997 and this remained the basis for the excessive deficit procedures until a convergence, stability and growth programme (PCEC) for 1998 to 2000 was approved by the ECOFIN in May 1997.

As Portugal was absent from international financial markets, the lack of credit familiarity would have been bad enough for enterprises and citizens in relatively calm periods. In the turbulence which followed the entry into the ERM, things were of course much worse and this may have contributed to a slowing down of the learning process, especially in the midst of a severe recession and the domestic political instability which preceded the 1995 elections.

Figure 1 presents nominal and real effective exchange rates of Portugal relative to the OECD average. It shows a rather pronounced nominal and real appreciation until 1992, when we joined the exchange rate mechanism. As implied above, it was the very last moment for entry into the original ERM, since the crisis broke out a few months later[4]. Before the turbulence began, and also afterwards, we managed to avoid this nominal and real appreciation because we now followed a policy rule that was transparent, i.e. the ERM code of conduct. This was a very important point in the change of regime. Without loss of reputation, we were able to let the escudo follow —sometimes completely, sometimes partly, sometimes not at all — the realignments of the peseta. We were able to use the "geographic fundamentals" to our advantage which, of course, was only possible because we were in the ERM. After that, as one can see, there has been stability. The dampening of nominal and real rates, and the way in which it was achieved, is due to the fact that we had a stable exchange rate rule which allowed us to correct the overvaluation.

This is the major relative price for a small, open economy and Figure 2 shows factor prices relative to the EU average, such as the prices of labour and capital, and one can again see a pattern. There were increases in wages and interest rates before the decline, but let us go back to the evidence of Tables 1 and 2 and to how the currency risk premium disappeared. In 1993 when we actually followed realignments that were introduced by Spain, our risk premium dropped substantially. This means that the market suspected that we might devalue again if we had the chance. Portugal was the only country in 1993 whose credit rating was upgraded to AA-. This occurred when the risk premium dropped. There was some instability in 1995 when the former prime minister said he would not run for office and the next prime minister was very ambiguous about whether or not he would continue the stability policy. In fact he did, but there was some uncertainty. However, there was no loss of reputation because we followed the rules of the game and still managed to avoid real appreciation.

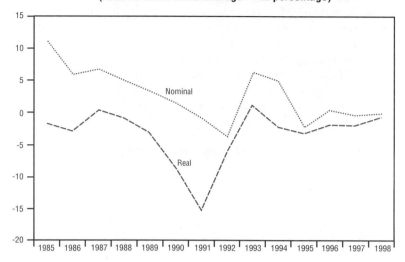

Figure 1. **Nominal and Real Effective Portuguese Exchange Rates**
(relative to the OECD average — in percentage)

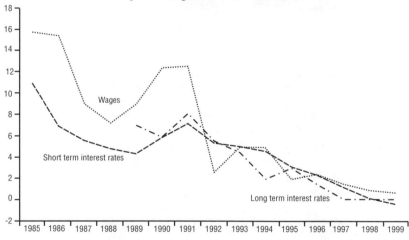

Figure 2. **Wage and Rental Moderation**

Figure 3 shows the fiscal deficit, and the straight line is the 3 per cent of the EU treaty. The deficit fell substantially in the early 1980s when Portugal embarked on its reform process. In 1989 it dropped slightly below 3 per cent due to a tax reform in which people paid the old and new taxes in transitional arrangements. The deficit increased again in 1990, and the peak was reached in the election year. That was also when wages and interest rates increased, as shown in Figure 2. The deficit fell again in 1992 under my first budget. I had just presented a convergence programme in Brussels which mapped out our non-interest expenditure until 1995. This was a very clear signal of our commitment to stability and a budgetary policy oriented towards the medium term. Thus my research staff persuaded me to forego the universal habit of finance ministers to underestimate revenue. This was a difficult time for innovation because of the single market. Customs could no longer collect a VAT and at the same time tax receipts plummeted due to the severity of the 1993 recession. Using Haussmann's terminology, the budget was counter-cyclical but the economic culture remained pro-cyclical. It is not surprising that the domestic press was highly critical of this, but the international market accepted the deterioration of the budget in its stride, as shown by the success of the Republic's global bond offerings in the autumn and winter of 1993.

Figure 3. **Double Dip Recession**

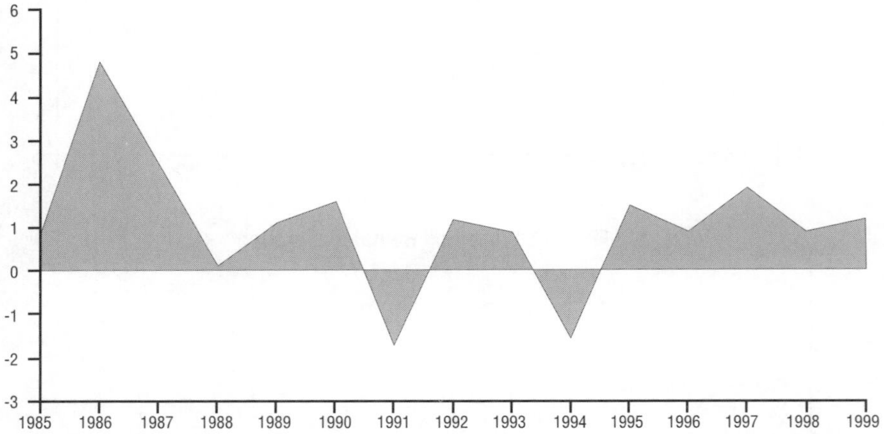

Again the markets really took 1993 very well, but public opinion, the parties and perhaps the voters, did not. They only were converted to the stability culture after the Socialist Party, which is now in power, followed exactly the same policy. The voters said in effect: "Gee, this is not just a couple of single-minded economists", to borrow the phrase of Ricardo Hausmann, "This policy may be here to stay". Figure 4 presents a very common indicator, the increase in Portuguese productivity relative to the average of the 15 EU members. At the beginning of 1985, Portugal had "Asian-type" productivity increases of 5 percentage points over the community average. Productivity then started falling but remained respectable. Thus before the recession, due largely to increased public sector wages, there was a dip in relative productivity increases. The economy recovered in 1992, partly because of the single digit wage agreement which consolidated the regime change. In 1993-94, however, the country experienced a second dip, which is the worst thing that can happen to employers, firms and trade unions. It then took a long time to recover and that is why the average voter and firms took so much longer than the markets to accept the regime change. They needed to be convinced, once again, that the stable environment was here to stay, and this only occurred during the first year of Socialist government in 1996, partly because there were so few changes in policy.

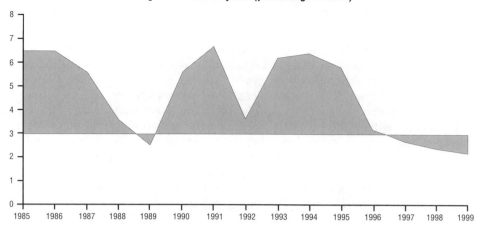
Figure 4. **Deficit Cycles (percentage of GDP)**

Even if the escudo manages to become the euro in 1999, major challenges must be met to sustain the financial reputation acquired thus far. They mostly concern public sector reforms that have been suspended since the 1993 local elections.

It is worth recalling the role that local elections had in implementing the regime change between 1989 and 1992. The gradual process was identified with the prime minister, but different persons had to stress international and domestic objectives alternately. This clarifies the roles of the four finance ministers: they either implemented structural reforms with high external visibility or were required to hold the line domestically. This outcome may not have been anticipated by each of the individuals but it is borne out by the pattern of the regime change.

The reconquest of stability implied changing the team who carried out the reforms before the local elections to stress the predominance of domestic objectives, but there were major differences between the two mid-term cabinet reshuffles. The 1990 reshuffle provided a second wind for the Social Democratic Party and allowed it to win the 1991 elections while the 1993 reshuffle did not have the same effect. There are surely other explanations for the differences besides resistance to the gradual extension of the stability culture, but the fact that the new economic regime was in place in 1993 made it less costly for the prime minister to halt reforms and simply attempt to finish his term. On the other hand, the economic recession and financial turbulence just after the entry into the ERM were ascribed to the government's obsession with stability at the expense of the political freedoms proposed by the country's Socialist president and the newly elected opposition leader, now the prime minister.

The challenge was successfully met: the Socialist government fully accepted the new economic regime and claimed the euro as one of its great achievements! While the Socialist prime minister carried out a mid-term reshuffle in late November as local elections approached, however, the minister of finance remained in the cabinet, unlike during his predecessor's reshuffles. As the results of the 1997 local elections were unfavourable to the parties of the extreme right and left, which oppose the euro and the stability culture, the pressure to step up structural reforms will have to come mostly from the Social Democratic Party.

A country can overcome "geographical fundamentals" and historical myths through sustained reform, and this is the last and perhaps the most disquieting point. Sustained reform is the name of the game. Whether a country is in the EU or not makes a big difference. The literature has now been identifying "the euro hold-up problem" which occurs when moving towards a single currency or when there is a stability culture without reform, retaining entitlements and avoiding unpopular reforms. In a sense, that is like being all dressed up but having nowhere to go. What should be done once inside the club? That is the main problem, and it is not exclusively a Portuguese problem. It is a problem for many European countries. The EMU is an extremely important reform, but it is also a condition for other reforms involving social security, education, justice, health, unemployment, etc.

Notes

1. This discussion is largely based upon, "Crises? What Crises? Escudo from ECU to EMU", Nova Economics Working Paper No. 313, December 1997, parts of which will also appear in a WIDER volume on "Short-Term Capital Flows and Balance of Payments Crises". The paper is available on line at: http://www.fe.unl.pt/~jbmacedo/papers/wider.htm.

2. The effect of European fiscal and monetary institutions on the Americas will be the subject of a session at the 12th International Economic History Congress, to be held in Seville in August 1998, for which a preparatory session was held at the University of San Andres, Buenos Aires, Argentina in April 1997. On that occasion I presented a paper, "War, Taxes and Gold: The Inheritance of the Real", co-authored by Alvaro Ferreira da Silva and Rita Martins de Sousa.

3. I introduced this expression in a paper written with Hervé Carré for the Reinventing Bretton Woods Committee in September 1994.

4. This is explained in the paper cited in note 1, where the variations in the daily volatility of the escudo-mark rate are used to provide evidence for the success of the ERM entry as a credible signal of regime change. The set-up is helpful for the "credibility tests" suggested by the Argentine experience. It also fits the simplicity criterion mentioned in the discussion by Mariano Tommasi.

Bolivia

Gonzalo Sanchez de Losada

Bolivia is a large country(1 000 000 km²) but a small economy with a gross national product of $7 billion and a population of 8 million people. However, the country's economic policies have been innovative on a number of counts. Bolivia has implemented some experiments comparable to "pilot-plant" projects which are not widely known.

Like most Latin American countries, Bolivia had been highly centralised since colonial times. When entering office, my administration initiated reforms aimed at encouraging decentralisation and, at the same time, a distributive economy. The biggest problem at that time was the lack of clear rules. For example, it had to be understood that economic problems have a political origin, and economic problems can only be solved when a political solution is found. Having recognised that, Bolivia was the first country to end hyperinflation under a democratic administration at a time when it was still generally believed in Latin America that hyperinflation could only be halted by an authoritarian regime.

Bolivia was able to do that for political reasons: we have a proportional representation system in which it is almost impossible for any political party to get a simple majority in Congress during the first round of elections. During the second round of voting the president is elected in Congress where political parties are obliged to form a coalition. Under such circumstances the biggest danger is federalism, and we have been struggling against this since independence.

Bolivia has nine departments, and I always asked the Bolivian people why they would want to have nine bad governments when there was already a government in La Paz that left something to be desired. The capitals of these departments are as disliked by rural local councils as is the central government, because small local urban elites have been trying to get more power since colonial times. We have learned from the experience of some other Latin American countries that a federal system is costly, inefficient and beyond our means.

Many changes are occurring in my country. A first major change is related to what may be called "popular participation". We have two levels of government in Bolivia: municipal and national. The municipal government was descended from the old colonial urban government that was like a medieval state in which landowners, tax collectors and *corregidores*, together with priests and the Church, exploited and generally oppressed the people in the countryside.

We have transformed these municipal governments into democratically elected ones with authority and responsibility, and we have also extended their territorial jurisdiction. Today there are 311 municipal governments (or territorial governments) which together receive 20 per cent of the country's total fiscal revenue. A major change in this respect is that we have introduced a fixed rule: we now distribute this 20 per cent to the municipalities according to their population. Under the previous system of revenue sharing based on tax collection, the capitals of three departments spent 92 per cent of the total revenue, while the rest was shared by the other poorer but more populated six departments. This simple rule has made people clearly understand what has changed on the fiscal account. This is based on the old concept of "one man, one vote. That is, revenue sharing has become equitable and also automatic at the time of tax collection.

There was some worry about whether local governments could really spend this money properly. This leads to my second point. The very reason for decentralising fiscal decision making is to enable local people to set priorities on the expenditure side. Generally, the first thing local governments did was to repair their central squares because this is symbolic in a town, but the second thing they did was to spend their money on local public services, such as primary education and health care, drinking water and country roads. This is because the central government gave them responsibility for primary education, health care, culture and sports, together with local roads and productive activities such as small irrigation works and other small community projects. It is very interesting that they have invested most in education and health care; the central government had been letting the buildings deteriorate, now the local governments have started to fix their schools and health centres.

One of the difficulties we are facing at the local level, and this is my third point, is how to contain corruption in a democratic and increasingly decentralised political system. Corruption is deeply rooted in the society. Before decentralisation it was largely confined to the central government, but now it can occur at the local level. We have tried to bring some control to the local budget process through monitoring by oversight committees made up of representatives of rural communities and urban neighbourhoods, since there is no way the central government can exercise this control directly itself. This has still not solved the problem because these oversight committees have been created by the civil society but were not been granted any legal power to stop disbursements.

My fourth and final point. When turning to the revenue side, we think that the only taxes that can be collected locally are taxes on urban and rural property, on vehicles and on the transfer of these assets. Under our new constitutional system the local governments cannot impose any broad-based taxes; only the central government can impose such taxes for distribution to local governments.

In addition to "Population Participation" we established "Administrative Decentralisation", executed by Prefects appointed by the President in the departments. They preside over a council of representatives named by the municipal council members, as part of the effort to achieve administrative decentralisation of the central government with social control from local governments.

At the beginning of my administration 75 per cent of the investment decisions were taken at the central level. Today, only 25 per cent are taken at that level. Furthermore, revenue sharing in the departments was established based on a formula that divides 50 per cent equally among the nine departments and 50 per cent according to population.

It is important to emphasize that decentralisation works best when responsibility and authority are transferred but also when revenue is shared. This enables the decentralised administration and local government to decide their priorities and have to achieve efficiency in order to satisfy the needs closest to the everyday problems of the people and within a pre-established budget constraint.

Eighth International Forum on Latin American Perspectives

PROGRAMME

Eighth International Forum on Latin American Perspectives

Thursday, 20 November 1997

Opening Remarks by co-Chairmen of the Forum	Jean Bonvin, President, OECD Development Centre Ricardo Hausmann, Chief Economist, Inter-American Development Bank

Session I. Fiscal Performance in Latin America: What Needs to be Explained?

Chair:	Jean Bonvin, President, OECD Development Centre
Speakers:	Michael Gavin and Ricardo Hausmann, Inter-American Development Bank
Discussants:	Alfred Stepan, Oxford University, United Kingdom
	Ricardo Lago, European Bank for Reconstruction and Development

Session II. Fiscal Decentralisation and Government Size in Latin America

Chair:	Helmut Reisen, OECD Development Centre
Speaker:	Ernesto Stein, Inter-American Development Bank
Discussant:	Bruno Frey, University of Zurich, Switzerland

Session III. Fiscal Decentralisation and Macroeconomic Stability: The Experience of Large Developing and Transition Economies

Chair:	Ricardo Hausmann, Inter-American Development Bank
Speakers:	Kiichiro Fukasaku, OECD Development Centre Luiz R. de Mello Jr., University of Kent, United Kingdom
Discussant:	Mariano Tommasi, University of San Andrés, Argentina

Session IV. Fiscal Federalism in OECD Member Countries

Chair: Kumiharu Shigehara, Deputy Secretary-General, OECD

Speaker: Jon Blondal, OECD Public Management Service

Discussant: Rudolph Hommes, University of Los Andes,
                  Colombia

Session V. Electoral Institutions and the Budget Process

Chair: Ricardo Hausmann, Inter-American Development
                  Bank

Speakers: Jürgen von Hagen, University of Bonn, Germany

                  Mark Hallerberg, Georgia Technological
                  Institute, United States

Discussant: Rémy Prud'homme, University of Paris XII, France

Friday, 21 November 1997

Panel Session. Fiscal Institutions for Decentralising Democracies:
Which Way to Go?

Chair: Gonzalo Sanchez de Losada, former President, Bolivia

Speaker: Ricardo Hausmann, Chief Economist, Inter-American
                     Development Bank

Panel Discussion: Carlos Ominami (Senator and former Minister
                     of Economy, Chile)

                     Jorge Braga de Macedo (Former Minister of Finance,
                     Portugal)

                     Rudolph Hommes (Former Minister of Finance,
                     Colombia)

                     Ariel Buira (Former Deputy Governor of the Central
                     Bank, Mexico)

                     Marcelo Piancastelli de Siqueira (Ministry of Finance,
                     Brazil)

                     Andrew Powell (Central Bank, Argentina)

                     Harald Rehm (Federal Ministry of Finance, Germany)

LIST OF AUTHORS AND PARTICIPANTS

Co-Chairmen

Jean Bonvin   President, OECD Development Centre

Ricardo Hausmann   Chief Economist, Inter-American Development Bank

Authors

Jon Blondal   OECD Public Management Service

Luiz R. de Mello, Jr.   University of Kent, United Kingdom

Kiichiro Fukasaku   OECD Development Centre

Michael Gavin   Inter-American Development Bank

Mark Hallerberg   Georgia Technological Institute, United States

Ricardo Hausmann   Chief Economist, Inter-American Development Bank

Ernesto Stein   Inter-American Development Bank

Jürgen von Hagen   University of Bonn, Germany

Discussants

Bruno Frey   University of Zurich, Switzerland

Rudolph Hommes   Rector, University of Los Andes, Colombia
Former Minister of Finance, Colombia

Ricardo Lago   Deputy Chief Economist, European Bank
for Reconstruction and Development

Rémy Prud'homme   University of Paris XII, France

Alfred Stepan   Oxford University, United Kingdom

Mariano Tommasi   University of San Andrés, Argentina

Panellists

Jorge Braga de Macedo   Former Minister of Finance, Portugal

Ariel Buira   Former Deputy Governor of the Central Bank, Mexico

Rudolph Hommes   Rector, University of Los Andes, Colombia
Former Minister of Finance, Colombia

Carlos Ominami   Senator and former Minister of Economy, Chile

Marcelo Piancastelli de Siqueira   Ministry of Finance, Brazil

Andrew Powell   Central Bank, Argentina

Harald Rehm   Federal Ministry of Finance, Germany

Gonzalo Sanchez de Losada   Former President, Bolivia

Other participants

Stephen Fidler	*The Financial Times*, United Kingdom
Ingrid Haar-Stöhr	Austrian National Bank, Austria
Olivier Lemaigre	Citibank, New York, United States
Alessandro Merli	*Il Sole - 24 Ore*, London, United Kingdom
Giuseppe Mureddu	Università degli Studi "La Sapienza", Rome, Italy
Françoise Nicolas	Institut français des relations internationales, Paris, France
Jozef Van't Dack	Bank for International Settlements, Basel, Switzerland

Diplomatic Representatives

Argentina

Archibald Lanus	Ambassador, Argentine Embassy, Paris
Felipe Gardella	Counsellor, Argentine Embassy, Paris

Austria

Doris Bertrand	Minister, Plenipotentiary, Delegation of Austria to the OECD

Belgium

Adelin Hudsyn	Embassy Counsellor, Delegation of Belgium to the OECD

Brazil

Denis Fontes De Souza Pinto	First Secretary, Brazilian Embassy, Paris

Chile

Alexis Guardia	Economic Counsellor, Chilean Embassy, Paris

Colombia

Rodrigo Pardo Garcia-Pena	Ambassador, Colombian Embassy, Paris
Olga Bula	Minister-counsellor, Colombian Embassy, Paris
Fernando Pabon Santander	First Secretary, Colombian Embassy, Paris
Jimena Garzon	Second Secretary, Colombian Embassy, Paris

Ecuador

Juan Cuedva	Ambassador, Ecuadorean Embassy, Paris

Finland

Kirsti Aarnio — Counsellor, Delegation of Finland to the OECD

France

Patrick Boursin — Sous-directeur Amérique du Sud, Ministère des Affaires étrangères, Paris

Germany

Horst Wetzel — Counsellor, Delegation of Germany to the OECD

Guatemala

Patricia Mendoza — First Secretary, Guatemalan Embassy, Paris

Honduras

Adriana Ariza — Minister-counsellor, Honduran Embassy, Paris

Ireland

Patricia Cullen — First Secretary, Delegation of Ireland to the OECD

Italy

Alessandro Vattani — Ambassador, Delegation of Italy to the OECD

Guido Latella — First Counsellor, Delegation of Italy to the OECD

Japan

Miho Kawahatsu — Technical Assistant, Delegation of Japan to the OECD

Mexico

Francisco Suarez Davila — Ambassador, Delegation of Mexico to the OECD

Héctor Manuel Rodriguez — Second Secretary, Mexican Embassy, Paris

Alfredo Genel — Economic and Financial Affairs, Delegation of Mexico to the OECD

Rogelio Arellano — Trade, Investment and Industry, Delegation of Mexico to the OECD

Netherlands

Paul Sciarone — Counsellor, Delegation of the Netherlands to the OECD

Nicaragua

Virginia Delgadillo Cuadra — Chargé d'affaires, Nicaraguan Embassy, Paris

Panama

Aristides Royo — Ambassador, Panamanian Embassy, Paris

Peru

María Luisa Federici Soto — Ambassador, Peruvian Embassy, Paris

Aelin Perez — Minister-counsellor, Peruvian Embassy, Paris

Turkey

Akin Altuna — Ambassador, Delegation of Turkey to the OECD

Ali Koprulu — Minister-counsellor, Delegation of Turkey to the OECD

Osman Emed — Counsellor, Delegation of Turkey to the OECD

United States

Lee Roussel — Minister-counsellor, Delegation of the United States to the OECD

Uruguay

Miguel Angel Semino — Ambassador, Uruguayan Embassy, Paris

Venezuela

Francisco Kerdel-Vegas — Ambassador, Venezuelan Embassy, Paris

Martha Ramos de Kerdel-Vegas — Economist, Venezuelan Embassy, Paris

European Commission

Ulrike Hauer — Administrator, European Commission, Brussels

International Monetary Fund

Julius Rosenblatt — Advisor, International Monetary Fund, Paris

World Bank

Michèle Bailly — Senior Counsellor, Relations with OECD, European Office, Paris

OECD Secretariat*

Kumiharu Shigehara — Deputy Secretary-General

John West — Principal Administrator, Private Office of the Secretary-General

William Nicol — Head of Division, Development Co-operation Directorate

214

Sara Johansson	Development Co-operation Directorate
Katia Michaelowa	Development Co-operation Directorate
Michael Engelschalk	Directorate for Financial, Fiscal and Enterprise Affairs
H. Peter Sturm	Head of Division, Economics Department
Kathryn Gordon	Economics Department
Andrea-Enrico Goldstein	Economics Department
Bernard Wacquez	Economics Department

Chairman of the Development Assistance Committee

James H. Michel	Ambassador, Chairman of the DAC

Inter-American Development Bank*

Rod Chapman	Senior Press and Information Officer, IDB European Office
Ziga Vodusek	Senior Economist, IDB European Office

OECD Development Centre*

Giulio Fossi	Head, External Co-operation Programme
Helmut Reisen	Head of Division, Research
Colm Foy	Head of Publications/Communication Unit
Charles Oman	Principal Administrator, Research
Catherine Duport	Principal Administrator, Administration and Support Services
Henny Helmich	Administrator, External Co-operation Division
Monika Queisser	Administrator, Research
Olga Salgado	Consultant, Research
Akiko Suwa-Eisenmann	Consultant, Research
Adèle Woods	Consultant, External Co-operation Division

* Except those listed as authors or discussants.

MAIN SALES OUTLETS OF OECD PUBLICATIONS
PRINCIPAUX POINTS DE VENTE DES PUBLICATIONS DE L'OCDE

AUSTRALIA – AUSTRALIE
D.A. Information Services
648 Whitehorse Road, P.O.B 163
Mitcham, Victoria 3132   Tel. (03) 9210.7777
                         Fax: (03) 9210.7788

AUSTRIA – AUTRICHE
Gerold & Co.
Graben 31
Wien I   Tel. (0222) 533.50.14
                   Fax: (0222) 512.47.31.29

BELGIUM – BELGIQUE
Jean De Lannoy
Avenue du Roi, Koningslaan 202
B-1060 Bruxelles Tel. (02) 538.51.69/538.08.41
                         Fax: (02) 538.08.41

CANADA
Renouf Publishing Company Ltd.
 5369 Canotek Road
Unit 1
Ottawa, Ont. K1J 9J3   Tel. (613) 745.2665
                         Fax: (613) 745.7660

Stores:
71 1/2 Sparks Street
Ottawa, Ont. K1P 5R1   Tel. (613) 238.8985
                         Fax: (613) 238.6041

12 Adelaide Street West
Toronto, QN M5H 1L6   Tel. (416) 363.3171
                         Fax: (416) 363.5963

Les Éditions La Liberté Inc.
3020 Chemin Sainte-Foy
Sainte-Foy, PQ G1X 3V6 Tel. (418) 658.3763
                         Fax: (418) 658.3763

Federal Publications Inc.
165 University Avenue, Suite 701
Toronto, ON M5H 3B8   Tel. (416) 860.1611
                         Fax: (416) 860.1608

Les Publications Fédérales
1185 Université
Montréal, QC H3B 3A7 Tel. (514) 954.1633
                         Fax: (514) 954.1635

CHINA – CHINE
Book Dept., China National Publications
Import and Export Corporation (CNPIEC)
16 Gongti E. Road, Chaoyang District
Beijing 100020   Tel. (10) 6506-6688 Ext. 8402
                     (10) 6506-3101

CHINESE TAIPEI – TAIPEI CHINOIS
Good Faith Worldwide Int'l. Co. Ltd.
9th Floor, No. 118, Sec. 2
Chung Hsiao E. Road
Taipei   Tel. (02) 391.7396/391.7397
                     Fax: (02) 394.9176

**CZECH REPUBLIC –
RÉPUBLIQUE TCHÈQUE**
National Information Centre
NIS – prodejna
Konviktská 5
Praha 1 – 113 57   Tel. (02) 24.23.09.07
                     Fax: (02) 24.22.94.33
E-mail: nkposp@dec.niz.cz
Internet: http://www.nis.cz

DENMARK – DANEMARK
Munksgaard Book and Subscription Service
35, Nørre Søgade, P.O. Box 2148
DK-1016 København K   Tel. (33) 12.85.70
                         Fax: (33) 12.93.87

J. H. Schultz Information A/S,
Herstedvang 12,
DK – 2620 Albertslung   Tel. 43 63 23 00
                         Fax: 43 63 19 69
Internet: s-info@inet.uni-c.dk

EGYPT – ÉGYPTE
The Middle East Observer
41 Sherif Street
Cairo   Tel. (2) 392.6919
                     Fax: (2) 360.6804

FINLAND – FINLANDE
Akateeminen Kirjakauppa
Keskuskatu 1, P.O. Box 128
00100 Helsinki

Subscription Services/Agence d'abonnements :
P.O. Box 23
00100 Helsinki   Tel. (358) 9.121.4403
                         Fax: (358) 9.121.4450

*FRANCE
OECD/OCDE
Mail Orders/Commandes par correspondance :
2, rue André-Pascal
75775 Paris Cedex 16 Tel. 33 (0)1.45.24.82.00
                     Fax: 33 (0)1.49.10.42.76
                     Telex: 640048 OCDE
Internet: Compte.PUBSINQ@oecd.org

Orders via Minitel, France only/
Commandes par Minitel, France
exclusivement : 36 15 OCDE

OECD Bookshop/Librairie de l'OCDE :
33, rue Octave-Feuillet
75016 Paris   Tel. 33 (0)1.45.24.81.81
                         33 (0)1.45.24.81.67

Dawson
B.P. 40
91121 Palaiseau Cedex   Tel. 01.89.10.47.00
                         Fax: 01.64.54.83.26

Documentation Française
29, quai Voltaire
75007 Paris   Tel. 01.40.15.70.00

Economica
49, rue Héricart
75015 Paris   Tel. 01.45.78.12.92
                         Fax: 01.45.75.05.67

Gibert Jeune (Droit-Économie)
6, place Saint-Michel
75006 Paris   Tel. 01.43.25.91.19

Librairie du Commerce International
10, avenue d'Iéna
75016 Paris   Tel. 01.40.73.34.60

Librairie Dunod
Université Paris-Dauphine
Place du Maréchal-de-Lattre-de-Tassigny
75016 Paris   Tel. 01.44.05.40.13

Librairie Lavoisier
11, rue Lavoisier
75008 Paris   Tel. 01.42.65.39.95

Librairie des Sciences Politiques
30, rue Saint-Guillaume
75007 Paris   Tel. 01.45.48.36.02

P.U.F.
49, boulevard Saint-Michel
75005 Paris   Tel. 01.43.25.83.40

Librairie de l'Université
12a, rue Nazareth
13100 Aix-en-Provence   Tel. 04.42.26.18.08

Documentation Française
165, rue Garibaldi
69003 Lyon   Tel. 04.78.63.32.23

Librairie Decitre
29, place Bellecour
69002 Lyon   Tel. 04.72.40.54.54

Librairie Sauramps
Le Triangle
34967 Montpellier Cedex 2 Tel. 04.67.58.85.15
                         Fax: 04.67.58.27.36

A la Sorbonne Actual
23, rue de l'Hôtel-des-Postes
06000 Nice   Tel. 04.93.13.77.75
                         Fax: 04.93.80.75.69

GERMANY – ALLEMAGNE
OECD Bonn Centre
August-Bebel-Allee 6
D-53175 Bonn   Tel. (0228) 959.120
                     Fax: (0228) 959.12.17

GREECE – GRÈCE
Librairie Kauffmann
Stadiou 28
10564 Athens   Tel. (01) 32.55.321
                     Fax: (01) 32.30.320

HONG-KONG
Swindon Book Co. Ltd.
Astoria Bldg. 3F
34 Ashley Road, Tsimshatsui
Kowloon, Hong Kong   Tel. 2376.2062
                         Fax: 2376.0685

HUNGARY – HONGRIE
Euro Info Service
Margitsziget, Európa Ház
1138 Budapest   Tel. (1) 111.60.61
                         Fax: (1) 302.50.35
E-mail: euroinfo@mail.matav.hu
Internet: http://www.euroinfo.hu//index.html

ICELAND – ISLANDE
Mál og Menning
Laugavegi 18, Pósthólf 392
121 Reykjavik   Tel. (1) 552.4240
                         Fax: (1) 562.3523

INDIA – INDE
Oxford Book and Stationery Co.
Scindia House
New Delhi 110001   Tel. (11) 331.5896/5308
                     Fax: (11) 332.2639
E-mail: oxford.publ@axcess.net.in

17 Park Street
Calcutta 700016   Tel. 240832

INDONESIA – INDONÉSIE
Pdii-Lipi
P.O. Box 4298
Jakarta 12042   Tel. (21) 573.34.67
                         Fax: (21) 573.34.67

IRELAND – IRLANDE
Government Supplies Agency
Publications Section
4/5 Harcourt Road
Dublin 2   Tel. 661.31.11
                         Fax: 475.27.60

ISRAEL – ISRAËL
Praedicta
5 Shatner Street
P.O. Box 34030
Jerusalem 91430   Tel. (2) 652.84.90/1/2
                     Fax: (2) 652.84.93

R.O.Y. International
P.O. Box 13056
Tel Aviv 61130   Tel. (3) 546 1423
                         Fax: (3) 546 1442
E-mail: royil@netvision.net.il

Palestinian Authority/Middle East:
INDEX Information Services
P.O.B. 19502
Jerusalem   Tel. (2) 627.16.34
                         Fax: (2) 627.12.19

ITALY – ITALIE
Libreria Commissionaria Sansoni
Via Duca di Calabria, 1/1
50125 Firenze   Tel. (055) 64.54.15
                         Fax: (055) 64.12.57
E-mail: licosa@ftbcc.it

Via Bartolini 29
20155 Milano   Tel. (02) 36.50.83

Editrice e Libreria Herder
Piazza Montecitorio 120
00186 Roma   Tel. 679.46.28
                         Fax: 678.47.51

Libreria Hoepli
Via Hoepli 5
20121 Milano   Tel. (02) 86.54.46
                            Fax: (02) 805.28.86

Libreria Scientifica
Dott. Lucio de Biasio 'Aeiou'
Via Coronelli, 6
20146 Milano   Tel. (02) 48.95.45.52
                            Fax: (02) 48.95.45.48

JAPAN – JAPON
OECD Tokyo Centre
Landic Akasaka Building
2-3-4 Akasaka, Minato-ku
Tokyo 107   Tel. (81.3) 3586.2016
                            Fax: (81.3) 3584.7929

KOREA – CORÉE
Kyobo Book Centre Co. Ltd.
P.O. Box 1658, Kwang Hwa Moon
Seoul   Tel. 730.78.91
                            Fax: 735.00.30

MALAYSIA – MALAISIE
University of Malaya Bookshop
University of Malaya
P.O. Box 1127, Jalan Pantai Baru
59700 Kuala Lumpur
Malaysia   Tel. 756.5000/756.5425
                            Fax: 756.3246

MEXICO – MEXIQUE
OECD Mexico Centre
Edificio INFOTEC
Av. San Fernando no. 37
Col. Toriello Guerra
Tlalpan C.P. 14050
Mexico D.F.   Tel. (525) 528.10.38
                            Fax: (525) 606.13.07
E-mail: ocde@rtn.net.mx

NETHERLANDS – PAYS-BAS
SDU Uitgeverij Plantijnstraat
Externe Fondsen
Postbus 20014
2500 EA's-Gravenhage   Tel. (070) 37.89.880
Voor bestellingen: Fax: (070) 34.75.778

Subscription Agency/Agence d'abonnements :
SWETS & ZEITLINGER BV
Heereweg 347B
P.O. Box 830
2160 SZ Lisse   Tel. 252.435.111
                            Fax: 252.415.888

**NEW ZEALAND –
NOUVELLE-ZÉLANDE**
GPLegislation Services
P.O. Box 12418
Thorndon, Wellington   Tel. (04) 496.5655
                       Fax: (04) 496.5698

NORWAY – NORVÈGE
NIC INFO A/S
Ostensjoveien 18
P.O. Box 6512 Etterstad
0606 Oslo   Tel. (22) 97.45.00
                            Fax: (22) 97.45.45

PAKISTAN
Mirza Book Agency
65 Shahrah Quaid-E-Azam
Lahore 54000   Tel. (42) 735.36.01
                            Fax: (42) 576.37.14

PHILIPPINE – PHILIPPINES
International Booksource Center Inc.
Rm 179/920 Cityland 10 Condo Tower 2
HV dela Costa Ext cor Valero St.
Makati Metro Manila   Tel. (632) 817 9676
                       Fax: (632) 817 1741

POLAND – POLOGNE
Ars Polona
00-950 Warszawa
Krakowskie Prezdmiescie 7 Tel. (22) 264760
                           Fax: (22) 265334

PORTUGAL
Livraria Portugal
Rua do Carmo 70-74
Apart. 2681
1200 Lisboa   Tel. (01) 347.49.82/5
                            Fax: (01) 347.02.64

SINGAPORE – SINGAPOUR
Ashgate Publishing
Asia Pacific Pte. Ltd
Golden Wheel Building, 04-03
41, Kallang Pudding Road
Singapore 349316   Tel. 741.5166
                            Fax: 742.9356

SPAIN – ESPAGNE
Mundi-Prensa Libros S.A.
Castelló 37, Apartado 1223
Madrid 28001   Tel. (91) 431.33.99
                            Fax: (91) 575.39.98
E-mail: mundiprensa@tsai.es
Internet: http://www.mundiprensa.es

Mundi-Prensa Barcelona
Consell de Cent No. 391
08009 – Barcelona   Tel. (93) 488.34.92
                            Fax: (93) 487.76.59

Libreria de la Generalitat
Palau Moja
Rambla dels Estudis, 118
08002 – Barcelona
            (Suscripciones) Tel. (93) 318.80.12
            (Publicaciones) Tel. (93) 302.67.23
                            Fax: (93) 412.18.54

SRI LANKA
Centre for Policy Research
c/o Colombo Agencies Ltd.
No. 300-304, Galle Road
Colombo 3   Tel. (1) 574240, 573551-2
                      Fax: (1) 575394, 510711

SWEDEN – SUÈDE
CE Fritzes AB
S–106 47 Stockholm   Tel. (08) 690.90.90
                            Fax: (08) 20.50.21

For electronic publications only/
Publications électroniques seulement
STATISTICS SWEDEN
Informationsservice
S-115 81 Stockholm   Tel. 8 783 5066
                            Fax: 8 783 4045

Subscription Agency/Agence d'abonnements :
Wennergren-Williams Info AB
P.O. Box 1305
171 25 Solna   Tel. (08) 705.97.50
                            Fax: (08) 27.00.71

Liber distribution
Internatinal organizations
Fagerstagatan 21
S-163 52 Spanga

SWITZERLAND – SUISSE
Maditec S.A. (Books and Periodicals/Livres
et périodiques)
Chemin des Palettes 4
Case postale 266
1020 Renens VD 1   Tel. (021) 635.08.65
                            Fax: (021) 635.07.80

Librairie Payot S.A.
4, place Pépinet
CP 3212
1002 Lausanne   Tel. (021) 320.25.11
                            Fax: (021) 320.25.14

Librairie Unilivres
6, rue de Candolle
1205 Genève   Tel. (022) 320.26.23
                            Fax: (022) 329.73.18

Subscription Agency/Agence d'abonnements :
Dynapresse Marketing S.A.
38, avenue Vibert
1227 Carouge   Tel. (022) 308.08.70
                            Fax: (022) 308.07.99

See also – Voir aussi :
OECD Bonn Centre
August-Bebel-Allee 6
D-53175 Bonn (Germany) Tel. (0228) 959.120
                        Fax: (0228) 959.12.17

THAILAND – THAÏLANDE
Suksit Siam Co. Ltd.
113, 115 Fuang Nakhon Rd.
Opp. Wat Rajbopith
Bangkok 10200   Tel. (662) 225.9531/2
                            Fax: (662) 222.5188

**TRINIDAD & TOBAGO, CARIBBEAN
TRINITÉ-ET-TOBAGO, CARAÏBES**
Systematics Studies Limited
9 Watts Street
Curepe
Trinidad & Tobago, W.I. Tel. (1809) 645.3475
                         Fax: (1809) 662.5654
E-mail: tobe@trinidad.net

TUNISIA – TUNISIE
Grande Librairie Spécialisée
Fendri Ali
Avenue Haffouz Imm El-Intilaka
Bloc B 1 Sfax 3000   Tel. (216-4) 296 855
                       Fax: (216-4) 298.270

TURKEY – TURQUIE
Kültür Yayinlari Is-Türk Ltd.
Atatürk Bulvari No. 191/Kat 13
06684 Kavaklidere/Ankara
                       Tel. (312) 428.11.40 Ext. 2458
                       Fax : (312) 417.24.90

Dolmabahce Cad. No. 29
Besiktas/Istanbul   Tel. (212) 260 7188

UNITED KINGDOM – ROYAUME-UNI
The Stationery Office Ltd.
Postal orders only:
P.O. Box 276, London SW8 5DT
Gen. enquiries   Tel. (171) 873 0011
                            Fax: (171) 873 8463

The Stationery Office Ltd.
Postal orders only:
49 High Holborn, London WC1V 6HB
Branches at: Belfast, Birmingham, Bristol,
Edinburgh, Manchester

UNITED STATES – ÉTATS-UNIS
OECD Washington Center
2001 L Street N.W., Suite 650
Washington, D.C. 20036-4922
                            Tel. (202) 785.6323
                            Fax: (202) 785.0350
Internet: washcont@oecd.org

Subscriptions to OECD periodicals may also
be placed through main subscription agencies.

Les abonnements aux publications périodiques
de l'OCDE peuvent être souscrits auprès des
principales agences d'abonnement.

Orders and inquiries from countries where Dis-
tributors have not yet been appointed should be
sent to: OECD Publications, 2, rue André-Pascal, 75775 Paris Cedex 16, France.

Les commandes provenant de pays où l'OCDE
n'a pas encore désigné de distributeur peuvent
être adressées aux Éditions de l'OCDE, 2, rue
André-Pascal, 75775 Paris Cedex 16, France.

12-1996

OECD PUBLICATIONS, 2, rue André-Pascal, 75775 PARIS CEDEX 16
PRINTED IN FRANCE
(41 98 05 1 P) ISBN 92-64-16060-4 – No. 50033 1998